ON HUMAN SYMBIOSIS
AND THE VICISSITUDES OF INDIVIDUATION

Infantile Psychosis

ON HUMAN SYMBIOSIS
AND THE VICISSITUDES
OF INDIVIDUATION

Infantile Psychosis

MARGARET S. MAHLER, M.D.

In Collaboration with
Manuel Furer, M.D.

INTERNATIONAL UNIVERSITIES PRESS, INC.

New York

Acknowledgments

I wish to express my basic indebtedness to Anna Freud, as well as to the late August Aichhorn, Alice Balint, and Willi Hoffer.

For my composite ego ideal as a psychoanalytic theoretician and clinician, I am indebted to Phyllis Greenacre, Heinz Hartmann, Edith Jacobson, Max Schur, and Bertha Tumarin; as a teacher, to August Aichhorn and Ernst Kris.

During the span of my involvement with the topics of this first volume, there was a mutual germinal influence and stimulation between Dr. Paula Elkisch and myself. I took note early of her gifts as a profound thinker and an imaginative and talented clinician. Her exceptional work with a child patient suffering from tics and psychosis, as well as her pioneering venture in treating successfully a young psychotic child and his mother, greatly inspired the direction of my work contained in this volume.

In addition to the stimulus I received from the atypical cases I had encountered in child analytic practice in Vienna before 1938, my research interest in childhood psychosis and schizophrenia received a decisive impetus when I was invited by Drs. Nolan D. C. Lewis, Irville McKinnon and William Horowitz to become a consultant to the Children's Service of the New York State Psychiatric Institute and Columbia University. Dr. Lillian Kaplan, senior resident at the time (1940-41), was the first to recommend that I be invited to assist in the reorganization of the Children's Service, and I am particularly grateful to her. This was the immediate consequence of a paper I presented at the New York Psychoanalytic Society in January, 1940 on "Pseudoimbecility: A Magic Cap of Invisibility" (Dr. Lillian Powers, presiding).

My everlasting appreciation belongs to Dr. Nolan D. C. Lewis for his also entrusting Dr. Jean A. Luke and myself with a research project: the study of tics and impulsions in children. In this study we were later joined by Dr. Wilburta Daltroff. The project was partly financed through the National Committee for Mental Hygiene, from funds granted by the Committee on Research in Dementia Praecox, founded by the Supreme Council 33° Scottish Rite, Northern Masonic Jurisdiction, U.S.A., which I would like to thank on this occasion.

My interest in this study of "motor neuroses" ripened during many years of psychotherapy of a young boy begun at Mount Sinai Hospital, continued on an outpatient basis at Psychiatric Institute, who suffered from Gilles de la Tourette's disease. I am indebted for diagnostic work-up and initial discussion of this case to Dr. Leo Stone, from whose broad knowledge of psychopathology I profited greatly during my short attendance at Mount Sinai Hospital.

In 1943, Dr. Leo Rangell co-authored, and in particular contributed the neuropsychiatric assessment of this case, in our much quoted article: "Psychosomatic Study of a Case of Maladie des Tics" (Gilles de la Tourette's Disease). I remember our collaboration with pleasure.

Several papers were the product of the happy joint endeavor with Drs. Luke and Daltroff and I wish to thank both of them most heartily for their enthusiasm and cooperation. The follow-up study of former tic patients of Psychiatric Institute, which Dr. Luke and I undertook and wrote up, "Outcome of the Tic Syndrome," brought the disorganizing effect of generalized tics on the ego of the growing personality into the focus of my interest, so that my work centered thereafter on the immediate study of psychosis in children.

Other authors with whom I worked at that time and who contributed to a special issue of *The Nervous Child*, entitled "Tics in Children," of which I was editor, included Dr. Samuel Ritvo who furnished a careful and complete survey of the literature on tics, and Dr. Bernard L. Pacella, who also wrote an article for that issue. Another co-author of a paper during the period of my tic studies was Dr. Irma Gross Drooz, whose untimely death saddened all who knew her.

The first product of my "Clinical Studies of Benign and Malignant Cases of Childhood Psychoses (Schizophrenia-like)" was a paper with that title jointly written with Drs. John R. Ross, Jr. and Zira De Fries, both residents at that time to the Children's Service. I thank them sincerely for their cooperation.

I have often expressed my gratitude, and I wish to do so again, to Dr. Leo Kanner, the discussant of our paper at its delivery at the February, 1948 meeting of the American Orthopsychiatric Association. His unexpectedly high praise as well as his recognition of the significance of our research efforts did much to encourage this work. His opinion was to a great measure responsible for my continuing the pioneering task of trying to conceptualize childhood psychosis within the frame of reference of psychoanalytic theory.

My thanks go to Bernard L. Pacella, head of the Children's Service for several years during my consultantship, as well as to all the interns and residents of the New York State Psychiatric Institute—such as, Jacob A. Arlow, Louis Gilbert, Theodore Lipin, Betty Allen Magruder, Ruth Moulton, Kathryn Prescott, Margaret Olds Strahl, and many others, too numerous to be recorded, who contributed to the unusually fruitful clinical conferences on the Children's Service of the Psychiatric Institute from 1941 to 1950, and who in their case presentations and in other ways helped in my conceptualization of the symbiosis theory of infantile psychosis. Special thanks also go to Dr. Marynia Farnham, co-consultant during my later years at Columbia University.

No one helped me more to clarify the concepts, elaborated in the paper which I was about to read at the Amsterdam Congress in 1951, than Lucie Jessner, then of Cambridge, Massachusetts. During our delightful sea voyage to that Congress, she checked these concepts against her own rich clinical material and sound diagnostic and therapeutic knowledge, and through her help I was able to formulate my hypotheses with far greater precision.

My lasting appreciation goes to Dr. Milton Rosenbaum, at whose invitation I joined the Albert Einstein College of Medicine and Bronx Municipal Hospital Center, when it was not yet even inhabited. The programs were still in the planning stage. I feel particularly privileged to have been able to witness the birth of this great institution and to participate in its fabulously successful development.

My thanks are due also to Dr. Joseph Cramer, Head of the Child Psychiatry Department, as well as to Dr. Morton Reiser, who always found time to help me with problems of research and methodology, and in many other ways, as did Dr. E. James Anthony of Washington University, St. Louis, Missouri.

Thanks are due to Dr. Manuel Furer, for his brilliant assistance in our first attempts at therapeutic action research at the Bronx Municipal Hospital Center (which we later had to abandon) as set forth in our first joint publication, "Observations on Research Regarding the Symbiotic Syndrome of Infantile Psychosis."

My very special thanks to the Board of Managers of the Masters Children's Center for their invitation to Dr. Furer and myself to use their premises at 75 Horatio Street, which were particularly well suited for setting up a flexible and entirely "un-institutional" method for the study of symbiotic child psychosis. It would not have been possible for that study to get under way (or for this book to be written), without the generous moral and, especially at the beginning, heavy financial support, of the Board of Managers from 1957 on. Their encouragement and understanding sustained us when, ever so often, the going became rough.

I could never succeed in expressing the extent of my gratitude to Granville Whittlesey, Chairman of the Board, and to my friend, Mrs. Mary J. Crowther, Chairman of the Program Committee, during those most important years of our research, as well as to the late Mrs. Mary Hall Furber, then Treasurer of the Board. My thanks are also due to Miss Mary Willis, Mrs. Jerry Metalene, Mrs. Jane Hills, and the other members of the Board from 1957 to 1963, as well as to our Executive Secretary, Mrs. Ruth Lambert.

Mrs. Ripley Golovin has my special devotion for the arduous and successful efforts that she and Mrs. Crowther expended in bringing the research in Symbiotic Child Psychosis to its fruition by helping Dr. Furer in establishing the Clinic for psychotic young children as a community mental health center, which is now growing and expanding its facilities.*

I also want to thank Mrs. Catherine Epler for her help in acquainting the Masters Board, as well as several lay and professional groups, with the significance of the research

---

* It should be noted that Dr. Furer, after our first plan to write a joint book, found it quite impossible, in the light of his commitments to the Clinic at the Masters Children's Center itself, with its innumerable organizational, fund raising, and professional responsibilities, as well as the increasing demands on his talents by the New York Psychoanalytic Institute and the American Psychoanalytic Association, to find either the time or the energy to continue with this endeavor, and therefore begged off from full co-authorship. Although the research project that contributed in part to this first volume of my two-volume work was undertaken and carried out with Dr. Furer as co-investigator, both he and I had agreed already at the end of the N.I.M.H.-sponsored research project, M3353, that he should be the one subsequently to direct the Clinic for the psychotic children, so that from 1963 on I could devote my energy as principal investigator in the study of the separation-individuation process (the subject of the second volume of this book). Hence, except for a few joint formulations in Chapter VII and a few sections of Chapters V and VI, the contents of this volume are entirely my own.

that Dr. Furer and I were carrying on at the Center—namely, a pilot study on normal individuation, as well as a study of symbiotic child psychosis. She did this in a particularly talented way that enabled her to be more clarifying than any of us could have been.

My deepest gratitude to Mrs. Miriam Ben-Aaron (now working in Israel) as well as Mrs. Anni Bergman, and Mrs. Emmagene Kamaiko, senior child therapists, without whose therapeutic insight, clinical acumen, and pertinent contributions to staff discussions this book would have lacked the more recent theoretical understanding contained in Chapter IV, and particularly the more recent case material in Chapter VI.

My greatest admiration and affection go to those colleagues who were co-authors of papers, until now scattered through the literature, on which I have drawn in the preparation of this book, in particular to Drs. Paula Elkisch, Bertram J. Gosliner, Manuel Furer, and Calvin P. Settlage.

I am grateful to the National Institute of Mental Health, U.S.P.H.S. for its major support in making possible the conceptualization and final formulations of my thoughts on human symbiosis and the vicissitudes of individuation, through its four-year Grant No. M 3353, to Dr. Furer and myself, from 1959-60 to 1962-63 for the study of the "Natural History of Symbiotic Child Psychosis," as well as for the lion's share of support of my work which will be contained in the second volume of this book, the latter through grant MH-08238.

Much of the evaluation of the material as well as its editing I owe to the capable, conscientious, and patient work of Mr. Harold Collins. My former secretary, Miss Diana Epstein, did more than secretarial work on this book; she also helped with the preliminary organization of this volume. Mrs. Carol Martin was helpful in the initial collecting and compilation of the extensive and complex bibliography, and Mrs. Marna Walsch of the Masters Children's Center helped with the prompt and flawless typing of large parts of the first draft of this volume in the summer of 1966.

The capable and self-effacing librarian of the Brill Library of the New York Psychoanalytic Institute, Miss Liselotte Bendix, contributed her profound knowledge of the literature, both unselfishly and tirelessly.

And finally, and most importantly, I cannot find the words to describe my indebtedness to Lottie M. Newman. I would not have undertaken writing what is essentially a new book if it had not been for my faith in her great talent, efficiency, and her assurance of assistance.

Contents

Volume I

Infantile Psychosis

Introduction

This first volume of a two-volume book will be devoted to a detailed explication of my theory of human symbiosis and its most pathological vicissitudes. It is the result of historical circumstances that my concern with extreme disturbances of pathological symbiosis preceded my present study of "The Normal Separation-Individuation Process."

Ever since the early 1930s, in clinical child psychoanalytic practice, I have been encountering rare cases of severe emotional disturbances in children, the clinical picture of which did not fit into the nosological category of neurosis; at the same time they could not be forced into the wastepaper basket category of organicity. But there has been a great resistance, emotionally tinged, against acknowledgment of the existence of schizophrenialike derangement in little children!

I had already been pleading, in Europe (just as Schilder, Bender, and others were pleading in this country), for recognition of the fact that a few of the child patients who had been referred to me, as a child analyst, to be treated with child analytic methods, were really cases of a schizophrenialike condition. They therefore neither belonged in the child psychiatric ward, among the mentally defectives, nor could they be regarded as severe neurotics, and therefore could not be analyzed by the classical psychoanalytic method. I reported on them in the Schilder Society in 1947.

During the early 1940s, I had the good fortune to be asked to become a consultant to the Children's Service of the New York State Psychiatric Institute and Columbia University. There, with the most interesting case material I have ever encountered, I saw and reported on children whose clinical pictures were clearly reminiscent of those of adult and adolescent schizophrenics. But still, in accordance with the spirit of the time, the only concession that adult psychiatry would make was to acknowledge the existence of "early infantile autism," described by Kanner just a few years earlier.

This was at the time when Kanner's classical description and delineation of "early infantile autism" was starting to penetrate into the child psychiatric circles and to become very slowly accepted there. The findings of the Bellevue school were at the time generally ignored.

Looking upon these phenomena in terms of the dynamic and genetic approach of psychoanalysis and, in particular, of child analysis, however, I have come to see again and again that, especially among school-age psychotic children, early infantile autism was not the main and certainly not the only psychotic condition. I had come to recognize gradually that autism was a defense—albeit a psychotic defense— against the lack of that vital and basic need of the human young in his early months of life: symbiosis with a mother or a mother substitute.

It was both against the background of, and in contradistinction to, the very valuable, truly epoch-making description by Kanner of "early infantile autism" that I had been studying, from the psychoanalytic point of view, the clinical pictures of those older children, as well as a few younger ones. It was thus that the theory of *the symbiotic origin of infantile psychosis* took shape in my mind (cf. Fliess).

While my clinical psychoanalytic practice in Vienna had already taught me that some cases that were brought to me for child analysis did not fit into either the nosological group of neurotics or into that of organic amentia—i.e., that there were basic dynamic differences—my experience during the early 1940s at the New York State Psychiatric Institute was to teach me something new. Against the background of the more usual types of interaction of the organic group of the population of the children's ward (those children displayed a somewhat bizarre, but still, for the most part, clinging, definite, and realistic interaction with the adult), I was able • to observe a most striking inability, on the part of the psychotic child, even to see the human object in the outside world, let alone to interact with him as with another separate human entity. This often seemed to be the most conspicuous, indeed the cardinal feature of childhood psychosis.

In the early spring of 1948, I presented (in collaboration with John R. Ross, Jr. and Zira De Fries) a preliminary résumé of my findings in sixteen cases of child psychosis. As to the symptomatology of five of the noninstitutionalized children and eleven of the cases of institutionalized children, I delivered a report at the Meeting of the American Orthopsychiatric Association, under the title "Clinical Studies in Benign and Malignant Cases of Childhood Psychosis (Schizophrenia-like)" (Mahler, Ross, and De Fries, 1949).

In that paper, which Kanner discussed, I did no more than, to begin with, delineate those features of the manifest symptomatology of the "schizophreniclike" child that I felt were pathognomonic and that distinguished it from that of other nosological, dynamically interrelated groups of childhood disorders. All I attempted in that paper was to bring some meaningful order into the bewildering array of manifestations of these children's break with reality—their attempts at restitution—and particularly to highlight what I had already begun to recognize, i.e., their inability to form meaningful object relationships, to interact meaningfully with other human beings.

Even though my idea of the time of onset of the psychosis

was somewhat inaccurate, in that paper I already ventured the opinion that the onset of the psychosis—as far as one could trace it from the anamnestic data of those sixteen cases—took place during the first year of life and seemed to be due to, or else to coincide with, the infant's lack of normal "confident expectation" of rescue from, or gratification of, affect hunger by his mother. This onset I thought then (even though I did not spell it out) was mainly characteristic of "early infantile autism."

In the second crucial period of onset, later in infancy (second to fifth year), the hitherto narcissistic appersonation of the mother was no longer sufficient, as I said then, to counteract the overwhelming anxiety predisposition of these infants. The predetermined and inevitable maturational growth increased the challenge by and requirements of outside reality, as well as of the psychosexual conflict in those years. It was the emotional separation from the symbiosis with mother that acted as the immediate trigger for the psychotic withdrawal from reality. I felt already then, even though I again did not spell this out, that the more stormy panic-ridden restitution attempts with what I later termed symbiotic syndrome took their origin from that break.

During subsequent years, especially at the beginning of my studies, and through the middle '50s, I worked on the formulation of what I had come to feel needed to be clearly emphasized: the differences between "early infantile autism" (or the autistic syndrome, as I like to call it) and the *symbiotic psychosis syndrome*.

Certain developments and shifts in emphasis in my characterization of the autistic and the symbiotic psychosis syndromes will be dealt with in Chapters II and III of this book.

This shift occurred during the course of the systematic study of symbiotic infantile psychosis, which Dr. Manuel Furer and I carried on in the '50s. We had availed ourselves of the opportunity that the Board of the Masters Nursery offered us in their building, which was destined to become, from 1956 on, the Masters Children's Center. There we continued a pilot project that we had started earlier at the Albert Einstein College of Medicine and the Bronx Municipal Hospital Center. We felt that we needed for such a study the informal atmosphere of the Masters Children's Center, in contrast to an "institutional" setting. At first, we experimented with a special nursery kind of approach (cf. Mahler and Furer, 1960).

As is indicated in more detail in Chapters III and VI, however, we soon gave up that approach. We felt that we had to try to design what one could designate as corrective symbiotic experience in a one-to-one relationship with a therapist, which would then lead to a reconstitution of a more symbioticlike relationship with the mother herself (cf. Alpert's "corrective object relationship"). Only through such an approach would we be able to reconstruct the genesis and the dynamics of early infantile psychosis—both in those cases in which autistic mechanisms prevailed and in those in which symbiotic features were predominant.

In the course of our four-year intensive study of the natural history of symbiotic infantile psychosis, we encountered predominantly autistic and predominantly symbiotic symptomatology, the "types" depending upon the defense and restitutive structure. Both defenses were recognized as regressive distortions of very early states of the sensorium and of the psychotic ego's way of dealing with the drives and the environmental impingements.

Finally, we now believe that we are dealing with symptomatology along a broad spectrum, from complete autistic withdrawal from the human environment—for example, the cases of Lotta or Violet in Chapters IV, V, and VI—to seriously panic-stricken, almost incessant and for the most part ambitendent (Bleuler) attempts at reinforcement of the delusional fusion with and riddance mechanisms against the symbiotic engulfment (see the cases of Benny, Aro, Alma, and George in Chapters IV and V).

A few more words about why this first volume of a two-volume book *On Human Symbiosis* has taken so long to be written and has therefore been published later than I would have wanted it to be.

I had been working and lecturing on this question for some twenty-five years, during which I have written more than a score of papers that have dealt, directly or indirectly, with the problem of childhood psychosis. The published papers (some of them translated into other languages) are scattered in almost as many different journals and books as there are papers. The simple collection of my papers would have had this advantage: that the reader could have availed himself, far more readily than he could have otherwise, of any of my papers as they were originally written.

This venture, however, did not seem to be challenging enough, either to myself or to the publisher. These papers contained, as may be expected, much duplication, while the historical development of my thinking would not have been clearly demonstrated or explicated.

I decided instead to write a book, that is to say, to use my papers on the subject only as a basis, a guideline, so to speak, for an elaboration of the *symbiosis theory* of the *development of the human being,* and in this first volume to deal with its most pathological vicissitudes.

CHAPTER I

On the Concepts of Symbiosis and Separation-Individuation

The term symbiosis is borrowed from biology, where it is used to refer to a close functional association of two organisms to their mutual advantage.

In the weeks preceding the evolution to symbiosis, the newborn and very young infant's sleeplike states far outweigh in proportion the states of arousal. They are reminiscent of that primal state of libido distribution that prevailed in intrauterine life, which resembles the model of a closed monadic system, self-sufficient in its hallucinatory wish fulfillment.

Freud's (1911a) use of the bird's egg as a model of a closed psychological system comes to mind. He said: "A neat example of a psychical system shut off from the stimuli of the external world, and able to satisfy even its nutritional requirements *autistically* . . . , is afforded by a bird's egg with its food supply enclosed in its shell; for it, the care provided by its mother is limited to the provision of warmth" (p. 220n., my italics).

In a quasi-symbolic way along this same line, conceptualizing the state of the sensorium, I have applied to the first weeks of life the term *normal autism;* for in it, the infant seems to be in a state of primitive hallucinatory disorienta-

tion, in which need satisfaction belongs to his own omnipotent, *autistic* orbit.

The newborn's waking life centers around his continuous
attempts to achieve homeostasis. The effect of his mother's
ministrations in reducing the pangs of need-hunger cannot
be isolated, nor can it be differentiated by the young infant
from tension-reducing attempts of his own, such as urinating,
defecating, coughing, sneezing, spitting, regurgitating, vomiting, all the ways by which the infant tries to rid himself of
unpleasurable tension. The effect of these expulsive phenomena as well as the gratification gained by his mother's ministrations help the infant, in time, to differentiate between a
"pleasurable" and "good" quality and a "painful" and "bad"
quality of experience (Mahler and Gosliner, 1955).

Through the inborn and autonomous perceptive faculty
of the primitive ego (Hartmann, 1939) deposits of memory
traces of the two primordial qualities of stimuli occur. We
may further hypothesize that these are cathected with primordial undifferentiated drive energy (Mahler and Gosliner, 1955).

From the second month on, dim awareness of the need-
satisfying object marks the beginning of the phase of normal
symbiosis, in which the infant behaves and functions as
though he and his mother were an omnipotent system—a
dual unity within one common boundary.

My concept of the symbiotic phase of normal development
dovetails, from the infant's standpoint, with the concept of
the symbiotic phase of the mother-child dual unity which
Therese Benedek (1949, 1959, 1960) has described in several classical papers from the standpoint of both partners of
the primary unit.

It is obvious that, whereas during the symbiotic phase the
infant is *absolutely* dependent on the symbiotic partner,
symbiosis has a quite different meaning for the adult partner
of the dual unity. The infant's need for the mother is abso-

lute, while the mother's for the infant is relative (Benedek, 1959).

The term "symbiosis" in this context is a metaphor. It does not describe, as the biological concept of symbiosis does, what actually happens between two separate individuals (Angel, 1967). It was chosen to describe that state of undif- ferentiation, of fusion with mother, in which the "I" is not yet differentiated from the "not-I," and in which inside and outside are only gradually coming to be sensed as different. Any unpleasurable perception, external or internal, is projected beyond the common boundary of the symbiotic *milieu intérieur* (cf. Freud's concept of the "purified pleasure ego"), which includes the mothering partner's Gestalt during ministrations. Only transiently—in the state of the sensorium that is termed alert inactivity—does the young infant take in stimuli from beyond the symbiotic milieu. The primordial energy reservoir that is vested in the undifferentiated "ego-id" still contains an undifferentiated mixture of libido and aggression. As several authors have pointed out, the libidinal cathexis vested in symbiosis, by reinforcing the inborn instinctual stimulus barrier, protects the rudimentary ego from premature phase-unspecific strain—from stress traumata.

The essential feature of symbiosis is hallucinatory or delusional, somatopsychic omnipotent fusion with the representation of the mother and, in particular, the delusion of a common boundary of the two actually and physically separate individuals. This is the mechanism to which the ego regresses in cases of the most severe disturbance of individuation and psychotic disorganization, which I have described as "symbiotic child psychosis" (Mahler, 1952).

In the human species, the function of, and the equipment for, self-preservation is atrophied. The rudimentary ego in the newborn baby and the young infant has to be complemented by the emotional rapport of the mother's nursing care, a kind of social symbiosis. It is within this matrix of physiological and sociobiological dependency on the mother that there takes place the structural differentiation that leads to the individual's organization for adaptation: the ego.

Ribble (1943) has pointed out that it is by way of mothering that the young infant is gradually brought out of an inborn tendency toward vegetative, splanchnic regression and into increased sensory awareness of, and contact with, the environment. In terms of energy or libidinal cathexis, this means that a progressive displacement of libido has to take place, from the inside of the body (particularly from the abdominal organs) toward the periphery of the body (cf. Greenacre, 1945; Mahler, 1952).

In this sense, I would propose to distinguish, within the phase of *primary narcissism*—a Freudian concept to which I find it most useful to adhere—two subphases: during the first few weeks of extrauterine life, a stage of *absolute* primary narcissism, which is marked by the infant's lack of awareness of a mothering agent. This stage I have termed "normal autism," as discussed above. In the other, the symbiotic stage proper (beginning around the third month)— while primary narcissism still prevails, it is not such an absolute primary narcissism, inasmuch as the infant begins dimly to perceive need satisfaction as coming from a need-satisfying part object—albeit still from within the orbit of his omnipotent symbiotic dual unity with a mothering agency, toward which he turns libidinally (Schur, 1966).

Pari passu, and in accordance with the pleasure-pain sequences, demarcation of representations of the body ego within the symbiotic matrix takes place. These representations are deposited as the "body image" (Schilder, 1923).

From now on, representations of the body that are contained in the rudimentary ego[1] mediate between inner and outer perceptions. The ego is molded under the impact of reality, on the one hand, and of the instinctual drives, on

---

[1] It will be this author's privilege to refer in detail to the important clinical and experimental work of Seymour Lustman (1956) in the second volume of this book. See also Richmond and Lustman (1955).

the other. The body ego contains two kinds of self repre-sentations: there is an inner core of the body image, with a boundary that is turned toward the inside of the body and divides it from the ego; and an outer layer of sensoripercep-tive engrams, which contributes to the boundaries of the "body self" (M. Bergmann, 1963).

From the standpoint of the "body image": the shift of pre-dominantly proprioceptive-enteroceptive cathexis toward sensoriperceptive cathexis of the periphery is a major step in development. We did not realize its importance prior to psy-choanalytic studies of early infantile psychosis. We know now that this major shift of cathexis is an essential prere-quisite of body-ego formation. Another parallel step is the ejection, by projection, of destructive unneutralized aggres-sive energy beyond the body-self boundaries.

The infant's inner sensations form the *core* of the self. They seem to remain the central, the crystallization point of the "feeling of self," around which a "sense of identity" will become established (Greenacre, 1958; Mahler, 1957; Rose, 1964, 1966). The sensoriperceptive organ—the "peripheral rind of the ego," as Freud called it—contributes mainly to the self's demarcation from the object world. The two kinds of intrapsychic structures *together* form the framework for self-orientation (cf. Spiegel, 1959).

The two partners of the symbiotic dyad, on the other hand, may be regarded as polarizing the organizational and structuring processes. The structures that derive from the double frame of reference of the symbiotic unit represent a framework to which all experiences have to be related, before there are clear and whole representations in the ego of the self and the object world. Spitz (1965) calls the mother the auxiliary ego of the infant. In the same line, I believe the mothering partner's "holding behavior," her "primary ma-ternal preoccupation," to be the symbiotic organizer (Winni-cott, 1956).

THE SYMBIOTIC PHASE

Greenacre (1958) has remarked how "extremely difficult [it is] to say exactly at what time the human organism develops from a biological to a *psycho*biological organization." Schur (1966) puts the time at the point when the "wish" replaces the purely "physiological need."

The implications of new sleep-physiological studies about REM activity in very young infants are most interesting and challenging indeed (see Fisher, 1965; Roffwarg, Muzio, and Dement, 1966).

Experimental psychologists tell us that, in the first two months of life, learning takes place through conditioning. Toward the third month, however, the existence of memory traces can be demonstrated experimentally. This was referred to by Spitz (1965) as the beginning of learning according to the human pattern. Learning by conditioning is then gradually replaced by learning through experience. Here is then the first beginning of symbiotic relationship as well. We may say that, whereas during the quasi-prehistoric phase of magic hallucinatory omnipotence, the breast or the bottle *belongs to the self*, toward the third month, the object begins to be perceived as an *unspecific, need-satisfying part object* (A. Freud, 1965).

When the need is not so imperative, when some measure of development enables the infant to hold tension in abeyance, that is to say, *when he is able to wait for and confidently expect satisfaction*—only then is it possible to speak of the *beginning of an ego*, and of a symbiotic object as well. This is made possible by the fact that there seem to be memory traces of the *pleasure of gratification*—connected with the memory of the perceptual Gestalt of the mother's ministrations.

The specific smiling response at the peak of the symbiotic phase predicates that the infant is responding to the symbiotic partner in a manner different from that in which he responds to other human beings. In the second half of the first year, the symbiotic partner is no longer interchangeable; manifold behaviors of the five-month-old infant indicate that he has by now *achieved a specific symbiotic relationship with his mother* (Spitz, 1959).

Anna Freud (1954a) reminded us that we may think of pregenital patterning in terms of two people joined to achieve what, for brevity's sake, one might call "homeostatic equilibrium" (see Mahler, 1954b). The same thing may be referred to under the term "symbiotic relationship." *Beyond a certain, but not yet defined degree, the immature organism cannot achieve homeostasis on its own.* Whenever during the autistic or symbiotic phase there occurs "organismic distress"—that forerunner of anxiety proper—the mothering partner is called upon to contribute a particularly large portion of symbiotic help toward the maintenance of the infant's homeostasis. Otherwise, the neurobiological patterning processes are thrown out of kilter. Somatic memory traces are set at this time which amalgamate with later experiences and may thereby increase later psychological pressures (Greenacre, 1958).

Understanding of symbiotic phenomena, which I conceptualized initially through observation of mother-infant behavior in well-baby clinics, and also through reconstruction from systematic studies of severe symbiotic psychotic syndromes, I have since supplemented by way of our observational study of *average* mothers with their *normal* infants during the first three years of life. We follow them from symbiosis through the process of separation-individuation— and up to the period of the establishment of libidinal object constancy in Hartmann's sense (1964).[2]

[2] As I indicated in my Brill Memorial Lecture (1963), "Through a study of normal infants and their mothers, I have been trying, not only to complement my psychoanalytic work with neurotic adults and children, but also to gain additional perspective and to validate previous studies in the area

THE SUBPHASES OF THE
SEPARATION-INDIVIDUATION PROCESS

The concept of subphases has been fruitful in that it has helped to determine the *nodal* points of those structuralization and developmental processes. We have found them to be characteristic at the crossroads of individuation. Their description has greatly facilitated the ordering of our data into the psychoanalytic frame of reference, in a meaningful way.

For more accurate conceptualization and formulation of these still (up to the third year) essentially preverbal processes, we have tried to determine characteristic behavioral concomitants of those intrapsychic events that seem to occur regularly during the course of separation-individuation.

At this point, I wish to refer only to a few points that may illustrate and somewhat complement more recent metapsychological constructs. These have pointed to the significance of *optimal human symbiosis* for the vicissitudes of individuation and for the establishment of a *cathectically stable "sense of identity."*

I would like to mention a relevant physiological and experimental finding that bears upon the transition from the autistic to the symbiotic phase. Those findings set the *beginning* of this transition at the *end* of the first month. There are corresponding findings—for example, by the late John Benjamin (1961), which show that around three to four weeks of

---

of infantile psychosis." Edward Glover (1956), in his introduction to his paper on "The Significance of the Mouth in Psycho-Analysis" [1924], says: "The truth is that psychoanalytical terms tend to develop into clichés: once the rough generalizations have been accepted they are handed down from one generation to another without either very close inspection or adequate amplification . . . as if they were the result of direct analytical observation: whereas in fact they are merely loose inferences drawn partly from observational data and partly from the direct analysis of cases from the age of four years upwards. . . . [A]nalysts are at last prepared to make actual observations of infant behaviour and to draw from these observations such conclusions as to primary mental processes as their pre-conceptions permit."

age a maturational crisis occurs. This is borne out in electro-
encephalographic studies and by the observation that there
is a marked increase in overall sensitivity to external stimulation. As Benjamin said, "Without intervention of a mother
figure for help in tension reduction, the infant at that time
tends to become overwhelmed by stimuli, with increased
crying and other motor manifestations of undifferentiated
negative affect."

Metapsychologically speaking, this seems to mean that, by
the second month, the quasi-solid stimulus barrier (negative,
because it is uncathected)—*this autistic shell*, which kept
external stimuli out—begins to crack. Through the aforementioned cathectic shift toward the sensoriperceptive periphery, a protective, but also receptive and selective, positively cathected stimulus shield now begins to form and to
envelop the symbiotic orbit of the mother-child dual unity
(Mahler, 1967). This eventually highly selective boundary
seems to contain not only the pre-ego self representations,
but also the not yet differentiated, libidinally cathected symbiotic part objects, within the mother-infant symbiotic matrix.

At the height of symbiosis—at around four to five months—
the facial expression of most infants becomes much more
subtly differentiated, mobile, and expressive. During the infant's wakeful periods, he reflects many more nuances of
"states"—by now "ego states"—than he did in the autistic
phase.

By the "states" of the newborn—which Peter Wolff (1959)
and Escalona (1962) have described—we gauge, in a very
general way, the states of the sensorium. In the course of the
symbiotic phase, we can follow by the "ego states" of the infant the oscillation of his attention investment between his
inner sensations and the symbiotic, libidinal attractions. During his state of "alert inactivity" the infant's attention turns
toward the outer world; this, however, as yet, comprises

mainly percepts that are more or less *closely* related to the mother.

The First Shift of Libidinal Cathexis

The indicator of outward-directed attention seems to be the prototypical biphasic visual pattern of turning to an outside stimulus and then checking back to the mother's Gestalt, particularly her face. From this kind of scanning, elements of strangeness reaction patterns will develop. Outward-directed perceptual activity gradually replaces the inward-directed attention cathexis that was, only recently, almost exclusively vested in symbiotically disoriented inner sensations. The process by which this occurs—and which might be appropriately termed *hatching*—can now begin.

The gratification-frustration sequences promote structuralization. It is important, however, as several writers have pointed out lately, that in the early months of life, tension should not remain on an inordinately high level for any length of time! If such stress traumata *do* occur during the first five months of life, the symbiotic partner—this *auxiliary ego*—is called upon to save the infant from the pressure of having to develop *his own resources prematurely*. As Martin James (1960) put it: "Premature ego development would imply that the infant—during the phase of primary narcissism —took over functions from the mother *in actuality*, or started *as though to do so.*" Winnicott (1965) and other British analysts call such an occurrence development of a "false self"—by which I believe they mean *the beginning of "as if" mechanisms.*

As M. Khan, in his paper at the 23rd Psycho-Analytical Congress, put it, the auxiliary ego may be thought of also as the mother's role as a "protective shield." His hypothesis is that "character pathology which we encounter clinically in some . . . patients of schizoid regressive type is derived from ego distortion during early phases of . . . ego differentiation." He believes that as the result of breaches in the mother's role as the infant-child's protective shield, cumulative trauma occurs, which accounts for the ego distortion.[3]

When pleasure in outer sensory perceptions as well as maturational pressure stimulate outward-directed attention cathexis—while inside there is an optimal level of pleasure and therefore *safe anchorage* within the symbiotic orbit— these two forms of attention cathexis can oscillate freely (see Rapaport, 1960, 1959; Spiegel, 1959; Rose, 1964). The result is an optimal symbiotic state from which smooth differentiatior—and *expansion beyond the symbiotic orbit*—can take place.

The hatching process is, I believe, a gradual ontogenetic evolution of the sensorium—of the perceptual-conscious system—which leads to the infant-toddler's having a *permanently alert sensorium*, whenever he is awake.

It has been fascinating to observe how the prototype of outward-directed attention cathexis evolves—how the normal infant's differentiation process is guided by the pattern of "checking back" to the mother, as a point of orientation. This pattern of checking back, and also the behavior termed "customs inspection" (Brody and Axelrad, 1966), which consists in the baby's careful, more or less deliberate examination (visually and tactilely) of all features of the "not-mother's" face and comparing it point by point with the preobject or part-object representation of the mother—both these comparing and checking patterns recur, in an expanded edition, in the period from about ten to sixteen months of age, during the practicing subphase of separation-individuation. It then is supplemented by what Furer has called "emotional refueling."

[3] It will remain for me to discuss in the second volume of this book this and other pertinent papers on the concept of cumulative trauma by Khan (1963, 1964). See also E. Galenson's discussion of Khan's (1964) paper.

The Second Massive Shift of Cathexis

The peak point of the hatching process seems to coincide with the maturational spurt of active locomotion, which brings with it increased maturational pressure "for action," to practice locomotion and to explore wider segments of reality. From the fourth quarter of the first year on, this activity motivates the infant to separate in space from his mother, and to practice active physical separation and return. This will have a greatly catalyzing influence on the further development of the ego.

The more nearly optimal the symbiosis, the mother's "holding behavior," has been; the more the symbiotic partner has helped the infant to become ready to "hatch" from the symbiotic orbit smoothly and gradually—that is, without undue strain upon his own resources—the better equipped has the child become to separate out and to differentiate his self representations from the hitherto fused symbiotic self-plus-object representations. But even at the height of the second subphase of individuation—during the practicing period— neither the differentiated self representations nor the object representations seem to be integrated as yet into a whole self representation or a whole libidinal object representation.

Among the many elements of the mother-child relationship during early infancy, we were especially impressed with the mutual selection of cues. We observed that infants present a large variety of cues—to indicate needs, tension, and pleasure (Mahler and Furer, 1963b). In a complex manner, the mother responds selectively to only *certain* of these cues. The infant gradually alters his behavior in relation to this selective response; he does so in a characteristic way—the resultant of his own innate endowment and the mother-child relationship. From this circular interaction emerge patterns of behavior that already show certain overall qualities of the child's personality. *What we seem to see here is the birth of the child as an individual* (cf. Lichtenstein, 1964).

It is the specific unconscious need of the mother that activates, out of the infant's infinite potentialities, those in particular that create for each mother "the child" who reflects her own *unique* and individual needs. This process takes place, of course, within the range of the child's innate endowments.

Mutual cuing during the symbiotic phase creates that indelibly imprinted configuration—that complex pattern—that becomes *the leitmotif for "the infant's becoming the child of his particular mother"* (Lichtenstein, 1961).

In other words, the mother conveys—in innumerable ways—a kind of "mirroring frame of reference," to which the primitive self of the infant automatically adjusts. If the mother's "primary preoccupation" with her infant—*her* mirroring function during earlier infancy—is unpredictable, unstable, anxiety-ridden, or hostile; if her confidence in herself as a mother is shaky, then the individuating child has to do without a reliable frame of reference for checking back, perceptually and emotionally, to the symbiotic partner (Spiegel, 1959). The result will then be a disturbance in the primitive "self feeling," which would derive or originate from a pleasurable and safe state of symbiosis, from which he did not have to hatch prematurely and abruptly.

The primary method of identity formation consists of mutual reflection during the symbiotic phase. This narcissistic, mutual libidinal mirroring reinforces the delineation of identity—through magnification and *reduplication*—a kind of echo phenomenon, which Paula Elkisch (1957) and Lichtenstein (1964) have so beautifully described.

I have previously (1966b) described—and shall do so in some detail in Volume II—the second massive shift of cathexis in ontogenetic development, which seems to take place when the practicing period begins. At that point, a large proportion of the available cathexis shifts from within the symbiotic orbit to investing the autonomous apparatuses of the self and the functions of the ego—locomotion, perception, learning.

In our study, we observe the intrapsychic separation-individuation process: the child's achievement of separate functioning in the presence and emotional availability of the mother. Even in this situation, this process by its very nature continually confronts the toddler with minimal threats of object loss. Nevertheless, through the predominance of pleasure in separate functioning, it enables the child to overcome that measure of separation anxiety that *is* entailed by *each new* step of separate functioning.

As far as the mothering partner is concerned, the practicing period confronts her with the impact of the toddler's spurt in individual autonomy, which is buttressed by the rapidly approaching occurrence—important for intrapsychic separation and self-boundary formation—of the negativistic behavior of the anal phase (A. Freud, 1952a; Spock, 1963).

The practicing period culminates around the middle of the second year in the freely walking toddler seeming to feel at the height of his mood of elation. He appears to be at the peak point of his belief in his own magic omnipotence, which is still to a considerable extent derived *from his sense of sharing in his mother's magic powers.*

Many mothers, however, take the very first unaided steps of their toddler, who is, intrapsychically, by no means yet hatched, as heralding: "He is grown up now!" These mothers may be the ones who interpret the infant's signals according to whether they feel the child to be a continuation of themselves or a separate individual. Some tend to fail their fledgling, by "abandoning" him at this point, more or less precipitately and prematurely, to his own devices. They react with a kind of relative ridding mechanism to the traumatization of their own symbiotic needs. These needs have been highlighted by the fact that maturational pressure has both enabled and prompted the child, at the very beginning of the second year, to practice the new "state of self": physical separateness.

One example of this is the case of Jay, who, at ten and a half months, had already learned *precociously* to walk. At that time, his body schema and his spatial orientation were still at a stage of *symbiotic fusion* and *confusion*. One could see this by innumerable behavioral signs.

The infant of twelve to fourteen months, who is gradually separating and individuating, rises from his hitherto quadruped exercises, to take his first unaided steps—initially with great caution, even though exuberantly. He automatically reassures himself of some support within reach. He also relies on his own ability to slide safely down into the sitting position—when the going gets rough, so to say. Jay, however, even though he was most wobbly and unsure on his feet, did not do any of these.

Through maturation of the ego apparatuses—and facilitated by the flux of developmental energy (Kris, 1955)—a relatively rapid, yet orderly process of separation-individuation takes place in the second year of life. By the eighteenth month, the junior toddler seems to be at the height of the process of dealing with his continuously experienced physical separateness from the mother. This coincides with his cognitive and perceptual achievement of the permanence of objects, in Piaget's sense (1936). This is the time when his sensorimotor intelligence starts to develop into true representational intelligence, and when the important process of internalization, in Hartmann's sense (1939)—very gradually, through ego identifications—begins.

Jay did not improve his skill in locomotion during his second year. He still impressed us with the impetuousness and repetitiveness of his locomotor activity, as well as with the frequency with which he got himself into dangerous situations and fell. He climbed onto high places and ran about, and peculiarly disregarded any obstacles in his way. All this time, his mother consistently and conspicuously made literally no move to protect him. Jay's behavior was—at least in the beginning—a tacit appeal to the mother. We assumed this because his falls definitely decreased when the mother was out of the room.

Jay's precocious locomotor maturation—with which the other developmental lines did not keep pace—should have made it even more imperative for the mothering partner to continue functioning as the child's auxiliary ego, in order to bridge the obvious gap between his motor and perceptual cognitive development. The mother's inner conflicts, however, resulted in her appearing transfixed, almost paralyzed, at the sight of her junior toddler son's dangerous motor feats.

As I said before, many mothers fail their fledgling, because they find it difficult to strike intuitively and naturally an optimal balance between giving support—and yet at the same time knowing when to just be available and to watch from a distance. In other words, for many mothers in our culture, it is by no means easy to give up smoothly their "symbiotic holding behavior"—and instead to give the toddler optimal support on a higher emotional and verbal level, while allowing him to try his new wings of autonomy—in the second year of life.

Jay's mother demonstrated this conflict to a bizarre degree; she continually watched from a distance like a hawk, but could not make a move to assist him. I believe that it was Jay's developmental lag—which the precocity of his locomotor maturation had created in him, combined with the mother's continued failure to protect Jay's body—that resulted in seemingly irreversible damage to each of the three essential structures of Jay's individuating personality.[4]

The sixteen- to eighteen-month level seems to be a *nodal*

---

[4] Whether the obvious defect in his visual-motor coordination was on an organic or functional basis to begin with is a moot and, at this point, I believe, indeterminable question, even though interesting.

point of development. The toddler is then at the height of what Joffe and Sandler (1965) have termed "the ideal state of self." This is, I believe, the complex affective representation of the symbiotic dual unity, with its inflated sense of omnipotence—now augmented by the toddler's feeling of his own magic power—as the result of his spurt in autonomous functions.

Rapprochement and the Development of Object Constancy

In the next eighteen months, this "ideal state of self" must become divested of its delusional increments. The second eighteen months of life thus are a period of vulnerability. It is the time when the child's self-esteem may suffer abrupt deflation.

Under normal circumstances, the senior toddler's growing autonomy has already begun to correct some of his delusional overestimation of his own omnipotence. During the course of individuation, internalization has begun, by true ego identification with the parents.

Jay did not seem to be able to learn through experience. He continued to suffer his hard falls, and ever so often, without appropriate affective reactions. He seemed to be peculiarly lacking in sensitivity to physical pain. This *denial of pain* appeared to be in compliance with his mother's reactive belief that her son was indeed impervious to pain. Jay thus earned, in addition to his mother's pride, the epitheton: "Jay, the Painless Wonder," from the mothers of other children in the group.

Even at twenty months, Jay was conspicuous for his poorly developed ability to "inhibit the immediate discharge of impulse, and the attack on materials." His behavior could be characterized as impulsive, repetitive, and disoriented in space; it seemed to lag in age-adequate reality testing. In pursuing a goal in space, he seemed to overlook obstacles that lay between his body and the point of destination he had set himself to reach—he bumped into them.

Examinations ruled out any neurological disturbance—a question which, of course, concerned us all along. Dr. Sally Provence, who examined and tested Jay, felt, as did *we*, that Jay was basically a well-endowed child whose intellectual development was being impaired by his psychological problems.

One of the crucial findings, if not *the main yield* of our study, concerns the *time lag that exists in normal intrapsychic development—between object permanency (in Piaget's sense) and the attainment of libidinal object constancy*, in Hartmann's sense (see Mahler and McDevitt, 1968). Attainment of *libidinal object constancy* is much more gradual than the achievement of object permanency—and, at the beginning at least, it is a faculty that is waxing and waning and rather "impermanent." Up to about thirty months, it is very much at the mercy of the toddler's own mood swings and "ego states" and dependent on the actual mother-toddler situation of the moment.

In Jay's case it seemed there was by far too little *neutralized* cathexis available by the end of the fourth subphase of individuation—the subphase of the gradual attainment of *libidinal object constancy*.

To repeat: during the second half of the second year of life the infant has become more and more aware of his physical separateness. Along with this awareness, the relative obliviousness to his mother's presence, which prevailed during the practicing period, wanes (Mahler, 1963).

Instead, the toddler of sixteen to eighteen months may appear suddenly and quite conspicuously surprised by situations—for example, when he hurts himself—in which mother is not automatically at hand to prevent such an occurrence.

The previous relative obliviousness to mother's presence is gradually replaced by active approach behavior on a much higher level. As he realizes his power and ability to physically move away from his mother, the toddler now seems to have an increased need, and a wish, for his mother to *share* with him every new acquisition of skill and experience. We may call this subphase of separation-individuation, therefore, the period of *rapprochement* (Mahler, 1963, 1965b).

Jay's primary identity formation by thirty months of age showed, as if in a distorted mirror, the mother's unintegrated maternal attitudes, her schizoid personality traits.

The mother's perplexity seems to have been triggered by Jay's purely maturational spurt, in the physical sense, away from her. The mother was able to respond positively to Jay only when he went directly to her. But toddlers, especially in the period of rapprochement, do not run to their mothers to be hugged or picked up—they approach the mother on a higher emotional level by bringing things to her, making contact by gestures and words! Jay usually played at some distance from his mother, but would occasionally glance in her direction. Proximal contact between the two was quite infrequent. When it did occur, it was either that the mother went to Jay with an offer to read to him; or Jay, in turn, approached his mother with a book in his hand, which she would then read to him.

Thus, we could see Jay picking up, for example, this one cue—echoing and magnifying the mother's wish, which we knew from our intimate knowledge of the mother—that he be an "outstanding intellectual." One could almost predict one of the fateful variations of the *leitmotif* (Lichtenstein, 1961) that is so frequently conveyed to the children of our time, and which Helen Tartakoff (1966) has dealt with in her paper: "The Normal Personality in Our Culture and the Nobel Prize Complex."

Already at the age of two, Jay had had great pleasure in the use of words. For a while, this acquisition of language had made for better communication between Jay and his mother. Yet, by the end of his third and *the beginning of his fourth year*, it became more and more apparent that there was a serious discrepancy in Jay's "lines of development" in Anna Freud's sense (1965)—both as to their rate of growth and as to their quality. Thus there ensued a serious deficit in the integrative and synthetic functions of Jay's ego. By that time, the counterphobic mechanism (which we saw in Jay's second year)—the impulse-ridden discharge behavior—had given way to phobic avoidance mechanisms.

The point that I wish to make calls for conceptualization of certain elements of Jay's faulty individuation. The crucial deficiency was, we felt, Jay's disturbed body image, which robbed him of the core of primary identity formation, and thus of a reliably cathected self-feeling invested with neutralized energy. Furthermore, because the polarizing function of the symbiotic dual unity of this mother-child pair failed the individuating toddler, there was an obvious lack of a frame of reference for perceiving the extrasymbiotic external reality. In consequence, the intrapsychic representational world contained no clear boundaries between self and object—the boundaries between ego and id remained deficient and so did the boundaries and connections between the intersystemic parts of the ego. Thus, one might say, symbiotic confusion has been perpetuated. Two conspicuous behavioral signs were Jay's handling of his body in space and the disturbance he displayed, in words and actions, in projecting experiences in the dimension of time.

When Jay graduated from our study to nursery school, we predicted that he would attain a borderline adjustment with schizoid features—unless corrective emotional therapy in Alpert's (1959) sense could be instituted. We felt that he had no solid footing in the formation of his core identity; nor were the boundaries—between id and ego, between self and object world—structured firmly enough and sufficiently cathected with neutralized energy. Furthermore, there was not enough neutralized energy available for ego development—thus the establishment of libidinal object constancy was also questionable. The possibility of secondary identity formation, by true ego identifications and internalization, was greatly reduced.

In Volume II I shall elaborate on the findings from our follow-ups, which were done several times—until Jay was seven years old—and which validated our predictions. Our prediction *now* is that Jay will be compelled to develop as an adolescent and as an adult—as he has already started to do, at age seven—"as if" mechanisms, in order to be able to function with his "false self" in his social environment. Suffice it to say that Jay reminded me of several patients in analysis whose central problem was their incessant search for their place in life—their search for an identity (Ross, 1967).

He reminded me especially of one analytic patient, whom I had treated as a child abroad and in his adolescence in this country. Charlie's developmental history I could reconstruct with fair accuracy—through the material that his intermittent analyses have yielded, and with the aid of my intimate knowledge of his parents' personality.

I could reconstruct a very long symbiotic-parasitic phase with a narcissistic mother, who was highly seductive yet could accept Charlie only if she could regard him as a continuation of her own narcissistic self. She had no regard for the little boy as an individual in his own right. She constantly needed babies to cuddle and bore infants up to her climacterium.

After the symbiotic-parasitic relationship, the mother suddenly abandoned Charlie to his own devices, at the beginning of the third year. Subsequently, Charlie developed a strong mirroring identification with his father. The latter, however, suffered from a paralyzing depression, and went into seclusion when Charlie was three years old. This coincided with the time when the mother gave birth to one of her many babies. Thus, *both* primary love objects were unavailable to Charlie for object cathexis and for true ego identification, in the fateful second eighteen months of life.

Charlie never achieved libidinal object constancy. Instead, his identification with his mother was a total one—so much so that, when his mother, while taking him by car to the kindergarten, accidentally hit a man, Charlie behaved as if *he* was the one who had *deliberately* hurt the man. He refused to go on to school: he was afraid that the police would arrest *him*. From then on, he insisted on wearing dark glasses—to hide behind. He became intolerably destructive, and attacked his mother by throwing objects at her—obviously aiming at her eyes. At the same time, he developed a phobia of fire and a fear of going blind.

His symptoms were understood, in the course of his first analysis in Europe, as an attempt to re-externalize—to eject —the dangerous maternal introject. In view of the unavailability of the father figure, however, this left Charlie utterly depleted of object cathexis.

Between his child analysis and his early adolescence, I lost sight of Charlie for quite a while as he and his family continued to live abroad.

Charles was sixteen years old when his analysis was resumed, here in the States. During the interval he appeared to have undergone a profound personality change. The maturational and developmental process had transformed the exuberant, aggressive, and irrepressible Charlie of the prelatency and early latency period into a subdued, overcompliant, utterly passive, and submissive youngster with a well-hidden cruel streak, which he tried strenuously to conceal even from himself.

He had a lofty—and not internalized—ego ideal, and imitated his father, parroting his sayings. Even though he seemed to try ever so hard to extricate himself from the actual influence of his mother, his analytic material revealed that he was forever searching for the "good" need-satisfying mother of his symbiotic phase. Yet, at the same time, he dreaded re-engulfment in symbiosis. As soon as he found an object, he arranged somehow to lose her, out of fear that

she would engulf him and that he would thus *"lose himself."*
This was the same mechanism, I believe, with which he had
so strikingly fought to eject the maternal introject at the age
of five and six.

For lack of true identity formation through ego identifications, Charles seemed to be compelled to search for his
identity—to fill the painful void, the inner emptiness, about
which he continually complained.

He set himself the goal—as several of these borderline
cases do, either covertly or overtly—of becoming famous, or
at least important. His quite good performance, however,
measured up very unfavorably against his lofty ego ideal,
with the result that Charles was left with an excruciatingly
low self-esteem. For this discrepancy, Charles blamed his
mother because she was the one who had made him believe—
in his early childhood—that he was "a genius."

In adolescence, then, Charles displayed a peculiarly affect-
less state. He lacked the charm that Helene Deutsch (1942)
and others have found to be one of the characteristics of true
"as if" personalities (Ross, 1967).

He repeatedly changed his allegiance to people and to
groups, because he never did feel comfortable when he came
close to them—*he could only long for them from a distance.*
This intense longing was the strongest affect I have ever seen
in Charles.

Like Greenson's (1958) patient, Charles was continually
seeking the company of others; he was quite incapable of
being alone. *But he was also incapable of being "à deux" for
any length of time!* What Charles kept seeking were experiences that would reunite him with the lost symbiotic mother
whom he had never renounced—in the intrapsychic sense.
His affectlessness seemed to be a deep defense against his
anxiety—to ward off the feeling of emptiness at the loss of a
part of himself, at a time when the loss of the symbiotic
mother was still equivalent to losing part of the self!

During his analysis in adolescence Charles once complained: "I don't feel like anything—I start thinking a lot; and when I think, I am not very happy." At another time, he said: "I try to find out in how many ways we are alike with any person—anybody—but particularly with people I like and respect. First I did this with my parents, with their older friends, and now I do it usually with girls. I try to find out what kind of sports and songs they like."

Charles tried to compensate for the cathectic void by identification of the mirroring type. By literally mirroring others, and also himself, he tried to learn how to feel, how to have emotions. Here are some of the associations he made in analysis: "When I dance with a girl, she becomes just like all the other girls. I want to refresh myself that *she is the one who dances with me, and yet that she is still kind and sweet.* I put my head back to look at her face, and into her eyes." In another analytic hour Charles said: "I dance around by the mirrorglass door where I can look at my own face—see what I look like, *from the point of view of others;* and also I catch a glimpse of her face, to see whether she is enjoying the dance. One thing I notice—even if I enjoy dancing, I don't look too excited, so one cannot say whether I enjoy it. So perhaps this is not the way to find out about how the girl feels either."

This brief excerpt from Charles's analysis shows how he struggled with his lack of empathy and his lack of genuine affect. One can also see that he is searching incessantly for the girl who is still *kind* and *sweet*—the "good" symbiotic mother—whom he can reflect and whose eyes reflect love for him.

SUMMARY

I have brought these clinical sketches of Jay and Charles, because these patients illustrate—through their developmental failure—the significance of normal symbiosis, and the crucial necessity of gradual individuation—particularly in the vulnerable second and third years of life.

In Jay's case we observed this developmental failure *in statu nascendi*. His traumatization occurred in the second year, and, as a result, *both* his reality constancy (Frosch, 1966) and his object constancy suffered.

In Charles's case, we could fairly accurately reconstruct— through analytic material—the severe traumata, at vulnerable, nodal points of his separation-individuation process, particularly toward the end of it, when libidinal object constancy becomes established.

The fact that this traumatization occurred later than Jay's —in Charles's third year—is perhaps the reason why Charles's reality constancy remained fairly intact.

Both cases had to fall back to the primary mode—the "mirroring" kind of maintenance of identity—because of the failure of true identificatory and internalization processes.

CHAPTER II

The Symbiosis Theory of Infantile Psychosis

THE CORE PROBLEM OF INFANTILE PSYCHOSIS

As I have elaborated in the previous chapter, perception of the "good" part-object's ministrations as "reliably" satisfying an internally arising need hunger (need tension) paves the way for the human infant's sociobiological state of symbiosis with the mother.

This phase of extrauterine evolution, the symbiotic relationship, is either gravely distorted or missing in infantile psychosis, and it is this that represents, to my way of understanding it, the core disturbance in infantile as well as adolescent and adult psychosis.

The core disturbance in infantile psychosis is therefore, as I see it, a deficiency or a defect in the child's intrapsychic utilization of the mothering partner during the symbiotic phase, and his subsequent inability to internalize the representation of the mothering object for polarization. Without this, differentiation of the self from symbiotic fusion and confusion with the part object does not occur. In short, faulty or absent individuation lies at the core of infantile psychosis.

In other words: the psychotic infant seems to lack or fails to acquire in earliest extrauterine life the capacity to perceive and thus to use the mothering agent for maintenance of his homeostasis; nor can he later release her.

Many workers will argue that the core deficiency in infantile psychosis consists simply of a sensoriperceptual deficiency. This assertion, I feel, does not pinpoint anywhere nearly accurately enough the specifically human deficiency in the prepsychotic infant (the newborn who is destined to be or become psychotic).

For a fuller understanding of my main hypothesis, the symbiosis theory of psychosis, I must describe the deviational development of the prepsychotic infant in the context and against the background of individuation in the normal infant (that is to say, I must in part repeat my description of normal development, in order to highlight the deviations in psychosis) (cf. Fish, 1960).

The Deficiency of Mutual Cuing between Infant and Mother in the Symbiotic Phase

It seems that psychosis is the sad prerogative of the human species. (Not so long ago psychiatrists believed that it was confined to adults alone.) Animals are born with well-developed instincts, which guarantee their independent individual survival not long after birth. In the human young, however, these animal instincts (in terms of "sense of track") have atrophied and become unreliable and, as Freud (1923) has stated, the ego must take over the role of adaptation to reality that the id neglects. The somatic corollary of ego development is the central nervous system, which is in a very immature state at birth. The neonate appears to be an almost purely biological organism, whose instinctual responses to stimuli are not on a cortical but essentially on a reflex and thalamic level. There exist only somatic defense mechanisms, i.e., overflow and discharge reactions; cortical inhibition is undeveloped. Thus we may say that at birth there exists only a rudimentary ego, incapable of retaining stimuli in any degree of tension; or, to put it another way, the undifferentiated phase of personality development persists for a comparatively long period of extrauterine existence (Hartmann, Kris, Loewenstein, 1946).

Yet the psychobiological rapport between the nursing mother and the baby complements the infant's undifferentiated ego. This normal empathy on the part of the mother is the human substitute for those instincts on which the animal is able to rely for survival. In a quasi-closed system or unit, the mother executes vitally important ministrations, without which the human young could not survive. The intrauterine, parasite-host relationship within the mother organism (H. Deutsch, 1945) must be replaced in the postnatal period by the infant's being enveloped, as it were, in the extrauterine matrix of the mother's nursing care, a kind of *social symbiosis*.

As early as the first day of extrauterine life the full-term neonate displays a discriminatory grasping reflex (Stirnimann, 1947), which proves that he has a significant innate endowment for distinguishing in a sensorimotor way between the living part object and lifeless matter. This primal ability to discriminate between animate and inanimate was given the name *Urunterscheidung: protodiakrisis* by von Monakow (1923). Furthermore, most babies are born with an appropriate signal equipment for dealing with instinctual tensions when these mount beyond a tolerable degree. Their affectomotor reactions serve automatically to summon and use the mother as their external executive ego (Spitz). The mutual cuing between infant and mother is the most important requisite for normal symbiosis, and in normal circumstances it develops into mutual verbal communication.

The presymbiotic, normal-autistic phase of the mother-infant unity gives way to the symbiotic phase proper (from the second month on). During his wakeful hungry periods of the day, the two- to four-month-old baby seems to perceive, temporarily at least, and in a Gestalt kind of perception, that small part of external reality that is represented by the mother's breast, face, and hands, the Gestalt of her ministrations as such. This occurs within the matrix of the oral gratification-frustration sequences of the normal nursing situation. This dim awareness of the "need-satisfying object" marks the beginning of the *phase of symbiosis*, in which the infant behaves and functions as though he and his mother were an omnipotent system (a dual unity) within one common boundary (a symbiotic membrane, as it were). The symbiotic phase is followed by the so-called separation-individuation phase proper, which occurs parallel with the maturation and consolidation of autonomous ego functions.

The Ego Deficiencies in Infantile Psychosis and the Distortion of the Sense of Identity

All psychoanalytically oriented authors writing on childhood schizophrenia have emphasized the ego defects characteristic of psychotic children. Whether these or what I have called the "core deficiency" are primary is a moot question, as is the issue of hereditary vs. experiential (as will be demonstrated below). The salient feature in childhood psychosis is that individuation, i.e., a sense of individual identity, is not achieved. Identity formation presupposes structuralization of the ego and neutralization of the drives. These in turn have two prerequisites: (i) the enteroceptive-proprioceptive stimuli must not be so overwhelming as to prevent formation of structure; (ii) in the absence of an "inner organizer" in the human infant (Spitz, 1959), the symbiotic partner must be able to serve as a buffer against inner and outer stimuli, gradually organizing them for the infant and orienting him to inner vs. outer world—that is, to boundary formation and sensory perception. Freud (1923) emphasized that "For the ego, perception plays the part which in the id falls to instinct" (p. 25). Hartmann has pointed out that formation of structure and neutralization of drives constitute a circular process: structure is formed by perceptual turning toward the outside world, and vice versa. If the two afore-mentioned conditions are not met, the ego's perceptual fac-ulty cannot gain ascendancy, nor can the ego's integrative and synthetic function develop (Hartmann, 1953; Hartmann, Kris, Loewenstein, 1946).

THE BODY EGO

The beginning of the sense of individual identity and sep-aration from the object is mediated by our bodily sensations. Its core is the body image, which consists of a fairly stabilized and predominantly libidinal cathexis of the body in its cen-tral and peripheral parts (Greenacre, 1953).

Proprioceptive inner stimuli as well as contact perceptions, deep pressure sensitivity and thermal interchange, in addi-tion to kinesthetic experiences (equilibrium) in the nursing situation—these contribute much more importantly and im-mediately to the body image than do the later maturing distance-perceptive visual and auditory images. The latter contribute primarily and most importantly to the recognition of and the distinction from the object world. Integration of our bodily feelings and unconscious fantasies about the body self, especially its contents, with visual, auditory, and kin-esthetic data about it, is a relatively late accomplishment of the ego. This coincides with the first level of integration of the sense of identity, which is one product of the ongoing separation-individuation process (A. Freud, 1952a).

THE BODY IMAGE AND PERCEPTION

The steps leading to individuation are mediated by per-ceptual processes, engaged in the search for the need-satisfy-ing object, which is strongly cathected with libidinal energy. We may use Freud's simile of the pseudopodi of the amoeba and say that: the "self" extends toward the object, takes it into its own orbit, assimilates (introjects) part of it, only to retract from it temporarily. It re-externalizes the object representation to which certain traits of the self representation have been attached. The formation of primitive, previsual engrams is mediated through *contact impressions* via the mother. Perception of inner processes, for instance, those linked with feeding, contact reception, complemented later by distance perception, form the basis of the mental representations of the body as *body image*. All this constitutes *the core* of the idea of *I*, the center around which memory traces, feelings and ideas about the self become crystallized, structured, and organized. These are gradually distinguished from the intrapsychic representations of the object world (Jacobson, 1954).

The fact that we ordinarily do not think about our self identity indicates that there is a balanced synthesis between the central images of the self, the boundaries of the body self, the self representations, and the object representations—the latter two clearly demarcated from each other. A comparison from the organic field seems appropriate here: under normal conditions we neither feel nor watch the tonus or the functioning of parts of our musculature; only if we are tense, anxious, or tremulous do we observe changes in innervation in our muscles. The normal muscle tonus is maintained by the balanced interaction of agonist and antagonist muscles. In the same way, we can visualize the normal state of *entity* and *identity* to be maintained by the cohesive cathexis which results from *centripetal* and *centrifugal* processes of silent cathectic and countercathectic processes.

My thesis is that serious disturbances of a permanent as well as of a transitory nature of the sense of identity are due to massive cathectic changes of this intricate regulatory process. Under certain circumstances, at particular crossroads of self-differentiation, cathectic shifts of such magnitude take place that the contributions to and hence our feeling of identity may become dissociated (Mahler, 1960). There may be narcissistic withdrawal, a massive shift of libido from object representations to self representations only; or there may be depletion of the neutralized cathexis of object and self representations in favor of body-organ cathexis (as in "psychosomatic" organ neurosis); or there may be massive cathectic redistribution of unneutralized energy onto the representation of the sexual part of the self image; there may be grave, premature overstimulation leading to polymorph-perverse symptomatology as in the cases of fetishism described by Greenacre (1953), but with more severe splitting of the self representations. Defusion of instincts always seems to generate surplus unneutralized aggression.

Studies in child psychosis bear out Bak's (1954) assumption that the schizophrenic process may be due to physiological changes in terms of "aggressivizations" occurring in the body image, which in turn may stem from an unsatisfactory early mother-infant relation and result in a "brittleness" of the ego. The centrifugal momentum of primitive aggressive discharges (compare Hoffer, 1949, 1950a) is in the presymbiotic and symbiotic phases mitigated by the libidinal aspects of centripetal countercathexis, the pleasurable contact perceptions through the mother's nursing care. Contact perceptions include warmth, turgor, smooth tactile impressions, light pressure sensations, smell, and gustatory impressions. If the perceptual faculty of the ego has, for intrinsic or extrinsic reasons (e.g., because severe sickness generated an excess of enteroceptive-proprioceptive stimulation during the early months of life) not gained ascendancy, then structuralization of the ego suffers greatly from the disruptive and disorganizing surplus centrifugal force of unneutralized aggression. In the process of centripetal perceptual structuralization it would seem important that the aforementioned contact perceptions within the symbiotic orbit should not augment the relative traumata of external stimulation but be allowed to become integrated with distance perceptions. In other words, contact impressions must not crowd out, stifle, or delay the distance-receptive perceptions; on the other hand, if they are too vague and deficient, they lack the force to secure a stable body image.

—We conceive of the sense of self-identity as arising from alternation of two kinds of experience, namely, pleasurable bodily contact with the nursing mother and pleasurable hallucinatory reunion with her during sleep, alternating with interpolated periods of wakefulness. During the gradually prolonged periods of wakefulness, there probably occur libidinization of the body surface and all those transitory phenomena which form the perceptual ideational borderland between the self and the object world (Winnicott, 1953a). The distance receptors play a comparatively minor role, it seems, in bodily self-finding, whereas they play a great role in "object finding."

The young infant is the almost completely passive recipient of the intensive stimuli impinging upon his organism. These stimuli are potentially traumatic in view of his hitherto sheltered intrauterine existence. In the first few weeks there is a relative stimulus barrier (*Reizschutz*) in that the perceptual conscious system, "the sensorium," is not yet cathected (Benjamin, 1961). The stimuli of the infant's internal physiological processes are potentially traumatic, particularly in the absence of an "inner organizer."

Hartmann (1952) emphasized the body's "double position": it is "part of the inner and also of the outer world" (p. 166; see also Hartmann, Kris, Loewenstein, 1946). By virtue of this characteristic, it stands out for the infant from the rest of the world and thereby enables him to work out the distinction between self and nonself. The sum of representations of his own body and its organs which this process of distinction yields to him, his "body image," is of fundamental importance for the further development of his ego. It does not coincide with the objective body, since, for instance, clothing and amputated limbs may be included in it (compare Mahler and Silberpfennig, 1938).[1]

Important aspects of the perceptual-emotional development and the differentiation of the body ego in the first eighteen months of life were described by Willi Hoffer (1949, 1950b) and by Winnicott (1965). Whereas the former described steps in the development of the body ego, the latter has examined the role which the first inanimate object— as he calls it, the "not-me object," the "first possession"—and other transitional objects and phenomena play in the development of individual identity. According to Winnicott (1953b) it is the inanimate first "not-me possession" which the baby can mouth and handle at will, which via oral and tactile contact-perceptive and kinesthetic as well as distance-perceptive experiences, helps to convey the three kinds of experiences forming representations of the (1) "I," (2) the libidinal object, and (3) the rest of the outside animate, semianimate and inanimate reality. On the basis of body-ego

---

[1] Hartmann and Schilder (1927) found that "Sensations, the subjective experiencing of our body, do not derive as such from or of the surface of the body. They derive from zones *near* the surface of our body, about 1/5 to 4/5 of an inch deeper than the surface. Also, the orifices of the body are located subjectively *under* the surface. Our *immediate* experience about the inside of our bodies contains nothing about organs. We perceive merely a heavy mass. We have only a sense of gravity as far as the parts of the body are concerned. To these gravity sensations are added bodily sensations around the orifices or zones." Schilder and Wechsler (1935) studied "What Do Children Know about the Interior of the Body?" Though their sampling of children is not large and representative enough, it seems to bear out the following: the normal child seems to pay little attention to the inside of his body. We all turn our attention toward the periphery of our bodies. For children from four to ten there exists inside the body only what one puts into the quasi-hollow organ: the body. It is interesting to note that some older children, however, when asked what there is under their skins and inside their bodies, said: "I, myself!" Schilder and Wechsler remark: "it is one of the paradoxes of our bodily experience that our sensations relate to the surface of the body, and yet we do not regard this [the actual surface] as our body proper. The skin can be removed. . . . We are inside our skins and know nothing directly of the interior of our bodies." As far as integrated body feelings go, the skin "is merely the envelope of our true self and of what is inside us. But in the deep, infantile strata of our minds we are not perfectly certain whether there *is* anything inside us except what is crammed into us from outside."

differentiation in the first year of life, the feeling of separateness from the object, of the object's separateness from the "I," receives a strong maturational spurt with the functioning, the coming-of-age of locomotion, as will be shown below. After quasi-bodily experimentation (from the end of the first year), firmer cathexis and thus differentiation of the boundaries of the body self seem to occur. It is the time when, after the normal shifts of cathectic distribution from the inside of the body (the viscera) in favor of the periphery of the body image, particularly the libidinal zones, clearer intrapsychic representations of the "I" begin to form. A crucial factor in this development is played by locomotion.

THE MATURATIONAL ACHIEVEMENT OF LOCOMOTION

Locomotion enables the child to separate, physically to move away from the mother, when emotionally he may be quite unprepared to do so. The two-year-old child very soon experiences his separateness in many other ways. He enjoys his independence and exercises mastery with great tenacity, and thus large quantities of libido and aggression are utilized by the ego. On the other hand, there are junior toddlers who show adverse reactions and increased clinging to the mother in reaction to their own autonomy. The awareness of separate functioning may elicit intense anxiety in these vulnerable toddlers; they try desperately to deny the fact of separateness, and at the same time struggle against re-engulfment by increased opposition to the adult partner.[2]

Experimental and academic psychologists also found the phase of individuation in which the child develops "self-awareness" an uneasy period in his life. Wallon and his pupil, Zazzo (1953), have studied the young child's recognition of his own image in three different situations: in the mirror,

[2] Ekstein (1954, 1955) and Ekstein and Wallerstein (1954, 1956) have described similar mechanisms, the "distancing" in space, against the dread of re-engulfment.

on photos, and in films (p. 174f.). They found that recognition of the mirror image does not occur until two years and two or three months.[3] A few weeks before this occurs the observers noticed "a kind of disorganization as if a sudden state of awareness of self had caused an affective upset" (Zazzo, 1953). Up to the end of the third year the child displays a certain fearfulness and at the same time a certain pleasure in looking at himself in the mirror. At about two years and ten months the image has become familiar and no longer causes uneasiness. It is at the same time, that is, two years and ten months to three years of age, that the personal pronoun "I" begins to be used without hesitation and grammatically.

The normal negativistic phase of the toddler is the accompanying behavioral reaction of this process of individuation or disengagement from the mother-child symbiosis. The fear of re-engulfment threatens a recently and barely started individual differentiation which must be defended. The less satisfactory or the more parasitic the symbiotic phase has been, the more prominent and exaggerated will be this negativistic reaction (A. Freud, 1952a; Loewald, 1951; Mahler and Gosliner, 1955). An ego which is unable to function separately from the symbiotic partner tries to re-entrench itself in the delusional fantasy of oneness with the omnipotent mother, by coercing her into functioning as an extension of the self. Of course, this device usually fails to halt the process of alienation from reality (a reality still represented almost exclusively by the mother).

[3] There seem, however, to be some exceptions to the rule of timing of this self-identity recognition. Such an exception (premature recognition) was observed in the case of a monozygotic twin (Mahler and Silberpfennig, 1938).

Experiments and observations of John McDevitt seem to indicate much earlier intermittent awareness of visual and Gestalt-wise recognition of the self (body) image. This seems to develop in a gradual way; the waning and waxing quality of the awareness finally disappears.

THE CRUCIAL IMPORTANCE OF "MOTHERING" AND OF PERCEIVING THE "MOTHERING PRINCIPLE" AS GOOD

We wish to use the term "mothering principle," or "mothering agent," to stand for the perception of, and seeming acceptance of, the relieving ministrations coming from the human partner which, though vague and unspecific, are pleasurable need satisfactions from the mother (or the therapist). The first step in development from the autistic to the symbiotic phase (and in treatment, the improvement of a child with a predominantly autistic syndrome to symbiosis) is the cathexis of the "mothering principle." It should be remembered that with this development, there does not yet occur the differentiation of the maternal object as a separate mental representation from the self; it does occur much later when the separation-individuation process is much further advanced.

From the point of view of the instinctual drives and the formation of psychic structure, we may describe the newborn's waking life as centering around his attempts to reduce tension. To ameliorate his unpleasure, the infant has two avenues: his own body (Hoffer, 1949) and his mother's ministrations. The effect of his mother's breast and her ministrations in reducing the pangs of need hunger cannot be isolated, nor can it be differentiated by the young infant from tension-reducing attempts of his own, such as urinating, coughing, sneezing, spitting, regurgitating, vomiting, and all the different ways by which the infant tries to rid himself of unpleasurable tension. The consequences of these expulsive phenomena, as well as the gratification gained by his mother's ministrations, help the infant, in time, to differentiate between a pleasurable or good quality and a painful or bad quality of experiences.

When the mother is a source of satisfaction, the infant

responds positively to her, as may be observed in the tension reduction that is manifested in quiescence and sleep. When body tension or mothering manipulations are a source of pain and unpleasure, the infant deals with them as he deals with noxious stimuli in general: he draws away from them, tries to expel them, to eliminate them. In other words, the infant's first orientation in his extrauterine life is according to "good-pleasurable" vs. "bad-painful" stimuli. Since hunger is the infant's most imperative biological need, these qualities of "good" and "bad" seem to become equated with "edible" and "inedible" substances.

Through the inborn and autonomous perceptive faculty of the primitive ego (Hartmann, 1939), deposits of memory traces of the two primordial qualities of stimuli occur. We might visualize these scattered foci of memory deposits as forming little islands within the hitherto "oceanic feeling" of complete fusion and oneness with the mother, in the infant's semiconscious state. These memory islands, which contain imprints of "pleasurable-good" or "painful-bad" stimuli, are not yet allocated either to the self or to the nonself. We further may assume that these primitive memory deposits are cathected with that primordial undifferentiated drive energy that Fenichel (1945) and Edith Jacobson (1954) have described.

The young infant is exposed to one rhythmically and consistently repeated experience, namely, that hunger and other need tensions that arise inside the body cannot be relieved, beyond a certain degree, unless relief is supplied from a source outside of his own orbit. This repeated experience of a need-satisfying good outside source that relieves him of a bad inside tension eventually conveys to him a vague affective discrimination between "self" and "nonself." It is at this point of differentiation that the predominantly "good" and predominantly "bad" memory islands become vaguely allocated to the self and the nonself. The qualities of "pleasure-giving" or "pain-inflicting" become anchored to the mother, but also to these primitive memory islands which were formed through "pleasurable" and "unpleasurable" sensations from within his own body. This seemed to be the beginning of the formation of scattered part images of the object and part images of the body self as well (Jacobson, 1954). I wish to emphasize that the self images are endowed with the same qualities of prevailingly "good" and predominantly "bad" as are the scattered part images of the mother (cf. Hendrick, 1951a).

I would propose that out of the primordial undifferentiated drive energy, libido and aggression become differentiated *pari passu* with the infant's primitive reality orientation, and in accordance with the above-described differentiation of the "good" and "bad" scattered part images of mother and self. "The mother in the flesh," as Bowlby (1951) calls the real mother, is both a source of pleasure and a source of unpleasure, just as the infant's own body is. To "bad" stimuli coming from inside or outside, the infant reacts with impetuous aggressions, by ridding and ejective mechanisms; to "good" stimuli coming from inside or outside, the baby reacts with quiet bliss and, later on, with reaching out. Both pleasure and unpleasure manifestations, however, are overshadowed by the still undifferentiated and unneutralized impetuous drive of aggressive and indiscriminate incorporation of good and bad, which reaches its peak at the period of oral aggression.

The infant has the tendency to suck in, to mouth, to incorporate, to devour, as much of the outside object as possible. His expulsive, ejective, ridding tendencies alternate with this tendency to engulf.

The generally accepted psychoanalytic hypothesis that the infant relegates unpleasurable feelings to the nonself, to the outside world, is difficult to demonstrate. Negative hallucination in the infant is even more difficult to observe than is its positive forerunner. What we can observe are the two distinct groups of phenomena just described. The infant tries to expel, to sever from his own body orbit, all painful stimulation, irrespective of whether it has originated from the outside or from the inside. Second, we can also observe, particularly from five to six months on, an indiscriminate incorporative tendency which is familiar to all of us. In both observable groups of phenomena, the surplus of unneutralized aggression as against libido seems evident.

Hoffer (1950b) drew attention to the fact that deflection of surplus unneutralized aggression from the body ego is of utmost importance for normal body ego development.

Libidinal cathexis, on the other hand, should gradually shift from the visceral, particularly abdominal, organs in a cranial and peripheral direction (Ribble, 1941; Greenacre, 1945; Mahler, 1952). With the libidinal shift of cathexis to the sensoriperceptive system, great progress is achieved, and clearer demarcation of the infant's own body from that of the mother thus evolves.

We may assume that confluence and primitive integration of the scattered "good" and "bad" memory islands into two large, "good" and "bad" part images of the self, as well as split "good" and "bad" part images of the mother, do not occur before the second year of life. This is attested to by the normal emotional ambivalence (and behavioral ambitendency) that is clinically discernible at this age.

Only now, from twelve to eighteen months on, during the process of separation-individuation, are the rapidly alternating primitive identification mechanisms possible and dominant. We owe their description to Melanie Klein (1932).

In the further course of normal development there is unification of the split images of objects and of the self, and a unified object representation becomes demarcated from a unified self representation.

Solid integration, in which there is a blending and synthesis of "good" and "bad" mother images, even in normal development, is not achieved during the symbiotic phase of the mother-child relationship, nor is it completed during the next eighteen-month period of life, the separation-individuation phase. If the symbiotic and the separation-individuation phases are normal, however, from three or three and a half years on, the child is increasingly able to respond to the "whole mother," to realize that one and the same person can both gratify and disturb him. With the advent of the latency period the child should clearly perceive and recognize not only that mother is separate and complex, but that other important love objects and he himself are separate and complex as well. He should begin to be able to modulate feelings within himself, appraise "good" and "bad" by "trial acting" (i.e., thinking). In brief, he should go through the process of establishing object constancy and increasingly accept the reality principle.

Freud (1924a, 1924b) considered the ego's alienation from reality to be the pivotal disturbance in adult and adolescent psychosis. In transposing this idea to infantile psychosis, one has to stress the fact that the infant has to *become acquainted* with reality, very gradually, via the mother.

As elaborated earlier, the infant's reality, his acquaintance with the world, comes about through his discovery during the symbiotic dual-unity stage that his needs derive satisfaction from his symbiotic partner outside his "self." Therefore, the psychotic child, in the light of his core deficiency, namely, his inability to use the mother to arrive at even the most primitive sense of reality, i.e., the sense of her as a need-satisfying object, cannot be thought of as having *become* alienated from reality. The fact is that he never attained a solid sense of external reality.

THE CONSTITUTIONAL (NATURE) VERSUS EXPERIENTIAL (NURTURE) CAUSATION (ETIOLOGY) CONTROVERSY

From the preceding pages, it must be abundantly clear that I regard the issue of nature-nurture a moot one. Looking at autistic and symbiotic psychotic children, one cannot help but feel that the primary etiology of psychosis in children, the psychotic child's primary defect in being able to utilize (to perceive) the catalyzing mothering agent for homeostasis, is inborn, constitutional, and probably hereditary, or else acquired very early in the very first days or weeks of extrauterine life. In other words, there seems to be a predispositional deficiency (N. D. C. Lewis).

My own observations do not bear out the theories that implicate exclusively or even mainly the "schizophrenogenic" mother. I believe it is more useful to approach this problem in terms of a complementary series *(Ergänzungsreihe):* (a) If, during the most vulnerable autistic and symbiotic phase, very severe, accumulated, and staggering traumatization occurs in a constitutionally fairly sturdy infant, psychosis may ensue, and the human object in the external world loses her catalyzing, buffering, and polarizing capacity for the infant's intrapsychic evolution and "hatching." (b) On the other hand, in constitutionally greatly predisposed oversensitive or vulnerable infants, normal mothering does not suffice to counteract the innate defect in the catalytic, buffering, and polarizing utilization of the human love object or mothering agency in the outside world for intrapsychic evolution and differentiation.

In my opinion, this whole complex issue gains in clarity if we compare the nature of the tie to the mother in different types of children: the normal, the neurotic, the impulse-ridden, the moderately organically brain-damaged, the severely emotionally or physically deprived children, and the group of psychotic children.

Here I shall single out only a few categories, namely, the anaclitically depressed children, institutionalized infants, and children brought up in a concentration camp or in constantly changing foster homes. I do this because these children have one factor in common—that is, object loss in *reality.* If the infants who suffered actual object loss are juxtaposed with the psychotic children, the nature of "object loss" in psychosis will become apparent.

Provence and Lipton (1962) have established that all primitive faculties showed up at a predetermined point (even if they were delayed) in those mother-deprived infants in institutions. These faculties appeared in accordance with the *inherent maturational timetable,* and were to a great extent independent of environmental factors. On the other hand, however, very shortly after they appeared, these faculties "withered on the vine," as the authors described it, because they did not receive what Piaget calls "nutrients," that is to say, stimulation by the human object. Even though the emotional development of these institutionalized infants seemed to lag far behind as early as the second half of the first year, they seemed to have the innate (inborn) endowment to extract every drop of human nutrient, every bit of stimulation available.

I have stated repeatedly that in the nonpsychotic normal infant the libidinal availability of the mother (or a mother substitute), because of the emotional dependence of the child, facilitates the optimal unfolding of innate potentialities. In the average infant with the average expectable environment—that is to say, with an "ordinary devoted mother" being available—the rich abundance of developmental energy, particularly during the individuation process, accounts for the regeneration of developmental potentialities to an extent never seen in any other period of life (except perhaps in adolescence).

We know from Spitz's investigations (1945b, 1946a, 1946b), for example, that his anaclitically depressed infants, who suffered loss of the (symbiotic) love object in the second half of the first year, did attempt to regain the lost object world, which in infancy involves finding a substitute object. On the other hand, when the symbiotic object was not restored, and when no substitute mothers were available, the anaclitically depressed infants succumbed to inanition and literally died as a result of the symbiotic object loss. Yet, in those cases in which the mother *was* restored to the anaclitically depressed baby, and when this occurred within a reasonable period of time (after separation), before the infants' vulnerable ego had suffered irreversible damage, *the infants did recover.*

One is amazed at the normal infant's striking power of recovery. One is equally impressed by the institutional infant's inborn endowment to extract every drop of human stimulus, of environmental nutrient, every bit of human contact available.

The experiences of two other groups of babies bear on the issue of the impact of experiential vs. hereditary factors. The infants I am thinking of were subjected to unusually frequent substitution of need-satisfying (symbiotic) objects. Concurrently, they had to cope with the permanent loss of the original love object—the mother. I refer to the infants described by Anna Freud and Sophie Dann (1951) and the group studied by William Goldfarb (1945).

The children described by Anna Freud and Sophie Dann had spent their first years of life in concentration camps. Their mothers had been brutally taken from them. In addition to the extreme material deprivations, they were constantly exposed to new people who again disappeared and who themselves were under the constant pressure of terror. Thus, these infants were unable to establish any stable symbiotic relationships. While these experiences left their traces on these children's object relationships, the children developed strong ties to each other and none of them suffered from a childhood psychosis.

The babies in William Goldfarb's studies, referred to by Bowlby (1951), had been placed in foster homes and moved from one home to another with great frequency. Yet, amidst the most trying circumstances, these infants were able to extract, as it were, substitutions for the actual loss of mothering. Although they may have paid the price for this object loss with neurotic disorders, character distortions, or psychopathic difficulties later in life, they *never* severed their ties with reality. We must assume that their rudimentary egos were able to sustain some kind of memory trace of earlier need satisfaction from an external human source, that some vestige of "confident expectation" remained operative, that they could integrate whatever meager substitute maternal care was available, and that they were able to utilize to the utmost the autoerotic resources of their own bodies and probably also of transitional objects (Winnicott, 1953b). In other words, they were able to create a nondehumanized narcissistic orbit for themselves.

In contrast, the anamneses of children with predominantly autistic or primarily symbiotic psychosis did not indicate, or only very rarely, that separation of any significant duration from the mother had actually occurred. In the majority of these cases, there was no real loss of the symbiotic object, beyond those brief separations that most normal infants experience during the course of the first two or three years of life. I refer to such ubiquitous traumata as transient separation from the mother due to the birth of a sibling or due to hospitalization of either mother or child. When such events occur at the end of the first year of life (or during the crucial separation-individuation phase), there is no doubt that the infant suffers considerably. However, most babies are able to accept substitute love objects if these are at all available during the mother's absence. They seem to be able to develop and sustain the mental image of the original symbiotic object. This enables them to enjoy need satisfaction from a substitute temporarily and then to restore the original image after reunion.

Since real and prolonged separation from the mother was conspicuously absent in the anamneses of our psychotic children, it must be emphasized that actual object loss was not an etiological factor in their psychotic break with reality.

This is so because the psychotic child's tie to the mother is of an entirely different order (see also Mahler, 1968).

PSYCHOTIC SUBSTITUTIONS FOR OBJECT RELATIONSHIP AND DEFENSE

Inasmuch as the psychotic infant cannot use his mother in the usual way, he has to resort to different ways in order to maintain his life. These substitute mechanisms are different from object relations as well as defense mechanisms used by any other group of children. The two main mechanisms which the psychotic child uses, in different combinations and admixtures, are essentially autistic and symbiotic—deanimation, dedifferentiation, devitalization, and fusion and defusion. These can be called neither defense mechanisms nor adaptive mechanisms in the sense in which these terms are used with any other group of children, normal or neurotic. For that reason, I would prefer to call them *maintenance mechanisms*.

These maintenance mechanisms do operate defensively against the object ties, if it is understood that "object" for the psychotic child has a different connotation. When we speak of object relationship in psychotics or of "psychotic object relationship," we must redefine and vastly broaden the concept of object relationship as the term was originally used in psychoanalysis. In the original, Freudian sense, object relationship meant one person endowing another human being with object libido. In this sense, object relationship is the most reliable single factor by which we determine mental health on the one hand and therapeutic potential on the other. In contradistinction to object relationship, we used to speak of relationships of a narcissistic nature.

It is obvious, then, that if we speak of "psychotic object relationships," we abandon such strict definitions. We must broaden and enlarge the concept of "object" as well as that of "relationship," and, as I shall show below, also that of "defense." In the broadest sense, we may speak of anything as an object which, in a field of interaction, physiologically or otherwise, impinges upon the organism, either *in utero* or in extrauterine life, as part of its environment. This broadened concept of object versus subject may prove invaluable in research into earliest ontogenetic development, as well as for the deciphering of some of the enigmas of psychosis. We must learn from modern ethology as well as from those workers who, to my mind, have correctly emphasized that in earliest development it is physiology rather than psychology that shows us the way.

Recent research into physiological interreactions between fetus and mother and neonate and mother, such as that of Greene (1958), elucidates some of the vascular-respiratory rhythmic interactions of the mother-fetus and mother-neonate dual unit. According to Greene's observations and hypothesis, the key configuration or Gestalt that enables the subject eventually to become aware of (to perceive) the object is this compatible rhythmicity, which renders the perceptual experience predictable.[4] It would seem that early incompatibilities may contribute to early failure of libidinization processes. This may be one of the factors at the root of regression to psychotic levels of object relationships in Winnicott's sense. In his paper on "Transitional Objects and Transitional Phenomena" (1953b), Winnicott described how optimal use of transitional, *inanimate* objects facilitates autonomy of the ego, whereas too rigid adherence to, or substitution of, transitional objects *in lieu* of human relationships may be the first—and a quite reliable—sign of later pathology.

The phenomenon that is more or less overtly common to

[4] At Pittsburgh University, Charney, Coleman, and Schossberger are doing microfilm analyses of congruent and incongruent rhythms, which may become quite relevant.

all psychotics is the blurring, if not complete failure, of distinction, of affective discrimination between the social, the human object world and the inanimate environment. In some cases, we find only a lack of or very tenuous emotional contact, phenomena of estrangement, complaints of derealization. In cases of acute severe psychotic breakdown, however, we find deanimation of the human object world with concomitant animation of the inanimate environment (see the case illustrations at the end of this chapter and in Chapter IV). Between these two groups of cathectic derangements there seem to exist fluent transitions (compare, for example, cases of fetishism).

What I said with regard to broadening the concept of "object relations" also applies to the concept of defense. As this concept is used in analysis, it refers to mechanisms operating against the instinctual drives and their internal representations. However, from what I have previously stated in great detail, it must be clear that neither the instinctual drives themselves, nor the drives and the ego, nor the object and the subject, are differentiated. For this reason, the psychotic "maintenance mechanisms" operate against an undifferentiated "drive-object," which persists far beyond the normal dual-unity stage.

Several formulations about infantile psychosis center around the idea that these pathological formations represent regressions to very early, yet normal phases of development: regression, that is, in the sense of a change in the relationship to the actual human object, and that this relationship is equivalent to that of, let us say, the three- to eight-month-infant and his mother in the normal symbiotic phase, or to the preobjectal relationship that is characteristic of the newborn and one- or two-month-old infant and his mother in the normal autistic phase.

The pathological formations, however, whether they are predominantly autistic or symbiotic syndromes, represent grave distortions that take place by way of a pathological intrapsychic process in which there has occurred, in the case of the symbiotic syndrome, a refusion of the maternal and self representations in a delusional mother-child omnipotent unit—with defusion of instinctual drives and predominance of aggression, that is, regression in the sense of a psychotic defensive regression of intrapsychic formations. The externalization of these regressive formations, their manifestation in observable behavior, is seen, for example, in the child's expectation that the mother will respond to his merest signal, as he gestures, vocalizes or thinks it. The prototype of this psychotic appersonation is the psychotic child's use of the maternal hand as a mechanical unindividuated extension of his own body, in an apparent belief that what he thinks is automatically and simultaneously the mother's thought as well.

This conceptualization allows, of course, for a dynamic interaction between the child's experiences and the intrapsychic process. In a certain phase of treatment, for example, the therapist may attempt to fit herself and the mother into this delusional unit. This is then followed, if further progressive development is to occur, by increasing distancing and frustration, by gradual disengagement of this pathological symbiotic tie.

It should be pointed out that, when the concept of the pathological syndrome of symbiotic child psychosis was formulated, the relationship between the mother and her psychotic child was described as a "parasitic symbiotic" union. This was stated in order to emphasize the mutually harmful nature of this intimate union, in contrast to the usage of the term "symbiosis" in biology, where the term implies a mutually beneficial relationship.

In short, it is worth restating that the intrapsychic situation in the psychotic child does not involve a regression to *any known phase* of development. The concepts of normal

autistic, normal symbiotic, and subsequent normal separation-individuation phases of development were partly derived by comparing the phenomenology of normal infant
development with genetic reconstructions that had been
made during the course of the study of symptom pictures
presented by children with psychoses. The behavior of children with the predominantly "symbiotic psychotic syndrome"
indicated the delusion of an omnipotent mother-child unit,
which was reminiscent of what one hypothesized as the state
of psychic organization of the three- to ten-month-old infant.
The withdrawal and other manifestations in the autistic
psychotic syndrome similarly brought to mind the hypothesis
of that stage of complete nondifferentiation of ego and id,
and of self and object world, that is assumed to be predominant in the newborn up to the end of the second month
of life: the *normal* autistic phase.

To illustrate the difference, however, between the two
psychotic syndromes and their parallels in normal development: in the four- to ten-month-old infant, as well as in the
symbiotic psychotic child, there is an awareness of the sensation of hunger as coming from inside the own body, and of
relief as coming from without. By contrast, we do not conceive of such an awareness, or, in other words, a differentiation or discrimination between inside and outside to any
extent at all either in the newborn up to the second month
of age or in the predominantly autistic psychotic syndrome.[5]

[5] As to the clinical symptomatology of autism, a clinical descriptive distinction has been of value: It seems that there is a dynamic difference between autism as a syndrome and autisticlike withdrawal as a temporary
defense. The latter state is one of temporary or partial fusion of self and
object representations involving a kind of intrapsychic, symbolic, symbioticlike libidinal refueling, yet distancing one's self. This is the opposite of the
autistic deanimation process, which is a rigid, unyielding autism and not a
temporary, intermittent, autisticlike behavior that seems to be in the service
of rest and recuperation of the ego, for example, during treatment. We conceive that during these periods there is a restitution of whatever ego structure has been formed in the course of therapy. This temporary regression
seems to serve that which Winnicott (1953b) describes as "the perpetual
human task of keeping inner and outer realities separate yet inter-related."

Case Illustrations

In what follows I shall illustrate the operation of maintenance mechanisms with case material. Sechehaye's (1950) patient, Renée, graphically described the subjective experience that is connected with the animation-dehumanization processes: "I was as if frozen. I saw . . . each thing separate . . . detached from the others, cold, implacable, *inhuman,* by dint of being without life. . . . These people . . . became void. . . . Mama I perceived [as] a statue, a figure of ice which smiled at me. And this smile, showing her white teeth, frightened me. . . . 'things' . . . began to take on life, suddenly the 'thing' sprang up. The stone jar . . . was there facing me . . . I looked away. My eyes met a chair, then a table; they were *alive*, too. . . ."

In other words, as in Schreber's *Weltuntergang* experience, or as in the case of my young patient George (see Chapter IV), one could reconstruct this acute, step-by-step failure of the perceptual-integrative capacity of the ego, which is eventually relegated to becoming the passive victim of the defused, rapidly deneutralized instinctual forces. The ego tries to ward off the onslaught of the two sets of stimuli, from without and from within, by a number of psychotic mechanisms, the outstanding of which are massive denial, displacement, condensation, and dedifferentiation. Complex stimuli, particularly those that demand a social-emotional response, are massively denied, autistically hallucinated away, so that ego regression may not halt before a level of perceptual dedifferentiation is reached at which that primal discrimination between living and inanimate (the *protodiakrisis* of von Monakow) is lost.

In Chapter IV, the case of George is presented in great detail. Here I wish to describe how seven-year-old George gradually lost this perceptual faculty of his ego upon the sudden loss of symbiotic possession of his mother. He exhibited bizarre preoccupations, among which was his feverishly seeking to find beer barrels near the brewery located near his home, in order to touch and feel their surface. These represented attempts to recapture, to mend by means of this primitive tactile perceptual experience, his broken tie with his pregnant mother's body. In his case, as in those of some other psychotic patients, the steps of this dedifferentiation demonstrably contained the elements of dehumanization, devitalization of the human living object world, including the patient's own body feelings, and relative animation, quasi-humanization of the inanimate environment. The phase in which his world appears to be populated with hallucinatory-delusional projections of preterhuman introjected objects is only one (better known, because conspicuous) phase in this regression of the psychotic (cf. Bychowski, 1956a, 1956b).

It would seem that the unpredictable acts of destruction, of cold, seemingly unemotional, yet calculated violence are based upon this fateful regression, this psychotic defense mechanism of the ego. In this regressed state, the impulse is experienced as a compelling command, which continually threatens the disintegrating ego from within. The ego experiences outside stimuli as acceptable only if they are simple, soothing, and predictable, and do not require an active and complicated emotional response. The more complex, variable, and unpredictable sensory stimuli are, the more threatening they become. Stimuli that reach the rapidly fragmenting ego from the living object world are much more complex, and appear to be much more dangerous. They seem to conjure up the demoniacal inner impulses (personified often as tormenting introjects). The psychotic child, as well as the psychotic adult, is often tormented by murderous impulses that are triggered by stimuli which come from residual human "love objects."

George, when he was eight years old, upon returning from his weekend visits at home, would imploringly say to me: "I'm afraid of killing my mother. I have ideas of killing her, and these thoughts upset me so! That gives me bad feelings in my head. It makes me so upset when I am home. Doctor, you are supposed to take them out."

The case of Alma (Chapter IV) is another illustration of psychotic alienation from reality. She clearly described the devitalization, deanimation struggle against all elements of the social living object world, including her own self.

Here I should like to cite briefly the cases of six-year-old Barry and seven-year-old Betty, to illustrate the compensatory or restitutive *animation, "machine-ization"* of the inanimate object world. Barry, who had an IQ of 170 or more, had to be hospitalized at six years of age, when with determined purposefulness he attempted to apply a drill to the temple of one of his classmates in order to look into his head to see if the little boy had any brains. Barry was a strangely detached, brilliant little boy. His mother had had a postpartum psychosis and intermittently had episodes of (probably schizophrenic) depression. During these episodes she would keep Barry in the double bed beside her in a semidarkened room. This happened in Barry's second year of life. Whenever the little boy whimpered or fussed, his mother, in order to keep him occupied, would throw various picture books to him. Barry's father had great hopes and ambitions for his little son. He taught the alphabet to Barry who at two and a half surprised the adults by citing cautionary sentences he had read in magazines. He read and understood big words in the dictionary and talked with the vocabulary of an adult.

On admission, this intellectually so superior and very precocious boy acted with peculiar lethargy, had no emotional contact, and spoke in a private language. He seemed to live in a world that he called the "underground land," which was populated by animated quasi-personified symbols. In this world, people communicated by sign and gesture language. For example, they revealed maturity by lowering their eyelashes; they indicated emotions by changing the color of their skins, and so on. Barry would talk only about his underground people, of whom he was the master; and he displayed emotions only when someone tried to pull him away from the land of the underground people. (Later on, in an unemotional tone of voice, he parroted what he must have heard his father say: that his mother had no love for him; for this reason, Barry said, he preferred and loved the underworld people so much.) In other words, Barry was somehow aware that his replacement of the human object world with these self-created creatures was due to the failure of his primary love relationship. Barry had annihilated the real people, by drawing all the libido away from their representations and substituting for them delusional creations.

In rare cases, the steps taken by the ego regressively to counteract murderous impulses can be reconstructed after years of analytic work. The analytic treatment of Betty, a seven-year-old child, had been preceded by so-called "release therapy" with a noted child psychiatrist, who had succeeded, when Betty was four years old, in luring her out of her mutism which she had maintained from the age of three years on. At the end of the second year of analytic treatment, Betty started spontaneously to enact and demonstrate in a peculiarly emotionless way the release therapy sessions of five and a half years before. She set "the stage" as it had previously been set for her by her former psychiatrist to help her express and "abreact" hostile feelings and impulses. In the typical way of the psychotic child, Betty had not repressed, but still remembered minute details of how she had wanted to bite off her brother's penis and push him into the river, etc.[6] After re-enacting all this, Betty paused, and then, in the same recitative voice, remarked: "And isn't it sad for a little girl to want to do all that to her own brother?"

Still, to a child like Betty, the difference between life and death—that is to say, rendering things inanimate that had

---

[6] Noteworthy also was Betty's failure to repress affect-laden situations of the past. This was similar to the case of Stanley (see Chapter IV).

been alive and, therefore, less "irritating"—did not mean emotionally the same as it does to normal people.

Betty attributed to the dolls of my doll collection all the emotions she thought their features displayed. These were constant and predictable features, whereas the emotions of living people she tried to, but could not, decipher. This was a child who wanted desperately to identify with people by mimicking them, by learning their emotions (compare Eissler's patient [1953]). For weeks she would greet me by asking: "Do I look sad today? Please say I look happy. . . ." Somehow she expected that my saying she looked happy would impart to her the feeling of happiness. Betty struggled against any unsolicited activity on the part of people in her environment. In her analytic sessions, she would fly into a rage whenever I tried to deviate from my role of a puppet whose strings Betty pulled. Betty had concretized and come to believe in the transfer of emotions and thoughts.

This concretization was characteristic of another patient of mine. Teddy, an adolescent, also believed I knew his thoughts, and he expressed his idea of the transfer of emotions and strength in his delusional system. He was preoccupied with the fear of losing body substance, of being drained by his father and grandfather, with whom his body, he believed, formed a kind of communicating system of tubes. At night the father-grandfather part of the system drained him of the "body juices of youth." Survival depended on who was most successful in draining more life fluid from the others, he or the father and grandfather part. He invented an elaborate heart machine which he could switch on and connect with his body's circulatory system so that he would never die. This much for Teddy's deanimation and concretization defense.

Betty's self-boundaries and identity were equally blurred, her self became fused with whomever she was with. She expected and believed, for example, that I concretely took part in her thoughts, intentions, and feelings—that therefore I could give them and take them away. Around Easter, Betty came home from the park bringing two twigs which she arranged crosswise and then asked her mother what she thought this was. Her mother answered: "I guess it is a cross." Thereupon Betty began to whip her mother furiously, crying all the while that her mother deliberately hurt Jesus' feelings, that she ought to have acknowledged that it was *the* Cross to which He was nailed and which, according to Betty, her mother knew. I took this up in Betty's analysis, where I learned that her sadomasochistic fantasies had undergone a number of psychotic elaborations. She employed in particular massive denial, condensation, and displacement. The crucified Savior's likenesses, which Betty had seen in church, and their miniature replicas on sale, she endowed with animation (life). There was identification with Jesus, and a condensation of the cruel persecution of and martyrdom suffered by Him, as well as her own suffering which she attributed to her mother's "meanness." Condensed sadomasochistic impulses were thus acted out in the above-described concrete way (Elkisch and Mahler, 1959; Bettelheim, 1959).

Betty's rage and panic reactions, for which she was brought to analytic treatment, concerned inanimate objects with which she was incessantly and at first lovingly preoccupied. As time went on, they became alive and persecuted her. At first she accused her brother of stealing her Japanese garden arrangement, then the contents of her beloved jewel box. At a later stage she had delusions and frank hallucinations about these things coming toward her at night. Her most persistent persecutor became the animated wastepaper basket. It may be of interest that even now, at the age of twenty, Betty still has this psychotic idea, even though she has succeeded in encapsulating and somewhat "distancing" (isolating herself from) the psychotic areas of her personality. (From adolescence on she has been in analysis with a colleague.)

So far I have presented a few short clinical illustrations of the mechanisms of dehumanization and reanimation, to which the disintegrating ego regresses in quest of adaptation when its perceptual integrative capacity fails. The ego then has become the passive victim of the deneutralized, defused drives, particularly of the unmitigated destructive impulses. In another case (to be described in Chapter IV) Elkisch and I (1959) observed psychotic mechanisms which we felt were infantile precursors of the "influencing machine" (Tausk, 1919). In this boy, Stanley, a similar dedifferentiation and a quasi-equation of animate with inanimate were at work. The dedifferentiation was based upon the massive denial of percepts, of stimuli coming from the *outside world*.

In the wake of this kind of negative hallucinatory psychotic denial, inner percepts, saturated with aggression, gain ascendency. Such inner excitations cannot be denied; they force themselves into the sensorium. In order to cope with these proprioceptive-enteroceptive stimuli the psychotic ego tries to dedifferentiate, to deanimate them. Emotions are equated with motion, via the perception of motor innervations and are also equated, it appears, with mechanical movements. These inner sensations of one's own body and of other life phenomena are then projected onto and confused with machine phenomena. The split of the ego into an intentional part and an experiencing part is frequently clearly discernible. The body image thus appears to be mechanically put together in a mosaiclike way, by fragments of a machinelike self image.

Since the psychotic child, like the normal one, sees the world in his own image, in the psychotic child's reality all objects take on the same machinelike, preterhuman quality that his own body image has.

Betty at first identified her own body self with the Japanese garden and, via the jewel box, with the wastepaper basket. At the next stage, she projected her own deanimated aggression-saturated self image onto these animated objects and felt persecuted by them.

SUMMARY

I should like to point to the lasting validity of what Freud regarded as the essential criterion for the psychotic break with reality—namely, the slipping away of the libidinal *human* object world. We can only rarely observe, but are often able to reconstruct, the prepsychotic struggle, the desperate efforts to cling, to hold on to the human object world. "Psychotic object relationships," whether with human beings or otherwise, and "psychotic defenses" are therefore no more than restitution attempts of a rudimentary or fragmented ego which serve the purpose of survival. No organism can live in a vacuum and no human being can live in an altogether objectless state (Rollman-Branch, 1960; Winnicott, 1953a; Spitz, 1965).

Because of the infant organism's lack of autonomous somatic defense functions, as well as because of the disorientation as to what is inside and what is outside of the organismic self, even the most primitive orientation and coping must be promoted and helped by the mothering partner. We are inclined to assume that in cases of early autism, organismic distress of such magnitude affects the organism at such an early stage of maturity that it certainly destroys the perception of the mother as functioning on his behalf. Fixation at or regression to an archaic type of perceptual dedifferentiation seems to account for the particular disturbance of autism in which the most conspicuous symptom is that the mother as representative of the outside world seems not to be perceived *at all* by the child. She does not seem to exist as a "living beacon of orientation" in the world of reality. Neither the self, nor even the bodily self, seems to be distinguished from the *inanimate* objects of the environment. Regression, therefore, does not occur to a *normal* phase of human development.

It may be argued whether this negative hallucinatory behavior, this turning a deaf ear toward mother and to the entire world, is or is not an acquired specific and active warding off of the mother. If it is an acquired somatopsychic defense, it develops so early (at or after birth) that psychic content and meaning are open to question. One might assume, as I believe Greenacre is inclined to do, that perhaps there exist severe intrauterine physiological incompatabilities between fetus and mother which result in this negative autistic reaction. These children seem to have managed to build up, or maintain and solidify, their original massive, negative hallucinatory stimulus barrier—of the first weeks of life—against the impingement of the outside world. These autistic children command the adult, with signals and gestures, to serve as an executive extension, an inanimate mechanical switch or a lever or a machine.

In contrast, the symbiotic psychotic child has some awareness of the mothering principle. However, he alternates between wanting to fuse with the "good" part object and warding off re-engulfment with the "all-bad" part object. His maintenance mechanisms, though they are less archaic, are much more bizarre, varied, and wrought with panic.

In neither syndrome can one speak of true object relationship. Only object relationship with the human love object, which involves partial identification with the object as well as cathexis of the object with neutralized libidinal energy, promotes emotional development and structure formation. Only libido that is neutralized by human "object passage" becomes deinstinctualized enough to be available to the ego.

CHAPTER III

Diagnostic Considerations

When I first presented my paper on child psychosis in Amsterdam in 1951 I maintained a sharp distinction between the two types of childhood psychosis, the syndrome of "infantile autism" (a term introduced by Kanner in 1944) and the "symbiotic syndrome" (first described by Mahler in 1952). The first two sections of this chapter are confined to a description of my classification of childhood psychosis as I saw it then. Since that time I have somewhat revised my ideas, and these revisions are presented in Chapter II and in the third section of this chapter.

THE AUTISTIC SYNDROME

As elaborated before, it is our hypothesis that the various types of psychoses in children can be understood as psychopathological distortions of normal phases of development of the ego and its functions within the early mother-child relationship.

From our sociobiological point of view, early infantile autism represents fixation at, or regression to, that first, most primitive phase of extrauterine life, which we have called the normal autistic phase. The most conspicuous symptom is that the mother, as representative of the outside world, seems not to be perceived at all by the child. She does not seem

66

to exist as a living beacon of orientation in the world of reality. The child's self, even the bodily self, seems not to be distinguished from the inanimate objects of the environment. There seems to be an innate, primary lack, or a loss of that primordial differentiation between living and lifeless matter that von Monakow called *protodiakrisis*. It may be argued whether or not this negative hallucinatory behavior—this "turning a deaf ear" toward mother and to the entire world —is an acquired, specific, and active warding off of the mother. If it is an acquired somatopsychic defense, it is so archaic and develops so soon—at or immediately after birth— that its psychic content and meaning cannot be discerned. The anamnesis of these children contains descriptions of their earliest behavior, which reveals that there was no anticipatory posture at nursing, no reaching-out gestures, and no specific smiling response (Spitz and Wolf, 1946).

It is characteristic of these children to become attached to a high chair or a toy, or to some other lifeless object. Mothers describe the infants' behavior in the following ways: "I never could reach my baby." "He never smiled at me." "The minute she could walk, she ran away from me." "It hurt me so when I saw other babies glad to be in their mothers' arms; my boy always tried to creep away from my lap as soon as he could." "He never greeted me when I entered, he never cried or even noticed when I left the room." "She never was a cuddly baby, she never liked to be caressed, she did not want anybody to embrace or kiss her." "She never made any personal appeal for help at any time." This last remark, by the very observant mother of an autistic child, describes quite succinctly the disturbance as it is seen in terms of social behavior.

The entire symptomatology and behavior pattern of the infantile autistic syndrome takes shape around the fact that the autistic infant or child is unable to utilize the auxiliary executive ego functions of the (symbiotic) partner, the mother, to orient himself in the outer or inner world. The most basic modalities of matter thus remain unintelligible to him, and he has to create substitutive modalities of orientation in order to cope with stimuli from within and from without.

To begin with, he must (and does) create and try to enclose himself within a small, utterly restricted world of his own. His most conspicuous and characteristic behavior patterns are the classical features described by Kanner (1942b, 1944): an obsessive desire for the preservation of sameness; a stereotyped preoccupation with a few inanimate objects or action patterns toward which he shows the only signs of emotional attachment. As a consequence, he shows utter intolerance of any change in his inanimate surroundings.

These features, then, may serve as differential diagnostic criteria in order to distinguish infantile autism from organic syndromes. Another characteristic of the primarily autistic child's appearance and behavior is his intelligent, even pensive, facial expression, in spite of the fact that he does not focus on you, but seems, rather, to look through you.

In his behavior, the primarily autistic child differs from the organic, as well as from the predominantly symbiotic psychotic child, by his seemingly self-sufficient contentedness —*if only he is left alone*. These autistic children behave like omnipotent magicians if they are permitted to live within, and thus to command, their static and greatly constricted segment of inanimate environment. Either they are completely mute (they "talk" to their inanimate fetish companion or imaginary objects by gestures), or, if they do speak, their language is not used for functional communication. Instead, it serves as a quasi-signal, such as is seen in earliest infancy. These autistic children, with signals and gestures, command the adult to serve as an executive extension of a semianimate or inanimate mechanical kind, like a switch or a lever of a machine. But they use the same gestures, sounds, or words, in trying to coerce—to conjure, as it were—the living part object as the thing they covet.

What is the meaning of this autism? What is its function?

It would seem that autism is the basic defense attitude of those children who cannot utilize the beacon of emotional orientation—the living primary love object, the mother—for whom she is functionally nonexistent as such. The child, being devoid of emotional ties, is unable to cope with the complexities of external stimuli and inner excitations that simultaneously threaten his very existence as an individual entity. Autism is an attempt at dedifferentiation and deanimation. It may be looked upon as the mechanism by which such patients try to shut out, to hallucinate away, the potential sources of sensory perception, particularly the infinitely variable ones of the *living* world, which demand emotional social responses.

One of the first reasons why parents seek help and frequently guidance is the failure of these children to heed or even to hear the parents' communications. The parents prefer to believe (notwithstanding other symptoms of autism) that their child is deaf or hard of hearing. But some form of massive cathectic withdrawal from the distance-perceptive sensorium seems clearly to be at work, as is borne out by the following diagnostic examination.

In order to establish a first tentative diagnosis, we may drop some metal object near the child, so as to make a loud noise. At that point, the autistic child behaves as if he heard nothing. One is sometimes reminded of the normal autistic phase, in which the distance receptors are not yet functionally tuned or, as we say in psychoanalysis, not cathected. That this lack of response (there is no startle reaction) is a kind of negative hallucinatory denial of perception, rather than real deafness, is proved by the fact that if one now turns on a record player and plays a familiar tune, the child will turn and listen with rapt attention. He may also move rhythmically, beat time to the record, or at least look at the revolving disk with fascination, having been made aware of it by the sound alone.

When we observe this type of psychotic child clinically,

the most striking feature is his spectacular struggle against any demand of human, of social, contact. It would seem that the capacity of these children to master their inner feelings, their own thought processes, their motility, their highly selective and restricted sensory awareness, all but overtaxes their undifferentiated, defective, and rudimentary egos. They cannot cope with unsolicited and unexpected stimulation from the external world. They are unable to mediate between external and internal stimuli. In short, it seems as though these patients experience outer reality, aside from their own stereotyped, constricted "reality," as an intolerable source of irritation, without any specific or further qualification. Therefore, these children seem to have managed to build up, and to maintain and solidify, their original massive, negative hallucinatory stimulus barrier against the impingement of the outside world. Their psychotic defense mechanisms aim at dedifferentiation and deanimation of inner and outer reality.

Psychoanalytic concepts help us to understand still other features of infantile autism and to differentiate it from organic syndromes and from symbiotic child psychosis as well. These children are, more often than not, toilet trained at the age when normal children are. This relative ease of toilet training seems, however, to stem from two factors: one of these seems to be an insufficient erotization of the body surfaces and orifices; the second is the paradoxical situation that it is precisely the lack of emotional involvement that makes toilet training an uncharged *conditioning* process for these children. The autistic child neither eats nor defecates to please the mother, nor does he refuse food or withhold his stools to spite her.

Most autistic children have a relatively low cathexis of their body surface, which accounts for their grossly deficient pain sensitivity. Along with this cathectic deficiency of the sensorium goes a lack of hierarchic stratification, of zonal libidinization and sequence. This is evident from the relative paucity of autoerotic activities, and the ease with which they substitute one for the other. Instead of autoerotic activities, these children show such aggressive habits as head knocking, self-biting or other self-hurting, mutilating activities, along with a mixing up of oral, anal, and phallic contents. In fact, these autoaggressive activities seem to serve the purpose of boundary cathexis of a distorted and deranged libido economy, constituting a pathological attempt *to feel alive* and whole. Autoaggressive manipulations seem to help these children to feel their bodies; some of these activities definitely serve the purpose of sharpening the awareness of the body-self boundaries and the feeling of entity, if not of identity.

THE SYMBIOTIC PSYCHOSIS SYNDROME

The immature ego of the symbiotic psychotic child, unlike that of the autistic child, seems to have progressed in its development to the symbiotic phase and, more often than not, shows beginnings of differentiation in terms of separation-individuation. The symbiotic syndrome represents fixation at, or regression to, a more differentiated stage of personality development than the autistic—namely, the stage of the need-satisfying part object. Therefore, the clinical pictures are infinitely more complex, mottled, and variable in children with this predominantly symbiotic psychosis than is the case in early infantile autism.

A close scrutiny of the developmental history of the predominantly symbiotic child often shows unusual sensitivities, such as Bergman and Escalona (1949) have described—an unevenness of growth and a striking vulnerability of the budding ego to any minor frustration. In the anamnesis of these children, one finds evidence of extreme reactions to the small failures that normally occur in the exercising, practicing period of partial ego functions. For instance, such children will give up locomotion for months because they once fell or sat down with a bump. There is usually a complementary environmental trauma, such as an abrupt, though probably unconscious, change of attitude on the part of one or both parents, which occurs at the onset of the separation-individuation period. These changing attitudes of parents at different ages of their children were particularly emphasized by Coleman, Kris, and Provence (1953) and form the basis of more recent research (see Anthony and Benedek, 1968). The acute break with reality is ushered in by what proves to be essentially a separation and annihilation panic, in response to such ordinary experiences as enrollment in the nursery school, hospitalization with physical separation from the mother, the birth of a sibling—all of them events that may in effect serve as triggers.

In symbiotic infantile psychosis, the mental representation of the mother remains, or is regressively *fused with*—that is to say, is not separated from—the self. It participates in the child patient's delusion of omnipotence.

Children of the symbiotic group rarely show conspicuously disturbed behavior during the first year of life, except, perhaps, disturbances of sleep. They may be described by their mothers as "crybabies" or as oversensitive infants. Their disturbance becomes apparent either gradually or fulminantly at those crossroads of personality development at which maturation of the ego would usually effect separation from the mother, and would enable the child to master an ever-increasing segment of reality, independently of her. As soon as ego differentiation and psychosexual development confront the child and thus challenge him with a measure of separation from and independence of the mother, the illusion of symbiotic omnipotence is threatened and severe panic reactions occur. These reactions usually manifest themselves during the third or fourth year, or else, at the height of the oedipal conflict. In other words, it would seem that a break with reality is touched off by the maturational growth of motor coordination, which harbors the inherent challenge of independence; later the complicated and differential emotional demands of the oedipal situation throw the symbiotic psychotic child into the described affective panic.

In symbiotic child psychosis, unneutralized libidinal and aggressive forces have remained narcissistically vested in fused systems of the mother-father-child unit, which is reminiscent of the primary unit (mother-infant). Landmarks of fragmentation of the ego are traumatizations through illness, separation (for instance, placement in a nursery school), birth of a sibling, but also all kinds of changes of a minor nature, which upset the precarious psychobiological balance of such children. Thus, the cumulative effect of previous traumata very often plays a role. The world is hostile and' threatening, because it has to be met as a separate being. Separation anxiety overwhelms the brittle ego of the symbiotic psychotic child. His anxiety reactions are so intense and so diffuse that they are reminiscent of the organismic distress of early infancy.

Clinically, such children show all the signs of abysmal affective panic. These severe panic reactions are followed by restitutive productions that serve to maintain or restore the narcissistic fusion, the delusion of oneness with mother or father. Restitution in symbiotic psychosis is attempted by way of somatic delusions and hallucinations of reunion with the narcissistically loved-and-hated, omnipotent mother image, or sometimes through hallucinated fusion with a condensation of father-mother images. In symbiotic infantile psychosis, reality testing remains fixed at, or regresses to, the omnipotent delusional stage of the symbiotic mother-infant relationship. The boundaries of the self and the nonself are blurred. Even the mental representation of the body self is unclearly demarcated. These are the cases, I believe, of whom Bender (1947) was thinking when she described the body of such a child as melting into one's own. The autistic child's body, by contrast, is uniquely unyielding, and feels like a lifeless object in one's arms (Rank and Macnaughton, 1950).

In the symbiotic psychotic syndrome, self-differentiation from the mother during the separation-individuation phase has failed, and the delusional symbiotic omnipotent fusion with the mother is still being maintained. In trying to understand the clinical symptomatology and dynamics of the primary symbiotic psychosis syndrome, it is most helpful to visualize the accelerated rate or *maturational growth* of ego apparatuses in the second and third years of life. This maturational growth of the central nervous system and of the ego apparatuses is preordained and rather independent of environmental and emotional influences (Hartmann, Kris, Loewenstein, 1946). The maturational spurt in the second year puts the *normal toddler* in a position of relatively advanced physical autonomy. His emotional, developmental growth and independence must catch up—must keep pace, as it were—with this somatic maturational spurt. The baby who for intrinsic or environmental reasons cannot separate gradually, whose ego cannot differentiate from that of the mother, cannot proceed beyond the symbiotic phase of normal development. Such babies have difficulty in functioning as separate individuals when their maturational growth enables them to do so, and experience the growing discrepancy between maturational and developmental growth with panic reactions. If the rate of growth of autonomous ego functions is greater than that of the emotional differentiation from the mother, the brittle ego structure of these children splits into fragments. This usually occurs when integration at the level of bisexual identification fails as the result of a fateful cathectic depletion of the ego.

Psychosexual maturation is also biologically predestined and thus proceeds, whereas object relationship and reality testing may not do so. It seems that the most consequential *maturational* processes occur during the phallic phase. The massive concentration of libido in the sexual parts of the body image takes place independently of environmental influences. It causes important shifts of cathexis, in terms of body-image representations emerging via pregenital libidinal phases, and bisexual identifications giving way to firm establishment of sexual identity. This second phase of integration of the body image seems to be dependent on a number of important conditions: (1) the successful integration of pregenital phases of development (the orderly stratification of zonal libidinization, and the neutralization of both libidinal and aggressive drives, but particularly of the latter); (2) successful identification with the parental figure of the same sex, in which the emotional attitude of both parents toward the child's sexual identity is of the utmost importance; (3) the ability of the ego to organize the memories, ideas, and feelings about the self into a hierarchically stratified, firmly cathected organization of self representations. The eventually distinct feeling of sexual self-identity, which receives decisive experiences at this second level, depends on cathectic shifts along the line of the solution of the oedipal conflict —beyond the more or less marked bisexual identification (cf. Greenson, 1964, 1966; Stoller, 1966a, 1966b). During latency, more complex and qualitatively distinct images of self and object world are formed. If the two phases of integration have been disturbed, representations of the self, belonging to one sex and integrated within the cohesive cathexis of the ego, become jeopardized by the hormonal upheaval of puberty.

THE RELATIVE RELEVANCE OF
ANAMNESTIC DATA

As I mentioned earlier, when I first presented my paper on child psychosis in Amsterdam in 1951, I made a sharp distinction between the autistic and the symbiotic psychosis syndromes. I postulated that the autistic psychotic child is one who has never libidinally cathected the mother and her ministrations, whereas the symbiotic psychotic child is fixated to or regresses to that stage of preobject relationship in which, presumably, the mental representation of the mother is fused with that of the self. All the symptomatology of the autistic child was understood as consisting of restitutive attempts, based on a fixation at the stage of preobject and part-object relationship, the first state of primary narcissism (cf. Chapter I).

During the course of our intensive diagnostic study and systematic "therapeutic action" research of nearly forty cases of psychotic children of preschool age, we came to realize that the earlier sharp distinction between autistic and symbiotic infantile psychosis should be modified. We proposed instead that infantile psychosis be categorized in terms of the predominance of one or the other primitive psychotic defensive organizations—that is, according to whether it is the autistic or the symbiotic defenses that are paramount.

Clinical experience has shown us that in those cases in which the mother as external gratifying object seems not to have been cathected in infancy, mental representations of the mother were established later, in a quasi-spontaneous development, even though that fact was often concealed by the presence of predominantly autistic mechanisms. On the other hand, cases that we have classified as symbiotic infantile psychotic syndromes frequently develop, at a later stage (as will be apparent in some of the case reports in Chapter IV), secondary autistic mechanisms. They do so either in the service of restitution, of spontaneous progress, or in the form of a transient mechanism arising during the course of therapy (and used in a beneficial way in the service of the ego!). In other words, by the age of three and one half to four years both autistic and symbiotic patterns seem to be present in the majority of cases,[1] and the anamneses generally reveal many, though at times slight, progressions and retrogressions to the earliest stages of preobject relationship —namely, the autistic and the symbiotic phases.

In short, our clinical experience over the past fifteen years has confirmed the impression that there are two broad descriptive categories of infantile psychotic syndromes, but the variations within these categories are great; that is to say, there is a broad spectrum of combinations of autistic and symbiotic features within the infantile psychosis syndrome.

At one end of the spectrum are those cases whose anamneses have clearly shown that autism prevailed in infancy. They are described as imperturbable, "good" infants, interested only in tiny objects in their cribs, and unresponsive to human contact, even to the mother. In some instances, lags in development were noted, especially in the motor area. Later on, deviations in verbal development became most conspicuous. At times, speech did not appear at all until the third year of life; in other instances, there are reports of babies of twelve months of age who could not walk, yet were able to repeat tunes and words to songs, and subsequently repeat, in an echolalic, singsong fashion, radio and TV commercials and the like. The most characteristic features of these children is that they do not use language signs functionally—that is, for normal communication.

Frequently, during the second year of life there are severe temper tantrums and sometimes severe sleep disturbances. In the third year of life, some of these children are reported by the parents to be coming out of their isolation, the reason for this assertion apparently being the fact that they have taken to imitating the parents' speech and gestures. It appears that the children use this mirroring of the parents, as

[1] Exceptions to this rule may be those child patients with early autism who in institutions remain in a daze of disorientation and become indistinguishable from the feebleminded group (Mahler, 1952; Kanner and Eisenberg, 1955).

well as other devices, as a way to exert magical command
over their environment (cf. Mahler, 1966b).

In other cases, the isolation remains unbroken; at the
chronological age of separation-individuation, their self-
limitation becomes even more rigid, so that autoerotic and
autoaggressive behavior manifestations come to constitute
these children's main repertoire of functioning. These manifestations include the whirling of objects as well as of the
child's own body around his own axis (Bender, 1947), head
banging and rocking, and stereotyped day-long preoccupation with the psychotic fetish (Furer, 1964). (Mother-child
pairs sometimes come for treatment at this stage, but more
often at the stage at which the mother's efforts have begun
to fail and a return to the "autistic equilibrium"[2] between
mother and child has asserted itself.) It is in these cases that
such primitive motor signs as teeth grinding, flailing, and toe
walking seem to become predominant.

At the opposite end of the spectrum we find those cases in
whom the symbiotic psychotic syndrome predominates: the
child's infancy is described by the mother as having been like
that of a normal child, without marked deviations in development and with what appears to her to have been affectionate
responsiveness. These children, during their second and third
years, experienced a more dramatic disorganization along
with loss of functions, such as deterioration of speech, often
associated with or ascribed to such events as a short routine
separation from the love object. By the third and fourth
year of life, reorganization took place, with a range of psychotic symptoms in the foreground. These include: loss of
boundaries of the self, and loss of intersystemic boundaries,
extreme reaction to any failure; magic gestures—"wipe away
if touched," "push away and cling"; extreme panic without
known cause; echolalia and echopraxia; psychotic preoccupations with an inanimate object, such as a fan, a record

---

[2] About autistic equilibrium between mother and child, see Chapter VI.

player, a baby jar, even a thread that one can wind around one's finger—in short, the "psychotic fetish." Through their speech, clear evidence emerges of primary process thinking and other thought disorders. There are also catatoniclike symptoms, such as posturing, waxen flexibility, etc.

During the course of treatment of the child with a predominantly symbiotic syndrome, we can more readily decipher the condensed intrapsychic conflicts and memory traces of psychotically elaborated traumata that are contained in these manifestations. However, as has already been noted, the entire picture may be hidden behind a secondarily autistic defensive organization, involving mutism and the shutting out of the human environment, much as one sees in the primarily autistic group. On the other hand, in some cases of primarily symbiotic psychoses, an intensive study, especially of home movies made during the child's first three years (Serota), can disclose evidence of disturbances in visual focusing and emotional contact. This suggests that an autistic withdrawal preceded the symbiotic picture in these cases as well.

The autistic defense is conceived of as primarily a response to the fear of human contact, an armor plating against such contact. It manifests itself behaviorally in the shutting out of the actual human object, in order to effect a delusional denial of the existence of the human object world and therefore of the danger of annihilation. Intrapsychically, an attempt is made to deanimate the mental representations of the object, whatever the forms in which they may exist—that is, even if only in the form of not integrated memory islands fused with part images of the self. Hence, the self also appears to be deanimated ("devitalized"). This is a psychotic mechanism that has no parallel in any phase of normal development. There is also regression to the complete nondifferentiation of the autistic phase, both of ego-id and of self and object—for example, such a child does not seem to become aware of the localization of sensations inside his own body, not even that of hunger (cf. Lotta's case in Chapter IV).

Children with a predominantly autistic defense organization show marked variations in their capacity to advance to the symbiotic organization. When, through therapeutic intervention, such a change does occur, we observe the development of a multitude of more understandable psychotic symptoms; on reconstruction these appear to involve investment of some portion of the "mothering principle" (the "good" object) as a mental representation. This points to the fact that what is involved is a regression rather than a total lack of cathexis of gratifying experiences.

We do not rule out the possibility, however, that what may be called a complete autistic state may persist, especially in neglected or deprived psychotic children (Mahler, 1952; Kanner and Eisenberg, 1955).

By contrast, the symbiotic defensive organization is conceived of as primarily a response to separation panic, which I call "panic" advisedly, because the extent of traumatic anxiety cannot be considered a part of the ordinary experience of normal infancy. The regression to the symbiotic defense involves aspects of a later stage in the normal development of the previously mentioned mother-child dual unity. This defense is therefore represented intrapsychically by poorly differentiated self and object representations. In the child's behavior one can observe an attempt on his part to externalize the omnipotent dual unit as a delusion onto the outside world—for example, to have the mother behave as though she were in reality an extension of the child's own body.

It is the failure of the symbiotic defensive regression that forces the child into the autistic position. More explicitly, we assume that the symbiotic disorganization carries with it the potential for an additional organismic panic, the fear of disintegration, of complete loss of the sense of entity and identity—that is to say, of re-engulfment by the symbiotic object. We conceptualize the fear of re-engulfment as a dread of dissolution of the self (loss of boundaries) into an aggressively invested dual unity that the child cannot magically control. The subsequent psychotic defensive effort—autism—should thus be thought of as a secondary defense.[3] This portion of the theory comes closest to maintaining the Freudian theory of the decathexis of object representations. In general, however, it derives from a genetic theory of object relations—or perhaps one would do better to call these "preobject relations."

[3] At this point it is proper to mention a clinical descriptive distinction that has been of some value—namely, that between the rigid, unyielding autism as a psychotic defense organization and another, quite different kind of temporary, intermittent, autisticlike behavior (the latter in the service of rest and recuperation during treatment). In the course of therapy, the patient at times seems to have the need to withdraw his libidinal cathexis from the object and seemingly from the outside world altogether. We conceive of these withdrawals as necessary intervals during which a restitution takes place of whatever ego structure has been formed in the course of therapy. This temporary regression thus seems to serve what Winnicott (1953b) describes as the perpetual human task of keeping inner and outer realities separate, yet interrelated. It seems that there is a dynamic difference between autism as a syndrome and autisticlike withdrawal as a temporary defense. The latter is a state of temporary or partial fusion of self and object representation, which involves a kind of intrapsychic, symbolic, symbioticlike libidinal refueling, yet at the same time a distancing of one's self—the opposite of the autistic deanimation process. This example re-emphasizes how carefully the distinction must be made between clinical description and inferred internal psychic events.

CHAPTER IV

Clinical Cases of Child Psychosis

In this chapter clinical cases of infantile psychosis will be described in considerable detail. They will illustrate in the area of clinical symptomatology the hypotheses which the previous chapters described theoretically.

STANLEY

The first case illuminates with particular clarity many basic disturbances of the ego; of its functions of defense, perception, affect modulation; its deficiency of cognition in terms of causality and of abstraction as well as of its integrative and synthetic capacities.

Stanley's case yielded much important material, because his therapist, Dr. Paula Elkisch,[1] is endowed with that rare and felicitous combination of clinical acumen and unprejudiced observational and therapeutic flair.

Stanley was brought for treatment when he was six years old and was in analytically oriented psychotherapy for more than three years. Both his therapist and I had the opportunity to follow his case till well into his teens when he was

[1] The observations communicated in this section were carried out during the first year of treatment. His therapist was Paula Elkisch, co-author of several papers dealing with Stanley (Mahler and Elkisch, 1953; Elkisch and Mahler, 1959).

a high school pupil with a fairly adequate scholastic record; but some of his psychotic mechanisms had persisted and his social maladjustment seemed to us quite conspicuous.

Stanley's case taught us important insights into a phenomenon that some psychotic children display: the so-called "fabulous memory," which revealed itself as due to the psychotic ego's crucial failure to execute its basic defensive function, namely, that of *repression*.

Parents of psychotic children frequently stress the "fabulous memory" these youngsters have. Closer examination of this phenomenon reveals that this memory for the smallest details of certain affect-laden situations of the past is precisely due to the psychotic child's inability to forget selectively.

In Stanley's case, for example, Paula Elkisch could observe that some extraneous or tangential quality of a detail of a subsequent experience would remind him of the past situation and elicit in him a sweepingly diffuse total reaction. Through a seemingly slight similarity, he was reminded of the past and became completely overwhelmed by the affect which the past experience had once evoked.

The case of Stanley illustrates his ego's inability to recall selectively and to react specifically to certain perceptive and affective stimuli.

Ever since the time when Stanley had first been read to, his mother used to read to him a book called, *When You Were a Baby,* which made him cry uncontrollably. His reaction to this story has never changed; at the age of six he still cried bitterly when he listened to the story, yet he often insisted upon hearing it. However, it was not only this book that elicited such a total emotional reaction; all other stories about babies also seemed to cause recall of the same total memory and affectomotor response. On several occasions when his kindergarten teacher read a story to her group in which a baby was mentioned, Stanley would burst into uncontrollable crying. He cried so hard and became so upset that his teacher found it necessary to telephone Stanley's mother and ask her to come and console him or else take him home.

In his book, *When You Were a Baby*, which originally made him cry every time it was read to him, there were two pictures on two facing pages. One picture showed "The Baby" in his playpen, of which one could see only the bars; the other picture showed "Panda" sitting in a cage, of which one also could see only the bars. The Baby cries, his toys are strewn outside the playpen, and he cannot retrieve them; Panda, on the facing page, has a bowl with food sitting beside him. For anybody, the two pictures suggest certain similarities, in addition to the dissimilarities, between the Baby's situation and Panda's. Both Baby and Panda are behind bars. The similarity is also expressed in the text, which reads: "And Mama thought: 'That baby looks like the fat Panda at the Zoo sitting in his cage.'" The interesting and unusual thing was what this little patient did with the situational similarity. He completely discarded, it seemed, each or both of the obvious motivations for the baby's crying. According to our observation in the treatment situation, whenever Stanley came in contact with either a baby doll or a baby picture, he called it "Panda." From the situational similarity Stanley equated Baby and Panda. Baby and Panda were together in that book, therefore they always belonged together. The image of one elicited the other; *the two "concepts" became fused and quasi-interchangeable.* Stanley was unable to separate or differentiate the two parts of the composite image he had once perceived. The two "personalities" of the picture book, whose image at one time happened to appear "syncretically" (Werner, 1948), became engrams, forever connected in his memory.

Furthermore, there was evidence in the material for the assumption that, to Stanley, *the perception and the affect,* "Baby and crying," had become *irreversibly* connected (Piaget, 1936). The crying baby in the book sat opposite the noncrying Panda, who had a bowl with food beside him. Stanley would often feed a "crying baby" whom he detected in another book. One might have assumed that Stanley's diligent bottle-and-spoon feeding of the "crying baby" was motivated by his wish to console both the "crying baby" and himself in identification with it. This was not so. Neither his reactions nor his answers to questioning bore out the slightest causality to this effect. On the contrary, in feeding the "crying baby" Stanley acted out a need for completion of restitution from a syncretically formed traumatic affective memory. (We shall see, in particular, that crying and being fed by mother belonged inseparably, irreversibly, but not *causally*, together.)

During our observation of this patient, we obtained proof of the fact that for Stanley the psychic representations not only of Baby and Panda, but of three figures—Baby, Panda, and mother—were blurred, undifferentiated from each other, and intermingled with the representation of his own self. In other words, the body image of the self and the images of objects, the intrapsychic representatives of himself (Baby), Panda, and mother were not clearly differentiated, a state of affairs that is so very characteristic of the symbiotic psychosis syndrome. Not only were the four representations Baby, Panda, mother, and he himself easily fused and confused with one another, but so were certain emotional (affective) qualities which had been connected with those four syncretically coincident images at the time when the conglomeration of concepts had originally occurred, very likely during the second half of the first year of his life. Clues for such an assumption were reconstructed from the following material and data.

At times, Stanley became quite absorbed in a children's book, *Fun with Faces*, which he found at his therapist's office. In this book there was a picture of a baby's face whose expression could be changed by pulling a little tag attached to the bottom of the face and then pushing the tag up. In other words, this tag worked like a "switch"[2] with which one could "turn on" one physiognomic expression and "turn it off" for another. One of the baby's expressions was "crying," the other was "not crying." Stanley "turned on" one expression and then "turned it off" for the other. That is, he switched the baby depicted as "crying" to the picture of the baby depicted as "not crying" and vice versa. He called the baby "Panda." When Panda, the baby, did not cry, Stanley said: "Now she[3] is happy!"[4] and he would insist that the mother substitute should "say she is happy." Stanley was satisfied for some moments only when the therapist said, "Now she is happy."

It seems important to interpolate here some data about this boy's general behavior during the treatment. Every time he was "switching" the baby's expression "on and off," he displayed paroxysms of excitement. That is, he threw up his stiffened and flexed arms, strained and tightened his arm muscles rhythmically in this position for some time, while twisting his head downward and to the left side. His face was bizarrely distorted with widely open mouth and protruding tongue. Grimacing in this way, Stanley jumped up and down like a rubber ball so that the whole motor behavior impressed the observer as a "performance" of a mechanical toy that had been wound up, rather than that of a human being.

This type of behavior (catatoniclike excitement) contrasted and alternated with another type of behavior. While Stanley exhibited the above-described catatonically excited behavior, his activity was concomitantly confined to one

[2] The significance of the switch, mechanical devices, and "the machine" in particular will be elaborated on later in this chapter (see also Elkisch and Mahler, 1959; Elkisch, 1952).

[3] Dolls, "octopuses," Pandas, etc., were girls to Stanley. For example, he always spoke about the "octopus girl."

[4] Actually, the "not crying" baby on that picture did not look "happy" at all. It looked sullen in terms of our perception and interpretation of emotional facial expressions.

single pursuit, for example, "switching the faces" of the baby picture. It was impossible to distract the child from this stereotyped pursuit or to "lure" him into any other. At times, however, he would behave in a diametrically opposite way; from the beginning of some treatment sessions, he would suddenly "fall" from the autistically stereotyped behavior into complete listlessness. Then all focus seemed lost; he would not play or "want to do" anything. Instead, he would fumble, as if in a dazed state, with whatever might be at hand. For example, he would finger some toys which lay around, drop them, and move lethargically back and forth from one place to another, without any aim or goal. At those times, he seemed to be no more than a quasi-part of the environment, a "particle" of the surroundings, in a state of cohesion with it and undifferentiated from it. Hans Volkelt attributes this state to the animal, about which he states that its "perceptions exist only in so far as they are part of a wider totality of action in which object and inner experience exist as a syncretic indivisible unit" (see Werner, 1948).

According to our observation, it was in this state of semi-stupor that Stanley would, all of a sudden, touch the arm of the mother substitute and, with this excitation, which was at first slight, the child would "switch himself on," it seemed, into an intense and diffuse affective state.[5] Such was the case with body contact, as well as with a trigger engram. For example, the word "baby" spoken or read to him from story books appeared to be just such a trigger engram. It seemed as though the patient was *very deliberately* seeking such a sweeping excitation, via the trigger stimulus, as if to defend himself against his apathetic state, as if to ward off the danger of symbiotic fusion through which his entity and identity would otherwise become entirely dissolved into the matrix of

---

[5] This case reminds one of Malcolm, whose transitory autistic withdrawal during treatment demonstrated the same alternation between symbiotic fusion and autistic withdrawal, even though seemingly in the reverse order (see Furer, 1964).

the environment. It appeared as if the child had switched himself into excited crying, or catatoniclike motor paroxysms as well, to gain momentum, as it were, like an engine, to counteract symbiotic dissolution of the boundaries of his "self." Although he could not stop once he had "turned on" these paroxysms of jumping, cramping, and twisting, he nevertheless sought the diffuse overcathexis of his ego, the increased body sensations, because they seemed to enable him to achieve some kind of self-identity (compare Eissler, 1953; Mahler, 1952, 1953b). His aim was, in short, delimitation of his self from his mother and from the environment by way of deliberately cathecting his "self" from without (as in touching the therapist) and thereby generating excitement from within. He used a mechanism which, though much less differentiated, to be sure, is nevertheless reminiscent of Eissler's adult patient (1953). This patient would use the mechanism of "feeling dead" in order to be able to engender emotions from within, to "pump up" a pretended emotion such as in the patient's estimation fitted the social situation.

The fascination which the two baby pictures in the book *Fun with Faces* had for Stanley corresponded to his quest for a rather primitive and undifferentiated mechanism of restitution (defense of psychotic children) with simple, learnable patterns, which he could imitate and then use to "switch on and off." By means of these patterns, he was endeavoring to orient and adapt himself in the disconcerting diversity of a highly structured social reality for which his unstructured and fragmented ego had neither the modulation capacity of affects, nor the prerequisites of selective perception, selective forgetting (repression), and selective recall. Psychotic child patients often seem somehow to realize that they cannot respond adequately to affective stimuli in reality, and therefore try to "learn" emotions or emotional reactions in the same way as one might learn a habit. (Compare this with Charlie, the case of an "as if" personality dealt with in Chapter I.) Thus Stanley showed evidence that he was desperately persevering in order to learn gestures, to "study" emotions mechanically and physiognomically,[6] as it were, so as to substitute for his ego's inability to react to real experiences specifically, and to recall them selectively and in a modulated way.

With his own baby book Stanley behaved like a traumatic neurotic who tries to overcome a trauma, bit by bit, through endless repetitions. Through treatment he seemed to have progressed in such a way that he began to master the overwhelming affect which had hitherto inundated his own self, by making the "baby face" (in the second picture book) cry, instead of crying uncontrollably himself. In other words, he was enabled to relegate (to project) his need to cry onto some other object (or image) with which he actively and even playfully identified. This was borne out by the fact that he accompanied the baby's "crying" physiognomic expression in the picture with the appropriate crying sounds of his own intonation. Is this not an attempt at restitution, and a successful one, with which Stanley expressed satisfaction by his paroxysmal, ecstatic jumping and elation?

On the other hand, it should be emphasized that when the "crying baby" was fed by Stanley (mother), "it" would not ever stop crying, even as a consequence of being fed. This made us aware of the fact that the nature of the ego defect and the restitution attempts with which we are dealing here are even more complex than we had at first thought them to be. Would one not assume that the "crying baby" upon being fed by his mother (personified by Stanley) would stop crying? Instead, for Stanley, being fed and crying both had to continue, to go on simultaneously. In trying to understand this, some references to the child's early history are relevant here.

As a baby, Stanley had suffered from an inguinal hernia. Reportedly, from the age of six months on, he had suffered in-

[6] Compare Kris's (1933) interpretation of the case of the sculptor Messerschmidt.

tense pain which would come on suddenly while the child was "happily" and quietly playing. "All of a sudden Stanley would break into violent crying." The abrupt and violent attacks of pain were not only distressing to Stanley's mother and father, the parents dreaded those attacks even more because of the possibility that the violent crying might in turn cause incarceration of the hernia. The parents were deeply worried about the crying possibly necessitating an emergency operation. Hence, upon the doctor's advice, and as a result of their own dread of the consequence of crying and pressing, they went about to prevent the child from crying, at all cost. Thus Stanley's need for crying was utterly frustrated. At the same time, and all along, Stanley was a feeding problem. He vomited a great deal and often refused to eat; but being fed by his mother while he was crying seemed to have merged in his memory into "one experience." Being fed and crying thus remained perceptibly as well as affectively synchronized in his memory, so that one might speak of "syncretic engram conglomeration."

Stanley continued to insist that the "crying" baby in the book *Fun with Faces* had to be fed while crying. Stanley himself fed the "crying" baby as though he wished actively to do to the baby what he had passively endured when he was a baby—being fed while in pain and crying. Now, when he played out his desire to feed the crying baby, which he did with diligence and glee, and amidst paroxysms of excitement, it was not in order to console the baby, as one would expect, but in order to overcome, it seemed, the other part of two simultaneously and passively perceived traumatic experiences of his babyhood. Just as they had happened to him together, so both experiences, pain-crying and feeding, remained connected and condensed in his memory. He therefore seemed compelled, as it were, to overcome the trauma of the total situation, pain-crying plus being fed, synchronically, *and not in terms of the laws of causality*. In this reaction, we could observe a specific disturbance in thinking and feeling, which had resulted from the failure of the selective repressive function of the ego.

This is only one of the many examples which demonstrates that this little patient could not connect situations which for normal people obviously belong together in terms of cause and effect, according to the secondary process. In Stanley, the mechanisms of the primary process—condensation, substitution, displacement, synchronicity, etc.—replaced the secondary process. Two simultaneously experienced emotions remained irreversible and inseparable. Hence, when he wanted to cope with one—being overwhelmed by crying when the trigger engram "baby" was touched—the same trigger seemed to call for restitution attempts for the simultaneously experienced displeasure of his early feeding situation.

Stanley's perceptive and affective disturbance (illustrated in one small segment taken from the wealth of material we gained in studying his case) resulted in a severe defect of the thinking process. This defect arrested him at the most primitive level of reality testing. He could not make the connection between two operations in such a way as to *conclude* that satisfying a need (being fed) might also result in cessation of pain and thereby render affectomotor discharge (crying) superfluous. Thus his development was partially arrested in the stage of primitive reversibility within action (Piaget), a level which babies at the stage of so-called "confident expectation" (Benedek, 1938) seem to be able to reach. He could not differentiate between two operations which occurred synchronically, for example, pain-crying and being fed, as different activities per se, with different connotations. The ability to draw such conclusions depends on the ability to abstract and to connect cause and effect. But Stanley was unable to grasp perceptions in their sequence and their relatedness to one another. He could not integrate perceptions into reversible thought operations (Piaget, 1936).

The material presented thus far demonstrates that the so-called "fabulous memory" of psychotic children has to do with their remembering minute details of affect-laden past events. This phenomenon is based on the proclivity of such patients to regress to much earlier ego states of their past infancy (Federn, 1952) and to recall undifferentiated affective-perceptive engram conglomerates, which seem to be stored, unchanged, in the patient's mind. The mechanism of syncretic memory storage might also be called "pseudo repression" because its content has not really been decathected and no countercathexis seems to have been established. According to Freud (1915), "the [different] mechanisms of repression have at least this one thing in common: *a withdrawal of the cathexis of energy*" (p. 154f.).

Stanley revealed that at the age of six and a half, he was still unable to combine, to blend, and to organize perceptions; his affective reactions were primary process reproductions of early infantile syncretic engram conglomerates, which appeared to be irreversible and irrepressible. It was to these early ego states that he readily regressed because they had never been decathected.

The pathogenesis of this ego defect, which amounted to a grave disability of learning, had at its root hereditary-constitutional factors, as well as early predispositional, somatic and environmental, causative ones. As to the hereditary-constitutional factors, there were manic-depressive and schizoid personalities in the extended family of this child. As to early predispositional factors: as early as 1915 Freud, in his paper on "Repression," pointed out that a painfully destructive stimulus (for example, organ pain) may acquire "far-reaching similarity to an instinct. . . . The aim of this pseudo-instinct, however, is simply the cessation of the change in the organ and of the unpleasure [pain] accompanying it." Freud went on to say, "Let us take the case in which an instinctual stimulus such as hunger remains unsatisfied [or pain in an organ remains unattenuated] . . . it keeps up a constant tension of need. *Nothing in the nature of a repression seems in this case to come remotely into question.* Thus repression certainly does not arise in cases where the tension produced by lack of satisfaction of an instinctual impulse is raised to an unbearable degree" (p. 146 f.; my italics).[7] There were many other traumata and a state of "silent traumata" in Stanley's earliest life which augmented beyond the threshold of repressibility, it seems, great segments of his inner and outer perceptions. We may assume that, concomitantly, this infant's tolerance to pain and unpleasure was diminished and his anxiety predisposition enhanced (Greenacre, 1941). The infant's "traumatized body as such does not easily provide the amount of stimulation, of body-ego experiences which the growing and recovering self longs for" (Hoffer, 1952, p. 38). It seems that if there are too great and chronic states of organismic distress, progress toward "me-experience" and object love as well as reality testing are impaired.

The conditions under which Stanley grew up during his first four years of life[8] seemed to render "me-experience" and "object experience" vague. Added to inherent constitutional proclivities was the early environmental condition that Stanley's mother was very much involved with her own father and mother at crucial periods of the infant's life. She seems to have been somewhat detached, or at least torn between her role as a mother and as a daughter. Although she functioned for Stanley as his "external ego" (Mahler, 1952, 1953b; Spitz, 1953), Stanley apparently did not experience her ministrations as a real and efficient rescuing from the trau-

[7] See also Anna Freud (1952b).

[8] At the age of three, several traumatic changes occurred in Stanley's life: (1) the family had to move from the familiar household which they shared with the maternal grandparents, because (2) the grandfather became acutely psychotic (agitated depression), and (3) the maternal great-grandmother to whom the maternal grandmother was morbidly attached died. Both the maternal grandmother and Stanley's mother reacted with depression. It was at the same time that Stanley's maternal uncle became so alarmed about Stanley's behavior that he called the parents' attention to the fact that Stanley seemed to be completely withdrawn and apparently was living in a world of his own.

matic situations that suffused his "rudimentary ego" (Greenacre, 1952a). Thus, as a consequence of his diffuse over-
sensitivities, in addition to the painful traumatic conditions
in the second half of his first year (Greenacre, 1953), over-
determined by "silent traumas" (Hoffer, 1952), and adverse
environmental influences during the phase of "normal separation-individuation," Stanley seemed to have become arrested, fixated, as it were, at the primary symbiotic stage
of mother-child relationship, so that he has not been able
to establish his individual identity separate from the mother's
self.

Another characteristic deficiency of the patient's ego followed from this: a defect in the faculty of abstraction. There
did not seem to exist for him any clear-cut differentiation
between the actual object and the mental representation
of it.[9]

It seemed that Stanley perceived external sensory stimuli
as very young babies do: in a physiognomic way.

In addition to the failure of the repression and the grave
disturbance of abstraction as far as cognitive development
was concerned, we learned much from Stanley's case and
similar cases about the elements and elementary disturbances
of the perceptual function of the ego. Those are the functions
which provide orientation as to what is inside and what is
outside, orientation in space and time, and differentiation
or discrimination between animate and inanimate.

This failure of the most basic perceptual discrimination
seems to be at the origin of the psychotic defense mechanism which appears to be the precursor of the phenomena of
the "influencing machine" described by Tausk (1919).

In 1923 Freud stated: "For the ego, perception plays the

[9] For example, one day during his therapeutic hour, Stanley looked
through the Baby book of his infancy. On some of the picture pages the
mother is absent. He became very anxious, saying, "Where is the Mommy?
Where is the Mommy?" While frantically turning the pages he "found" the
mother, yet he could not really quiet down until he ran out of the room to
his own mother, who was waiting for him in another room.

part which in the id falls to instinct" (p. 25). Hartmann (1939) has pointed out that structure is formed by perceptual turning toward the outside world and vice versa. Freud (1911b), in the Schreber case, described complete withdrawal of libido from the object world as the experience of *Weltuntergang*. The ego-regressive process in the psychotic child Stanley was akin to these *Weltuntergang* experiences which we studied.

We postulate that where there is a breakdown of the perceptual integrative capacity of the ego, external perceptions are massively denied, as Edith Jacobson (1957) has described in some of her borderline cases. In fact, regression seems to take place to that stage of reality testing which, we surmise, dominates the pleasure ego of the small infant: the stage of negative hallucination and projection of displeasure. However, massive denial cannot cope with those endogenous stimuli which are continually generated by physiological processes in the organism itself and which are very close to the instinctual drives not neutralized by the ego. There is no escape from the enteroceptive and proprioceptive excitations. These excitations gain predominance and force themselves continually into the sensorium. Whereas the external object world has been lost by delibidinization and thus has become deanimated, the endogenous excitations which have a predominantly aggressive momentum gain ascendancy. These stimuli undergo concretization and quasi-animation and replace the lost outside object world. They determine the psychotic child's concept of the self and constitute or seem to make up his body image. The delibidinized, quasi-animated forces are thence projected onto the external world. Delibidinization serves a defensive function to the fragmented ego of the psychotic child. The fragmented ego cannot cope with changeability and complexities. It cannot integrate and it cannot synthesize. Living objects are much more changeable, vulnerable, and unpredictable than inanimate objects: biodynamics are much more complex, subject to infinite modulations, and therefore much less predictable than are machines with mechanical dynamics. The internal psychotic reality dominated by the aggression-saturated proprioceptive-enteroceptive bodily sensations seems to be experienced as if the body were powered by more or less demoniacal, ego-alien mechanical forces (the introjects), and whatever object libido is available is in turn vested in inanimate objects or quasi-animate machineries. Dedifferentiation and aggression-saturated inner percepts give rise to the delusion of the "influencing machine."[10]

As stated earlier, at the age of six months Stanley suffered from an inguinal hernia. The pain came on suddenly while he was happily and quietly playing. "All of a sudden Stanley would break into violent crying." Throughout many months the child had these sudden attacks of intense visceral pains. The child and his parents lived in the maternal grandparents' house and the mother was forced to prevent violent crying by whatever means, partly because the pediatrician was afraid of possible incarceration of the hernia and partly because the grandfather had to remain undisturbed because of a beginning mental illness. Hence, the infant was carried back and forth by the mother so that his expressions of pain and rage were muted—a circumstance which was very similar to Steve's case (see Chapter V). In addition, in Stanley's case, however, at the height of the symbiotic phase there were those pain attacks that disrupted formation of a normal body image. Stanley had no opportunity to deflect aggression, to eject pain and discomfort, the "bad experiences," into the world beyond the body-self boundaries. The representation of his own body self became populated by painful and bad introjected objects. The early traumatic visceral sensations disrupted the continuum of the libidinization

---

[10] Several of the impulse-ridden tiqueurs show this phenomenon of experiencing their "impulsions," their involuntary tics, as ego-alien machinelike occurrences (cf. Mahler, 1944, 1949b; Mahler and Rangell, 1943; Mahler and Luke, 1946).

process; the child regressed to primary identification. This could be reconstructed. After having uttered a few words in the second half of the second year, Stanley stopped talking. As far as we could ascertain, he used his mother as an extension of himself, an inanimate or semianimate tool as it were, not as a love object. From the age of three, Stanley would lie limp on the floor, stare into space, never play; and though he clung tenaciously to his mother, the clinging differed conspicuously from that of a fairly normal, though overly dependent, small child. We recognize this clinical picture as that of primary symbiotic psychosis in which the mother becomes fused with the self again and belongs within the orbit of the symbiotic system. It was interesting to see how Stanley's mother was oblivious of the gross pathology, and denied its existence as long as possible. Such behavior is fairly typical of the mothers of symbiotic children. As stated earlier, the mother's brother drew her attention to the fact of Stanley's bizarre peculiarities. When finally the child was old enough to enter school, his pathology could of course no longer be denied.

Ever since we have known Stanley and even before that time, he has displayed a special "interest" in mechanical things.[11] For instance, in the city where he lived, there was an advertisement for beer, representing a mechanical robot riding a bicycle. This robot was in constant motion for twenty-four hours a day. Stanley frequently asked his parents to take him to the place where he could see "the man on the bike." His wish was usually granted and he often talked about his trips to "the man on the bike." Sometimes Stanley would move his legs as though he were riding a bike himself.

[11] We know that even normal children are interested in machines, an interest which seems to be fundamentally connected with their phallicity. On the occasion of an extensive study of drawings of normal schoolchildren, Elkisch (1952) pointed to the significance of the boys' projection of their body feelings onto the machine. In the art productions of twenty-two latency boys, there were only two whose subject matter did not include predominantly mechanical devices.

He would also "wheel" his arms around in a seemingly un-motivated robotlike fashion. This mechanical robotlike be-havior also occurred independently of his trips to "the man on the bike" and of his talking about them. One day he came from one of these visits directly to his analytic hour and, overcome by ecstatic joyousness, expressed in parox-ysmal movements, shouted: "He was off today, he was off—this is my luckiest day." The man who "stopped," the man who was "off" or "on" has become one of Stanley's endlessly repetitious topics ever since that day. It is noteworthy that at the age of five Stanley was given a tricycle on which he would sit but never pedal.

The "on" and "off" topic was also expressed in other ways: for hours and hours of his treatment Stanley would draw wheels that "spin" or "stop" spinning. He drew the wheels in such a way that each wheel had a man or a boy in the center; he also drew several "switches" which he pretended to turn "on and off." He would turn his wheels "on" by spinning his crayon in circling motion, and pressing it on the paper around and around with such violence that each crayon would be broken into bits. Again and again he would say, "It will stop soon," indicating his intention to stop crayoning, an intention that appeared as if it were dictated by an alien, isolated split-off part of his ego. And when he stopped crayoning, he would say, "Now *it* stopped." He seemed obsessed with what he was doing, overly excited—an excitement that he apparently "turned on" within himself (Eissler, 1953). In this state he could not be approached. If one asked him a question or tried to reason with him, for instance, saying that it was not the wheel that stopped "by itself," but that it was *he* who had stopped the wheel, by stopping crayoning, he behaved as if he did not hear and withdrew from contact. This confusion of the relation of the active subject and the passive object, the projection of his own intention onto a split-off part of his ego, was remark-able.

Stanley's obsession with "the man on the bike" became interwoven with another obsession about another machine-like object. In the treatment room there was a wall telephone which buzzed when someone pushed the button downstairs in order to get into the house. The noise of the buzzer, at a certain point of treatment, became the most startling, frightening, and fascinating experience to Stanley. From then on he entered the office with his ears covered by his hands, a most anxious look on his face, and rushed to the farthest corner, remaining there throughout the hour. If by chance he came near the telephone, he looked at it with fright and fascination, always covering his ears. No matter what topic was talked about, he inadvertently would ask the stereotyped question: "What will the wall telephone do today when the time is up?" When the therapist said, "It will ring," Stanley answered: "It will not ring." When the therapist further said: "What do you think will happen—because Benny will come and he will push the button downstairs, just as you did," Stanley said, "It will not ring." As Stanley remained so frightened, perplexed, and confused about the wall telephone, he was taken downstairs with all the doors left open so that he could both push the button downstairs and hear the simultaneous buzzing upstairs. In addition, someone else was asked to push the button for us while Stanley and his analyst "waited" for the buzzing upstairs. During this waiting period the boy looked at the wall telephone with apprehensive anticipation and, when it rang, he remarked, "It was not so loud today, because *it knew* we were waiting for it to buzz."

This remark indicates rather clearly the extent to which this patient projected his own tense anticipation onto the lifeless machinery's mechanical response. The machine "knew that we were waiting . . . ," the implication being not simply that an animation of the wall telephone would occur, as could be expected in the case of a normal small child, but the real belief of a seven-year-old that the machine functions in a human way, that the machine took his waiting into consideration and therefore deliberately did not ring so loudly. We can further see his complete confusion of the categories of time, space, cause and effect, besides the confusion of modalities concerning phenomena of life versus machine phenomena (Elkisch, 1956; Mahler, Ross, and De Fries, 1949; Mahler, 1958). Although the demonstrations of the function of cause and effect, as described above, were repeated innumerable times, Stanley could not bring into causal connection the button being pressed downstairs and the buzzer being affected by the electrical current upstairs. In fact, he remained anxious, confused, and startled as before.

This behavior is reminiscent of that stage of early ego development which Piaget (1923) described in the young child who cannot conceive of causal relationships unless cause and effect are in his "immediate perceptive field." In fact, there is a normal developmental stage—at the height of animism—in which the toddler to a greater or lesser degree and for a longer or shorter period of time is startled and frightened by such sounds or other mechanical occurrences, the source of which is not immediately perceivable. There is also a time when normal toddlers are afraid of buzzers, vacuum cleaners, an ironing board coming down from the wall, or other such mechanical devices.

In order to help Stanley overcome his anxiety and also to enable us to learn more about his ego's functioning, a simple electrical instrument was constructed, a board on which a button and a buzzer were installed close to each other, so that both the affecting and the affected thing, or "cause and effect," were in his immediate perceptual field. However, for Stanley, this device had no explanatory meaning whatsoever. He brought "*his* wall telephone," as he called the device, with him when he came to his hour, and he played with it the whole time. The board telephone had an electrical cord which had to be plugged into a socket; only then did the bell on the board ring by pressing the button. Stanley plugged the cord into the socket and then took the plug out, back and forth, which to him meant nothing else but switching something "on" and "off." When his wall telephone was "on," Stanley could push the button and the buzzer would buzz. This activity, intensely pursued and accompanied by orgastic jumping, alternated with the performance for which the machinery was originally devised, namely, the pushing of the button with the result of buzzing. Yet for him these two activities—the plugging and unplugging, on the one hand, and the pressing of the button and buzzing, on the other—seemed entirely disconnected from each other. Moreover, his "wall telephone" became just another machine to Stanley, a machine which permitted him to time and exert his own power: thus it did not arouse his anxiety. It is noteworthy that Stanley soon lost complete interest in his own gadget, but he continued to react to the wall telephone in the office with undiminished fright.

Stanley felt both fascination and fright at the surprising machineries. He displayed the same fascination and surprise at these machineries that he exhibited when he felt an inner impulse or intention. "It will stop soon." He treated his own impulses and reacted to them with the same emotional tone of passive experience as to a person in the environment, or outside force, as we saw him react to the machines: "it stopped"—meaning the wheel he was drawing. We can clearly see here the splitting of his ego into an isolated intentional part and a passive experiencing part. We can also see the equation of the inner impulse and the outside phenomena of machines.

Shortly after his "lucky" experience with the bicycling man "unable to move," Stanley became obsessed with switching lights on and off. For weeks he would arrive at the office, not paying any attention to anything or anybody, not taking off his coat and cap; rather, he rushed in wild excitement from one room to the other turning the lights on and off, an activity which seemed the most primitive realization of his own magic omnipotence, as we see in so many psychotic children. Stanley would turn the light on and then look at the bulb as though he had seen a light for the first time in his life; and then he would turn it off and look at the light-being-off with the same perplexed amazement. He would shout, "Now it is off," and give a smile to the therapist or hug her, jumping in great excitement. There were thirty-one switches all counted of which none was left unturned. His activity of switching on and off always found its climax in manipulating the light in the refrigerator, one of his greatest fascinations, as this was the place for food, in fact, as he verbalized it: "Spoiled baby food."

Very many of the machines with which Stanley was so obsessed and which he demanded to explore again and again seemed related to Stanley's desperate perplexities concerning his body image; they were quite conspicuously related to intense oral and anal preoccupations. For instance, when he was in a food market, he would not rest until his mother took him to one of the big freezers, which he "investigated." The "man on the bike" advertised beer, a fact which incited the boy to bring forth a flood of nonsense words, klang associations, all related to "beer," as, for instance, Esslinger-Beer, Beerlinger, Linger-Beer, Smear-Linger, Linger-Smear. About the wall telephone, Stanley remarked: "It will come down from the wall and take a bite out of you." He also developed an intense fear of the elevator, which was related to the fact that he might fall into the small gap between the elevator and the floor—a passive oral fantasy of being swallowed up, which he verbally related to manholes in the street, anxiously avoiding them, to the flushing of the toilet, and elaborate fantasies about his food going down the sewer.

Stanley's anxieties and panic reactions had always had a diffuse character. In this respect, too, he was a typical representative of similar cases of infantile psychosis. Their anxiety was more reminiscent of the organismic distress—the annihilation panic of the infant or else of the separation anxiety of the junior toddler—than of fear of loss of love or of castration anxiety. With his entire body being suffused with primitive aggression, the fear of exploding and disintegrating into bits seemed his basic fear. Moreover, Stanley's essential fixation occurred at the oral-sadistic level and most of these cases regress to that stage.

Freud (1938) postulated that in cases of splitting of the ego "by the help of regression to an oral phase, it [castration anxiety] assumed the form of a fear of being eaten by his father" (p. 277f.). Freud reminded us of the myth of Cronos, who swallowed his children. In Stanley's case, there was the typical fear of being swallowed, engulfed as it were —engulfed primarily by the mother who was perceived in his own image, deanimated, as if she had lost her human nature.[12]

The other fear encountered in older psychotic children in preadolescence and adolescence is the fear of losing body substance, of being drained of the "body juices of youth," as Teddy, a schizophrenic adolescent whom I analyzed, put it. Teddy was preoccupied with the delusion that father, grandfather, and he himself were a communicating system of glass tubes which competed at draining the life fluid from each other during the night. Survival would depend, so Teddy believed, on who was most successful in draining more from the others' life fluid at night. On the other hand, he worked hard on the invention of a "heart machine" which he could switch on and connect with his body's circulatory system so that he would never have to die.

Returning to Stanley: Stanley's most persistent delusional obsession concerned string beans going down the sewer. He

---

[12] In his paper on "The Delay of the Machine Age" (1933), Hanns Sachs commented: "Animistic man vitalized the inanimate world with such narcissism as he could find no other use for, the schizophrenic transforms his own body into something alien and inanimate (first, through 'feelings of alienation', in a further stage of regression into the 'influencing machine')" (p. 127).

had once eaten unusually long string beans at a meal in
school. Since that incident, Stanley asked every day his infinitely repetitious questions about the string beans: where
had they gone, where were they now, what did they look
like now, what would the sewer do to them, and so on.
Three months after this occurrence, Stanley still talked about
it: "The string beans I ate in Miss A.'s class—they have gone
down the sewer. Why should I worry about them? This is
silly, I know, for it is long ago and they give me strength,
they make my muscles strong and only the waste goes away.
What color do they have? I guess they have taken on the
color of my body—going down like that in the sewer. They
must have the color of my b.m.—I shouldn't worry about
them." These and similar verbalizations indicated Stanley's
intense hypochondriacal fears and perplexities, his complete
confusion between inside drives and outside powers, between
intentional and passive experiences, *particularly affectomotor
and motor phenomena.*[13]

Ever since the pain attacks in his first year of life Stanley
has been a feeding problem. He voiced unusually frequent
complaints concerning his stomach. Gas pains and the urge
to vomit, particularly at times of physical illness, became
very frightening experiences to him—so much so that for
periods after such illnesses when he had recovered sufficiently to be permitted to eat anything he wanted, he would
refuse to eat. We have earlier described Stanley's fabulous
memory as symptomatic of his ego's failure of repression.
Considering the facts that Stanley· was unable to forget

[13] In his discussion remarks, Dr. M. Schur emphasized that Stanley's case
illustrated Rapaport's conception of passivity (1958), namely, that the
transition from passivity to activity is an essential step to structure formation
and ego autonomy. At first there is no activity vis-à-vis the drives. It is only
with gradual development of structure that activity and with it all the
inhibitory functions vis-à-vis the drives come into being. States of regression
result in return to more or less complete passivity. This is clearly shown in
Stanley's case in whom the "complete" passivity toward the drives was so
obvious, and who in a very frantic and primitive way tried to turn the
drive on and off.

certain affect-laden situations of his past, and that he, like many of these children, seemed to have an uncanny *somato-psychic memory*, we might assume that the sensations or urges arising in his gastrointestinal tract, like the gas pains, abdominal distress or vomiting, recalled for him the sudden attacks in his babyhood. We are reminded of Tausk's reference (1919) to the case of Staudenmeyer, a man who "attributed every single peristaltic motion coming to his awareness to the activity of special demons allegedly located in his intestines" (p. 59). It would seem that because of the ego's fragmentation, the enteroceptive stirrings of the viscera and the hunger sensations of the oral cavity, the sensations experienced at defecation, the feeling of nausea, the urge to vomit—all these sensations and experiences remain unintegrated.

In his classical paper Tausk (1919) suggested that the end product, the "influencing machine" of his adult patient, Miss Natalija, must have forerunners in that "developmental stage in which one's own body is the goal of the object finding" (p. 72). In the case of Stanley, this very period of life was a time of intense pain and distress. In conjunction with the visceral pain attacks and the distortions of the early mother-infant symbiosis, Stanley's body ego was not sufficiently cathected with secondary narcissistic libido. The mother image remained fused or was regressively totally fused. The necessity of separate functioning in Stanley's case triggered a psychotic break with reality. When maturational growth confronted the child with the fact of separateness, the obligatory panic reactions with agitation which ensue in such cases at this crossroad were denied or perhaps went unnoticed by the symbiotic mother. Libido was withdrawn and stored in an undifferentiated form—in the inside of the body. Alienation, i.e., delibidinization and aggressivization of the body ego in its peripheral parts, could be seen in Stanley's manifest behavior: the peculiar mechanization of his own functions and movements, his own machinelike quality was striking.

Indeed, the endlessly repetitious preoccupation with the quasi-animated machines, so obviously identified with the dehumanized, devitalized representations of his oral, anal, and phallic functions, the split-up ego-alien introjects, expressed this child's struggle for finding a self-identity and some orientation and integration of internal versus external reality.[14]

In several other cases this utter bewilderment concerning boundaries and identity was spectacular and dramatic. For example, we have witnessed the behavior of psychotic children during defecation, which for them was a major crisis. They behaved as if the cyballum was a dangerous, ego-alien introject, a painful object inside, but which became even more dangerous when it passed the sphincter into the outside world. (I witnessed such situations in Lotta's case, which will be described later in this chapter.)

We return once more to Stanley. As mentioned earlier, Stanley appeared to be unable to express his emotions and affects in other than the most primitive and extreme forms. He had no capacity for modulation. If he displayed any emotions at all, they represented extreme affects, panic or else orgastic ecstasy (Mahler and Elkisch, 1953). At other times he showed complete apathy or even a catatoniclike stupor. These two crudely extreme forms of affective behavior sometimes alternated within one treatment hour, sometimes even several times back and forth; therefore it seemed to the observer as though the boy were switching himself, as it were, from one mode of behavior into the other. Once he had switched himself "on," it often seemed as if the motion were generated from within him, as from an engine—an engine gaining momentum and running so powerfully that the child

---

[14] For a more detailed description of this phase of Stanley's treatment, see Elkisch (1956).

had no way of stopping it. Moreover, the emotions which Stanley seemed to turn "on" and "off," like one of the switches, were created by him in a most peculiar and rather "unemotional" way. The child, evidently knowing that certain emotional expressions were expected of him by his environment, and, in his attempt to adapt and to comply with these expectations, at times gave the impression that he made himself "learn" emotions. Here is an example: on several occasions during his hour, the boy suddenly got up and, without the slightest provocation or detectable connection with what had gone on before, went from one place to another, took things which were within his reach, threw them on the floor, and tried to destroy them. He would look up smilingly and somewhat proudly say: "Today I want to be naughty." Even though such behavior could strike one as "aggressive," actually the boy could no more convince one of real aggressiveness than a very poor actor could. Another peculiar, artificial manipulation to satisfy, as it appeared, his affectively depleted sensory self image: he begged his father to spank him! We have seen and have described other cases in which a child resorted to bizarre modes to obtain greater libidinal and aggressive cathexis of the "rind of the ego" in order to obtain bodily self-demarcation. Stanley's father cooperated in a playful way, spanking the boy, but certainly without hurting him. But while he was, so to speak, "spanking" the child, Stanley started to cry. He cried and cried and his parents found it most difficult to stop him. The engine in him had gained momentum and had to be stopped by an outside operator. These "scenes" had to be repeated frequently.

Stanley's attempts to reach some kind of homeostasis and adaptation to reality expressed themselves in numerous other ways, all of which were mechanical and machinelike. The learning of emotions and the displaying of the learned emotions had an equivalent in the intellectual field. There they appeared to be less peculiar and less surprising than in the realm of affects. His way of communicating altogether had a quality of parroting. The child pretended to read without being able to read, running through the books which had been read to him, and which, through listening, he had learned by heart. He used phrases which he had picked up from others, mostly from the adults in his environment, and he used those phrases with the same tone of voice, sometimes even accompanied by the kind of mannerisms, gesture or posture or facial expression that the adult might have exhibited while speaking. With some exceptions, the phrases that Stanley parroted were not entirely inappropriate to the situations in which Stanley used them, so that his parroting speech and mannerisms actually constituted a bridge, a link between him and reality.

Stanley's intellectual learning in a narrower sense, however, did not afford him such a link with reality. There his "methods," because of their mechanical, mosaiclike quality, lacked the essential human features of learning by trial and error, by transfer and abstraction. As described earlier, Stanley commanded a fabulous memory, but this memory at close examination turned out to be a storage of disconnected engrams, unorganized as to the qualities of essential or unessential.

The child reacted as though a switch had been on in him and *the memory machine* was set in motion. Thus, when Stanley parroted someone in speech and mannerism, it seemed as though the content of the past conversation could not be divorced from certain qualities peculiar to that conversation or situation, or person who might have talked or read to him. Two or more things, images, concepts, affect and perception at one time experienced together, became engram conglomerates, syncretically and therefore forever connected with each other in his memory.

Summarizing what we learned from Stanley's case we can

say that the infantile precursors of the "influencing machine" are based upon:

delibidinization of the body image (especially its boundaries);

total introjection of the mother and withdrawal of libido from her and the rest of the object world.

The result is a narcissistic state, in which the ego becomes fragmented and the self-boundaries blurred, fused with the mother's.

The most essential failure of the fragmented ego pertains to the overall mechanisms of integration and synthesis of inside with outside stimuli. There is failure of repression as well.

In the place of these defense mechanisms, dedifferentiation is used (see also Peto, 1959, 1967).

Dedifferentiation is based upon massive denial of percepts—in the wake of which aggression-saturated inner percepts gain ascendancy. These inner stimuli or percepts undergo deanimation and machinization (Mahler, 1960).

The psychotic child—like the normal one—sees the world in his own image. Thus all objects in the psychotic child's reality take on the same machinelike, semianimate, preterhuman quality as his own body image.

The main difference between the adult and the child psychotic seems to be that in the adult the hallucinated (projected) outside machine influences the self, whereas in the child psychotic the influencing quality still manifestly pertains to his own self representation and is then projected (secondarily) to the outer world.

Stanley's case illustrated the sequelae of intrinsic (hernia-pain attacks) and early environmental (outside inhibition of crying) interference with the process of libidinization of the body surface, the skin, and the sensory-perceptive "rind" of the ego as well as the orderly sequence of zonal erotization (Fliess, 1957).

LOTTA

The case of Lotta was a heartrending demonstration of the outcome of insults suffered by a probably constitutionally vulnerable infant practically from the first day of her extrauterine life on all levels of zonal libidinization.

Lotta was, in Kanner's sense, a case of early infantile autism. She illuminated for me—like a cruel experiment of nature and more than any other case—the elements of the fabric of which human personality is woven, precisely because these elements appeared utterly fragmented and isolated in her makeup.

When I visited her to start treatment, Lotta was three years and two months old. I knew that to reach her it was essential that I approach her in her familiar home environment. She not only lacked the slightest trace of "confident expectation," her quest for sameness seemed to be the only principle by which she seemed able to exist.

Lotta had suffered multiple traumatizations by a mother who lived in a hateful dependency on her own mother. Lotta had experienced severe feeding deprivations; a lip injury at spoon feeding had occurred at a very early age. There was a strict and unloving regime of precocious toilet training. A vulvovaginitis followed the first signs of Lotta's beginning to "touch herself." Thus, traumatic overstimulation crowded out normal zonal libidinization in all areas of psychosexual development. Daily struggles over constipation, with digital removal of the feces, was just one indication of the kind of atmosphere that prevailed. At the age of three and a half Lotta had no language, no gestural communication, no hand, mouth, and eye integration (Hoffer, 1949). She neither fed nor handled herself, and she showed a terrified startle reaction at any chance touch *of* or *by* another person. By the usual intelligence rating she would have ranked among the lower imbeciles. However, Lotta's habits were compulsively neat, her motor and manipulative skills were age adequate, her knowledge of and her memory for her static inanimate environment were phenomenal.

During therapy, by using every conceivable device, she was slowly brought to sensory perception of the outer world, by gradually accepting contact with the analyst's body. Yet no normal identification occurred; instead there was extensive mirroring and parrotlike word formation. Word formation was autistic and speech was used not for intercommunication, but only for commands and signals—and it was used toward inanimate, especially machinelike, objects as freely as toward the analyst.

She seemed to catch up rapidly with isolated fragments of her arrested ego development. She went through repetitious aggressive exploration of her inanimate environment—banging the doors, switching the lights on and off, and fingering everything as blind people do.

At the stage of treatment when Lotta went through repetitious testing of her environment, she would indeed tax the patience of her mother. A little flashlight was provided for her by the analyst in order to drain away some of the disturbing behavior from the overstrained home situation. She became quite attached to the little flashlight, very much like a teething baby. When driving from the office that time, her mother, as usual, used the automatic lighter to light her cigarette. Lotta, unnoticed, got hold of the glowing lighter and put it to her mouth, causing severe scorching of her lips.

Without adequate reality testing Lotta seemed to want to reach out for the transitional object, the "psychotic fetish" which more than for the normal infant would help to bridge the void between her narcissistic isolation and the living object world, the beginning symbiotic relationship with her analyst and that with her parents. Lotta showed practically no reaction. Her pain sensitivity seemed grossly below normal. This, among other signs is, I believe, an indication of the lack or deficiency of peripheral cathexis in predominantly autistic child patients. In contrast, proprioceptive stimuli, visceral pain, were keenly felt and reacted to (Mahler, 1950).[15]

In Lotta's case, like in many other similar cases, it seemed unavoidable that autonomous ego functions emerged, were put together, and existed simultaneously like a patchwork of loosely connected parts, held together in a static way, without the specific matrix of "affective correlation" in the course of treatment. (Compare the previously described case of Stanley.)

This bizarre picture of scattered ego functions and the clinically clearly discernible lack of peripheral cathexis make us realize that in autistic infantile psychosis the vicissitudes of libido and aggression cannot be traced merely in terms of the hierarchy of zonal stages. Instead, we can in some cases trace during treatment the course of libido and aggression from the splanchnic-visceral position through progressive cathexis in cranial direction and outward onto the periphery of the body, the skin, and the sense organs, i.e., the perceptual conscious system (Mahler, 1950). The instinctual forces, both libido and aggression, exist in an unneutralized form, due to the absence or grave deficiency of the synthetic function of the ego. There is an inherent lack of contact with or warding off of perception of the human environment.

Whenever Lotta was in great distress, her whole little body shook with tearless sobs; yet she neither sought nor accepted help from anyone, but threw herself flat on the floor and pressed against the solid support of it. Likewise she would cling to the familiar high chair, but not to father or mother. This autistic psychotic child was characterized (as were all those whom I observed) by a peculiar inability

[15] When Lotta's mother, disregarding my request not to give Lotta laxatives, would give her some, I always knew about it because Lotta reacted in the therapeutic session as if possessed by demoniacal introjects to the enteroceptive internal peristaltic sensations and abdominal pain.

to discriminate between living and inanimate objects, even in a perceptual sense (compare Stirnimann, 1947).

As early as in 1952 I realized the inadequacy of treating the psychotic child who had regressed and organized his defenses for adaptation and survival within his secondarily created autistic shell, without full participation of the original symbiotic object, the mother. At that time I wrote:

> . . . if the [primarily or secondarily] autistic [child] is forced too rapidly into social contact . . . he is often thrown into a catatonic state and then [into a] . . . fulminant psychotic process . . . if such catastrophic reactions cannot be avoided, it seems that such autistic infants are better off if allowed to remain in their autistic shell, even though in "a daze of restricted orientation" they may drift into a very limited degree of reality adjustment only. Diagnosis of their "original condition," of course, then usually escapes recognition; they are thrown into the category of the feeble-minded [p. 303].

A most dramatic episode occurred in little Lotta's life at four and a half years of age, after she had established a symbiotic relationship with me in the second year of analytic treatment. The family moved to a distant suburb. As a result, her treatment was interrupted and her inanimate environment was radically changed. I subsequently received a call from her desperate mother, and visited them. Lotta epitomized the most heart-rending and tragic picture of utter bereavement. She was unable to focus on me; instead she behaved as if she wished to ward off the very perception of my presence by agitated creeping and sliding on her buttocks on the garden grounds, by rocking and throwing garden earth onto her disheveled little head with both hands; by whining pitifully, but without tears and without any signs of appeal to the humans around her. All the signals which she had learned in therapy, and which had enabled me to fulfill Lotta's needs, were lost. This signal language, syncretic in nature, but well libidinized, had involved confidence and pleasurable anticipation. Now Lotta warded off any approach from either her mother or me. Needless to say, it was most difficult and needed great effort to re-establish contact with Lotta when she was brought back for treatment.

Lotta's ego suffered a similar, but much more permanent, and, in fact, irreversible psychic damage when, at the age of about six, she was placed in an institution which housed autistic and organically brain-damaged children. Ironically, she was placed there after she had made a spurt of development in therapy and attained an extensive, though automatonlike, vocabulary. This vocabulary had been taught to her by her mother, who had also been able to teach her to perform automatized mental operations which were quite remarkable in their complexity, including the ability to read. Unfortunately, Lotta reached a plateau in this automatic learning, and her mother, preoccupied with a new pregnancy, was unable to meet Lotta's needs, which were manifested in the form of a very distorted and very delicate reaching out. Both parents decided it was just "no use."

Lotta's mother wrote to me about her visit to the institution. The description of Lotta in that letter sounded like the description of an adult in a state of acute melancholia. Lotta did not speak, merely pleaded desperately with her eyes. Her movements were slow and listless; she walked with a shuffling gait. The mother also reported that Lotta refused to eat. Lotta was subsequently taken home, and nursed back to life, so to speak, an utterly automatized and delibidinized life. Her mother was able to train her successfully enough so that Lotta was accepted and enrolled in the public school of the community.

Lotta was brought to my office to visit when she was nine. Her responses were automatic; there was no recognition of me as a person. She remembered syncretically the most minute details of the playroom, and enumerated, in primary process fashion, all the objects around her. There was an amazing execution of commands which her mother had obviously given her beforehand. For example, whenever I tried to say something personal to her, she would ward off an aggressive impulse from within by loudly reciting, in the voice of a town crier: "Always be polite"; "You should love all the children"; "Go to the blackboard"; "I can do long division, I can spell"; "The elevator will take you down"; "You will go home"; "You will sleep home." She used these internalized, but unintegrated commands to tame her anxiety and basic mistrust.

Precisely such experiences as those with Lotta and similar cases prompted us to design a therapeutic approach in which the mother can be fully engaged in the treatment process and thus helped to lend herself to her child for re-experiencing the missed and distorted developmental phases. Within this newly developed "tripartite therapeutic design," the therapist serves as the catalyst, the transfer agent, and the buffer between child and mother. Such an approach should forestall the irreversible and catastrophic reaction to the disintegration of a recently established therapeutically imposed symbiosis as we witnessed in Lotta's case (compare Chapter VI).

As David Beres (1960) stated succinctly: "Only with the development of . . . the capacity to create a mental representation of the absent object, does the child progress from the syncretic, sensori-motor-affective immediate response to the delayed abstract, conceptualized response that is characteristically human" (p. 334). This intrapsychic image, this mental representation of the temporarily absent symbiotic object, seems to serve as an indispensable catalyst in that it enables all the potentially autonomous capacities of the primitive ego to become functional. I consider it the spark which ignites the ego's capacity for human affect, for human social and emotional development.

In psychotic children, the breakdown of the ego's basic functions—of all or many of them—can be attributed to either one of the following conditions: (1) the ego's inability to create the relatively complex intrapsychic image of the human symbiotic object; or (2) the loss of a precarious mental representation of the symbiotic object which, because it is excessively linked to need satisfaction on a symbiotic-parasitic level, cannot grow toward object constancy, and which therefore cannot cope with the demands of the separation-individuation phase. We are all familiar with the chronic sequelae of these psychic events. *What we seldom see, and what is rarely described in the literature, is the period of grief and mourning which I believe inevitably precedes and ushers in the complete psychotic break with reality, that is to say, the secondary autistic withdrawal.*

Sadness and grief are the first signs of progressive development and seem to be obligatory accompaniments of the child's emergence from the deanimated autistic world through restoration of the libidinal object.

It is a well-known fact that the affective responses of the psychotic child who has regressed to a comfortably restricted autistic world of his own will be minimal unless this autistic, omnipotent, dedifferentiated world is upset. Thus, when both therapy and the unfamiliar, inanimate environment impinge upon his autistic withdrawal, his affective reactions may range widely from wandering off and searching,[16] to incessant, hyperactive, irritable restlessness and fretting, to abysmal panic reactions, fits of rage, temper tantrums, head banging, self-biting, and other grossly autoaggressive acts, until he reaches a state of exhaustion or extreme apathy. Then, as the child begins to retrieve the symbiotic object and to cathect its representation with libido, we observe more ego-filtered moods and emotions—sadness instead of desperation, anger instead of rage, longing and anxiety instead of panic. These manifestations of emotions mark the first stage of giving up and replacing autistic defenses; they also mark

---

[16] Compare Imre Hermann's work (1936).

the ego's emergence as a functional structure of the personality.

AMY

These processes could be observed in several children during therapy, one of which was the case of Amy. She was brought for therapy at the age of three and a half. At that time she was aimlessly preoccupied with such stereotyped activities as pouring water or sand all over. She was unable to focus, she seemed to look through people. She urinated and defecated whenever she was so prompted by an urge for bodily discharge; and darted about, snatching at objects. The slightest change in the environment evoked loud shrieks or prolonged whining.[17] Amy reacted to frustrations, however minor, with desperate temper tantrums and excessive hyperactivity.

In the course of our "therapeutic action research," Amy became noticeably attached to her therapist using the latter in a most primitive way as an extension of her ego, as a need-satisfying tool. Concomitant with this development, Amy retained her stools and held other tensions in abeyance as well. At this point the child who previously had alternated between reckless hyperactivity and exhausted lethargy occasionally began to display by her mien and gestures sadness and even grief.

By restoring the human object, therapy had helped Amy to form some representations of a symbiotic object. Yet, precisely in this phase of therapy Amy cried inconsolably at the sound of such trigger words as crib, blanket, lying down, going to sleep. Although her sleep itself was not disturbed, it seemed to us that Amy at this point showed a mechanism resembling those which transiently occur in the normal sleep disturbances of two-year-old normal toddlers.

[17] Amy's therapist was Mrs. Emmogene Kamaiko, one of our senior workers at The Masters Children's Center.

In a panel on Sleep Disturbances in Children (see Friend, 1956), Anna Maenchen considered "the *unspecified maturational reluctance* to retreat from all the activity and autonomy of waking life" in early childhood. Marianne Kris mentioned Liselotte Frankl's experience as a newspaper consultant in London. Frankl had "most requests for help with sleep disturbances in a two-year-old group." The intimate connection between the loss of object relationship and considerations of regression is important in these transient sleep disturbances. It is interesting that we, as well as other investigators of psychoses in children, have had the experience that predominantly autistic children did not suffer from sleep disturbances, while those who were predominantly symbiotic sooner or later did develop sleep impairments. Maenchen feels that the child, "once withdrawn into its autistic shell, is no longer afraid until he comes out of the withdrawal." Conversely, the appearance of sleep disturbances, according to her, could be an indication that progress in ego development is being resumed.[18] In Amy's case, I think her anxiety reaction and fretting when words reminding her of the state of ego regression in sleep were mentioned indicated a growing awareness of human object relationship. When Amy began to evolve the image or concept of a symbiotic object, she became aware of the danger which losing the symbiosis with this object in sleep entailed.

MALCOLM

This case was an unusual case. He suffered from a symbiotic psychotic syndrome in which the father was the sym-

[18] It is interesting to note that Lotta did develop a slight disturbance of her sleep at the time she became attached to a powder puff with which she soothingly stroked her cheek. She took the puff with her to bed and for a while would wake up crying when she lost it. As soon as somebody retrieved it for her, Lotta fell asleep again.

biotic object, whereas he reacted with autistic defenses to the mother.

When Malcolm, a three-and-a-half-year-old psychotic child, came to our attention, he had achieved a much higher level of integration than Amy. When he arrived with his "ordinary, devoted mother" at the Center, he wore at times the frozen expression which is so characteristic of primarily or secondarily autistic children. He was, however, the proto-type of a child suffering from a symbiotic psychotic syn-drome. He responded to his mother and usually was in con-tact with her—albeit in a rather primary process fashion. He later established a similarly patterned relationship with his therapist, provided his demands were correctly guessed and promptly fulfilled. His little face lit up immediately, how-ever, when someone suggested the game of telephoning his daddy. He assumed a longing, wistful expression while on the toy telephone he carried on his imaginary conversation with his father.

Malcoln also engaged in a passionate contact with Dr. Furer, a father substitute, snuggled up to him, and looked crestfallen and sad whenever the doctor left the room. Mal-colm's peculiar symbiotic relationship with his father gave way only very gradually—via a re-experiencing of the sym-biotic relationship with the therapist, and subsequently with his mother, by externalizing split-up representations of self and object, and by concentrating libido on the representation of the "good mother" and projecting his aggression onto the image of the "bad mother." Only after the delusional, patho-logical symbiotic tie with his father was loosened could Mal-colm experience, for the first time, the communion he had missed in his relationship with his mother. During this phase, which began after Malcolm allowed himself to spit at peo-ple, his therapeutic sessions involved endless babbling, coo-ing, and gurgling with his mother. Incidentally, his mother said to us: "Malcolm seems to be having the same experiences with me now that his two older brothers had with me when they were babes in arms."

The case of Malcolm has been described in great detail by M. Furer (1964), who focused on the problem of the psychotic fetish.

GEORGE

In the psychotic syndrome of George, bisexual identification and the urge for symbiotic fusion were paramount. George was just under seven when admitted to the Children's Service of the N.Y. State Psychiatric Institute and Columbia University with fulminant symptoms of delusions and hallucinations. He had developed fairly normally to the age of three, when his mother became pregnant. He then began to have night terrors and what his mother aptly described as "talking tantrums." He would pace the room, talking angrily to himself about something which seemed entirely irrelevant to his environment. Shortly after the baby sister was born, he became acutely disturbed. He wanted to wear her clothes, and often wanted to wear his mother's. He insisted that he wanted to be a girl, preferred female animals and asked his mother perseverative questions why he should not be a girl. At about the same time he began to be afraid of the holes in a fence which he passed, or wherever he encountered any. His father frequently used this fear as a threat, often telling him he would put him in a hole. George tried to get reassurance from his father by asking frequently: "Do you love me?"

George became a very good but asocial student. He often spoke of his sister, and again and again of his pet kitten in school. "I have a cat at home. It's a girl cat. I like my cat. I'm a girl cat." He had no contact with and was terrified by the other children, and could be kept in school, at least for a while, only because of the great appeal he had for his teacher. However, his behavior in school became so bizarre that the teacher referred him for hospitalization.

His fear of, and wish for, castration could be traced back to his mother's pregnancy. First he developed a strange interest in barrels. He stopped and touched barrels and looked at them with extreme interest. After his preoccupation with barrels (they lived next to a brewery) he became fascinated by pipes of all sorts, which again he would have to touch, commenting on their size, shape, or other characteristics. He would play with his father's pipes for long periods. After a few months he developed a similar preoccupation with electrical appliances. He would endlessly pretend to be plugging a cord into a socket. Later he developed an intense interest in fires, and this was dominant at the time of his hospitalization.

In the hospital his hallucinatory and delusional restitution attempts pertained to incorporative and destructive tendencies toward his sister and mother. In his most pronounced hallucinations, there was a fire destroying his little sister. At first George verbalized these fire hallucinations, and hence we knew how to read his agitated behavior when it betrayed these visions. In his clearer periods he would state: "I'm afraid of killing my mother. I have ideas of wanting to kill her. Yes, I think of killing her, and these thoughts upset me so. That gives me bad feelings in my head. It makes me so upset when I am home. Doctor, you are supposed to take that out."

At the same time his hallucinations also were attempts at restitution. While sitting next to the nurse whom he loved and hated most, he unzipped his overalls and began pulling at the nurse's skirt as though gathering up something. He then put his hands in his overalls as if pouring in what he had gathered. This went on for a short time; then he zipped up his overalls and sat there smiling. "I've got a Hollinger [name of the nurse] in there . . . that's what I've got in there." George was hilariously elated for the rest of the day and sat off in a corner, communicating with the introjected beloved (M. Klein, 1932).

It was thus obvious that this youngster in his childish way was also making restitutive efforts to solve, albeit psychotically, his bisexual conflict in a way that is comparable to the type of effort made by adolescent and adult schizophrenics.

George is an example of how the psychotic symbiotic defense of regressive refusion with the love object is used to ward off the erupting destructive instinctual drive which threatens to annihilate the self and the object world. In many cases, this defense alone is not sufficient, and secondary autism supervenes.

Only on rare occasions can we observe the slipping away of the object world, the actual process of loss of identity, and the fragmentation of the ego. It was possible to reconstruct some of the processes involved in George's case. (Compare also the case described by Kubie and Israel [1955] in the paper entitled "Say You're Sorry.")

Immediately after George's birth, the father left for the Navy. Mother and infant saw practically nobody but one another. When George was two, the father returned but was disinterested and morose. George had had no opportunity to experience and eventually overcome at the appropriate age the normal uneasiness of the infant and toddler about strangers. His father appeared suddenly and must have been an utter stranger to George. No wonder, then, that in his third year of life he seemed utterly to misunderstand the affective meaning of social situations, a misunderstanding further complicated by projection of his unneutralized aggression. For example, he would cry if greeted by an unfamiliar person wtih a friendly "hello," as if the word "hello" were a serious threat. If friends or relatives patted him on the shoulder or on the head, he became terrified, stated that they had hit him, and seemed frightened that they would harm him. His speech, which characteristically was not needed during his prolonged symbiotic relationship with his mother—because symbiotic partners communicate in a preverbal or nonverbal atmosphere—suddenly became overcathected. At the age of about two and a half to three, George's mutism abruptly changed to flighty and panic-stricken language, the "talking tantrums." At the end of George's third year of life, the mother became pregnant, and George began to have night terrors. During the last months of his mother's pregnancy he developed an absorbing, exclusive interest in examining his inanimate environment by touching. At this time he developed his compulsive interest in barrels, beer barrels in particular, and subsequently in pipes. Since his father was a plumber, he could play with the pipes in his shop for long periods. After a few months he developed a similar preoccupation with electrical appliances. Later George developed an interest in fires, and this was predominant at the time of his hospitalization.

George's case is only one example in which the slipping away of reality is ushered in by the loss of the innate human faculty of discrimination between the animate and the inanimate, the living and the dead. To this primal discrimination von Monakow has given the name *protodiakrisis*. It seems to depend on and consists of impressions of warmth, resiliency, turgor, deep tactile sensations between two living higher organisms in contact with one another.

In his third year George demonstrated his utter confusion about the workings of living bodies and inanimate systems. The nature of the sexual difference of bodies was particularly confusing to George.

After a far too exclusive and morbid symbiotic parasitic two-year period with his mother, George was suddenly faced in a hostile, extended environment with separateness from his mother in the functional-maturational sense, without being emotionally at all prepared to give up the delusion of omnipotent fusion with her. George seemed to have tried

frantically to adopt countercathectic devices against fragmentation of his brittle ego. He tried to counteract the
threatening loss of the libidinal object world by attempting
to recapture it in a concrete sense, by using the contact-
perceptive faculties of his ego. We see this kind of frantic
reality testing very frequently in this type of psychotic child.
George compulsively and feverishly tried to finger, "to feel"
things. He obviously tried to distinguish between—to compare—beer barrels with his pregnant mother's body. Later,
after his baby sister's birth, George compared, in this tactile
way, concrete symbols of male and female anatomy.

The bisexual problem augmented to a spectacular degree
this boy's struggle to regain his symbiotic completeness with
the "lost mother." Castration fear and envy of the intimate
relationship of the girl baby and the mother seemed to drive
George into intense body hallucinations which were characterized by psychotically destructive contents.

Patients like George, who began with an insoluble symbiotic problem, thus sever the ties with unbearable reality,
submerge into their self-created autistic inner reality, and
erect their own object world represented by the introjects.
These patients thus secondarily regress into autism to maintain their lives and entity in some dedifferentiated, deanimated form. In other words, continual separation-annihila-
tion panic being unbearable, children who begin with a
symbiotic psychosis will use autistic mechanisms as defensive
measures. This is a means of warding off the danger of losing
whatever minimal individual entity they may have succeeded
in attaining, either through development or through treatment. They try to preserve whatever autonomy they may
have attained by the mechanism of autism. To repeat, these
autistic reactions are secondary attempts to ward off the
threatened re-engulfment into a symbiotic relationship since
such fusion would destroy the individual entity the child
has barely attained.

CLIFFORD

This is another case of striking psychotic bisexual conflict. Bodily hallucinations of bisexual identity are characteristic of the older psychotic child.

Clifford, who had a mixed type of childhood schizophrenia, was also a patient of the Children's Service from the time he was six and a half years old. For the first fourteen months of his life, his development seemed normal, though he was never a cuddly baby and, in retrospect, seemed to have shown the characteristics of a case of early infantile autism during his second, third, and fourth years. At three and a half he became intensely jealous of his eight-month-old sister. His speech did not develop. He used stereotype phrasing, which he would perseverate in a sing-song voice, and spoke of himself exclusively in the third person. He became obsessed with mechanical and electrical equipment. At five, restitutive symbiotic mechanisms became increasingly marked. Whereas up to then he had defended his secluded, autistic world, now he insisted on sharing his parents' bed and sought close bodily contact with both of them. His bisexual conflict manifested itself in a way similar to that described in the case of George. Clifford began to bite the nurses, suddenly and impulsively, for example, when he passed them in the hall. He said he "loved" the nurses, called them each carefully by name, and sought their company for a type of ritualized conversation that consisted mostly in identifying them by name and telling his name, then naming other personnel on the ward. As his biting was discouraged, he began to dress in two handkerchiefs arranged as a skirt, a nurse's cap, and insisted, "Don't call me Clifford, call me Miss Clifford. I'm a nurse." He became anxious if this was not done, and for a period of time insisted on being called "Miss Clifford" or "Nurse Clifford."

This phase of behavior was introduced in the therapeutic

sessions by a denial. "I don't want to be a girl. Girls wear dresses, boys wear pants. I don't want to be like my sister. Girls and boys are different." The above was repeated at home, but was quickly followed, as in the hospital, by a period of insistence upon wearing his younger sister's clothes and being called "Miss Clifford" by his family as well.

ALMA

The following case illustrates the desperate attempt to perpetuate the symbiotic fusion when it conflicts with the struggle for separation and individuation, a struggle that is accompanied by the bisexual conflict in both the words and the behavior of an adolescent patient.

Alma came to our attention on the ward at the age of fourteen.[19] The onset of her psychosis could be traced back to the age of four and a half. At that time she had had a high temperature and had been hospitalized for ten days because of measles complicated by pneumonia. Her inclination to "somatization" and to bodily symbolization revealed itself in what seemed to be infantile pregnancy fantasies. These were indicated by the fact that during the entire period of ten days of hospitalization she had no bowel movement. After her return home, her abdomen protruded enormously, a fact that was verified by several observers. From then on, Alma seemed quite different: weak, sick, whimpering and crying. During her first three days at home, she defecated constantly so that her abdomen returned to normal size. Following this expulsion of feces, but not during it, she began to stutter. She became fussy about food, consistently refused all solids (warding off of oral-sadistic fantasies?), and vomited frequently. She began school at the age of six, but seemed to make no friends. At seven, according to her story,

19 I owe this material to the cooperation of Dr. William H. Cox, Jr.

an older man made sexual advances to her. It was difficult to determine whether there had actually been an advance of a sexual nature or whether she had interpreted the episode in that way.

At ten, following a bad dream, Alma became very disturbed. Her "nervousness" followed upon seeing the movie *Snow White and the Seven Dwarfs*. After this movie the patient had a dream from which she woke screaming and ran to her mother. It took a long time and much coaxing to persuade Alma to explain what was bothering her: *She had heard a voice saying: "Strangle your mother*, strangle your mother." She was therefore afraid to sleep in her own room and insisted on sleeping with her father, thereby displacing her mother to another room. At this point she was taken to a psychiatrist.

Alma began to feel that her friends did not like her because something was wrong with *her face. She felt* it was too skinny, later she felt that it *looked much older* than her age (approximately the age of her mother). She became overly solicitous about her mother's health, and also over-argumentative. On the ward she was constantly looking into the mirror and said that the whole ward (or world?) was a mirror image of herself. She said: "All things are two substances, soul and sex; some people and some things are primarily 'sex' (mainly women), some people combine the sex and soul feelings together (mainly men). The same feeling I have toward my mother pertains to sex feeling." In a letter she said:

Maybe then [at ten] *I for the first time separated from my mother and I was afraid of reality and therefore didn't give it a chance.*[20] And I cut myself off and forgot soul feelings. Like maybe *when I saw* "Snow White and the Seven Dwarfs,"

[20] We know from the anamnesis that the first real separation and the first prepsychotic reaction to facing reality apart from mother had in fact occurred when Alma was four and a half years old.

somehow I was the witch and fed the girl the apple—and I saw the prince and I saw soul and sex feelings which [feelings] in reality concern men.—*Maybe somehow I wanted to get my mother out of myself by strangulation and at the same time strangling or punishing myself* [for and by] *killing Snow White.*—All I know is after I said, "Strangle your mother," subconsciously *I equated my mother to the witch and sort of broke away from my mother.* I felt weird inside: strange, empty: an afraid weirdness. [Then] I was no more afraid of myself anymore for a few seconds. But *for a whole year I constantly threw up and always felt like dizzy.*[21] Maybe subconsciously I was strangling myself (as the witch) or was it mother—or was it Snow White—or was it the mice that Ma killed[22]—but I imagine it was me.—I thought I would sleepwalk and kill her.[23] After a few seconds I didn't feel empty but different.

One could hardly ask for a more explicit description of the steps which introduced the gradual loss of reality, the psychotic break with reality, and the subsequent development of restitutive mechanisms in this symbiotic psychosis. There is confusion between the self and the mother and a lack of direction between libidinal and aggressive tendencies. Both the mother and the self, as the objects of unneutralized instinctual forces, are confused and *fused*.

The introjected, persecuting mother makes Alma fear that she looks much older than she is; she has sex feelings toward the mother, has the impulse to strangle the mother—in herself and in the outside—and then she says either that she is her mother's mirror image or again that the world is her own mirror image. "It is as if I have to live with my reflection

[21] We again know from the anamnesis that the vomiting and her refusal of solids (in warding off obviously oral-sadistic incorporative fantasies by ejection) began at four and a half.

[22] Alma was horror-stricken when her mother actually exterminated mice in their kitchen.

[23] This was the rational reason Alma gave for sleeping with her father: to be protected from her dangerous impulse.

(like when I look in the mirror) [the mother in herself] and I have to face my reflection when I see people because they are my walking or live reflections." The fusion of all three representations—self, mother, and world—is expressed in her own words: "What if I am the living reflection of my mother and when I look in the mirror it is a double exposure. And I see my reflection in others and it makes me miserable. . . . I go around in circles. There is no escape. I live in a world that has a plane surface, flat like my reflection in the mirror, and the people I see in this world are the living reflection of myself, and this sex-person that I see in the mirror isn't me. I refuse to accept that person."

The crux of the pathogenic struggle to give up the symbiotic-parasitic fusion with the parental image is clearly expressed, and the Kleinian mechanisms are strikingly illustrated by the patient when she says: "After I said, 'Strangle your mother,' subconsciously I equated my mother to the witch and sort of broke away from my mother. . . . But for a whole year I *constantly threw up* and always felt like dizzy. Maybe subconsciously I was strangling myself [or the mother in herself] and felt guilty for strangling myself—or was it mother—or was it Snow White [whom the witch tried to kill] —or was it the mice that Ma killed—but I imagine it was me. After a few seconds I didn't feel empty, but I felt different."

This is only a brief excerpt from the wealth of material this young girl produced. Although these productions stem from the time when she was an adolescent, we cite them here because she was actually describing the genesis of her psychosis in retrospect (as verified by her mother, sister, and father) and because owing to her queer talent for introspection, she has described the most essential aspects and functions of the symbiotic-parasitic hallucinatory mechanisms of restitution.[24]

[24] They are identical with those seen in other symbiotic cases; e.g., George, who was described above, and Betty, who was analyzed from the age of five to eleven (see Chapter II).

ARO

This primarily symbiotic psychotic case illustrates the kinship between generalized tics and the struggle against re-engulfment and the persecuting introjects.

Aro was brought by his pediatrician for consultation at the age of nine and a half because of his incapacitating seizure-like paroxysms of generalized tics. He had been having tics with intermissions since the age of six. The referring pediatrician stated that Aro had been hypertonic and hyperkinetic from birth on. He had suffered from pylorospasm. Yet he is said to have been a happy, outgoing infant till the age of about two and a half. As an infant he is reported to have smiled at people, cooed, played pat-a-cake, how big, etc. At closer questioning the mother recalled, however, that Aro never could tolerate frustrations. He insisted that the mother or the nurse be closely at hand at all times. When, at the age of one and thereafter, Aro was put into a playpen, he would throw a temper tantrum.

In retrospect this was the first manifest sign—we believe— of a progressive disturbance in the neutralization of aggressive drive energy. The assumption is borne out by subsequent disturbed behavior: as soon as Aro could stand on his feet and walk, he manifested a "deadly" hostility toward his siblings, five and seven years older. He threw forks and knives and spit at them. This behavior, in turn, brought about a radical and abrupt change in the mother's attitude toward Aro. She was indignant and completely intolerant in the face of the small boy's bold, and what seemed vicious, attacks upon his so much older siblings. The mother unhesitatingly and completely sided with the siblings. Aro was often severely restrained, reprimanded, and ostentatiously left behind.

But there were objective signs and symptoms of a constitutional vulnerability of the ego, such as hypertonicity, in

Aro's case. At ten weeks Aro developed a severe pyloric stenosis. He would eagerly take his bottle and for a few moments would keep the milk down. Then there would be contractions of the stomach, observable through the abdominal wall. Unmistakable expressions of pain accompanied these contractions, and the milk was expelled by violent projectile vomiting. Very soon after he finished vomiting, Aro would be given another bottle; if he vomited again, this would be followed by forced feeding. He was weaned from the bottle to a cup at five months. From that moment on, he has put fingers, toys, and various objects indiscriminately into his mouth.

Attempts at toilet training were started unbelievably early by a strict nurse. At about the age of four, Aro began to retain his feces for a week at a time, complaining that it hurt to defecate. Against his protests and struggles, the mother gave the boy frequent enemas.

Aro began school at five and a half; a year later his tics began. At this time, the mother's father, who was devoted to the boy and to whom Aro was most responsive, died. A short time after the grandfather's death, Aro became depressed, and his tics became violent. Most disturbing to the family was a loud yelling tic. (Later, during a psychotic break, Aro was heard saying that he had a yell that could be heard around the world, that could bring the dead to life.)

At school Aro was unable to work up to grade, in spite of his normal IQ. At nine Aro suffered his first psychotic breakdown, which lasted six weeks. Aro insisted that he would not leave his room until his tics stopped. He would shriek prayers to God and announce that he and his daddy had a secret. "I'm practicing the loudest yell in the world. When I give that yell everything will come to life—even the picture in the room." Later, in his analysis, Aro elaborated this fantasy. In addition to the obvious wish to revive the dead grandfather, Aro fantasied that in response to his yell the most ferocious tigers in Africa would come to Aro, protect him, and kill his enemies.

The details of the onset of the psychotic breakdown are revealing. It happened in the midst of psychotherapy with a therapist Aro shared with his mother. The morning of the onset Aro was to be taken to the psychiatrist, and the mother noticed that Aro was crawling like a baby on the front lawn and that he was masturbating. She reprimanded him harshly. They then waited in their car for a friend. She remembers fearing an accident. Aro, who always was affected by his mother's moods, appeared tense and worried. The friend, a teacher, finally arrived and dramatically explained the reason for being late. One of her pupils badly cut her knee and they had to stop the bleeding. At that moment Aro slumped to the floor of the car, writhing about and uttering inarticulate cries and groans. His body appeared completely out of control and his clothes were drenched with sweat. The psychiatrist gave Aro a sedative which was ineffective, and following this Aro refused to leave his room. The friend's tale of the bloody accident that happened to the child triggered Aro's psychotic breakdown. At that time Aro was suffering from intense castration anxiety. His excessive masturbation indicated that repression of his oedipal strivings had not been successful. The mother's harsh reprimand, the fear of an accident, the bleeding accident of the pupil, and particularly the impending visit to the psychiatrist who belonged to mother and represented the punishing father—all these added to Aro's mounting terror. His psychotic breakdown represents a refuge for his disorganized ego from castration anxiety, a reunion with the good object on a regressive level. The almost totally disorganized child sought to obtain strength and nourishment from the higher good powers (God, father, etc.). Only the good objects are ego syntonic and can be tolerated within. Only by constant alternation of ejection of the bad object and incorporation of the good object can Aro succeed in replenishing his empty and disorganized self. It seems that during his psychotic episodes Aro's regressive behavior, entailing alternating primitive introjection-projection mechanisms, is similar to the patterning of the relationship between the normal symbiotic infant and mother, in which incorporative and ejective mechanisms alternate. The autism with its attendant megalomania connotes union and fusion with the good mother, whereas the tic paroxysms signify the loss of control in the struggle to eject the incorporated bad object.

Aro, an emaciated child of about ten, usually was brought to the office by his mother, who sat in the waiting room with an apologetic smile. Aro would sit as far away from her as he could get, and gaze away from her at the ceiling or wall. Frequently he would dart a look at her and then quickly avert his gaze. His body was racked with involuntary movements of arms, torso, neck, and face. The movements were particularly predominant in the mouth and jaw. We shall not give a detailed description of his tic paroxysms. Loud, guttural vocalizations frequently accompanied the tic movements. The boy would appear terrified and anguished during these episodes. At the completion of the tic paroxysm Aro would repeat it volitionally in an abbreviated form, with a look of nonchalant mastery. He might, during this purposive repetition, hum a little tune and move his body, as if in response to the rhythm. At these times he would attempt to maintain a contemptuous, mocking attitude which he would preserve until he was overcome by the next attack.

Applicable to Aro's tic syndrome is the description by Mahler (1944, 1949a) and Mahler et al. (1945, 1946) of the tic syndrome as a loss of control of the struggle against introjected objects, ego-alien demoniacal inner powers. To Aro, it was as if these powers gained possession and reduced the self to the status of a puppet. The voluntary repetition of the tic seizure indicates that ejection of the demon has been successful and that the ego-alien inner force has been banished. The child for the moment is once again in command.

His air of mastery during the volitional repetition of the tic movements, the rhythmic response of his body to his humming, indicates that his self-mastery is dependent upon the introjection of the good mother; he rocks and soothes himself.

Aro's defective ego alone is incapable of dealing with his inner needs. He constantly attempts to obtain strength and gratification from the outside by means of incorporation. His regressed patterning is that of an infant indiscriminately sucking in supplies from the outside. A consequence of this avid, incorporative striving is that the bad and painful as well as the good and pleasurable are ingested and introjected.

This cycle in the tic paroxysm—need, inner turmoil, loss of body control, on the one hand, and the attainment of gratification and quiescence through introjection, on the other— brings to mind Aro's experiences with the pylorospasm at ten weeks. Then the ingested food had caused actual pain and culminated in expulsion through vomiting. The vomiting was invariably followed by a fresh bottle until the infant attained satiety, even though at the expense of forced feeding. Or else quiescence through exhaustion ensued.

The fear of re-engulfment on the one hand and separation anxiety on the other are graphically demonstrated by the relationship of Aro and his mother. It was the mother who would ring the office and elevator bells, open the doors, greet and say good-by to the analyst. There was never any conversation or physical contact between mother and son. On occasion, when the mother came too close to him, Aro would suddenly lash out with his fist, striking her sharply on the breast.

Although mother and child did not converse, there was much communication by means of gestures, body movements and facial expressions. The mother was particularly adept at remaining at what, for Aro, was an optimal distance from him. He would indicate by tics or mouth-fingering, etc., when she was too far away and, as mentioned before, would strike her when she came too close.

The communication without words between Aro and his mother is illustrated by the following incident. In the waiting room on one occasion Aro lurched to his feet, looked at his mother, then looked toward the bathroom. He made a gesture toward his penis. His mother quickly arose, opened the bathroom door, and switched on the light. Aro urinated with the door open, looking back at his mother and chuckling happily. The mother flushed the toilet.

From the first, Aro willingly came into the consultation room alone. Without a sign of recognition he would move past the analyst with a curious propulsive gait and run through the open doors to the playroom. The social amenities were never responded to. He would cringe and shrink away from the slightest physical approach on the part of the analyst. Often Aro would look to one side, mutter to himself and then laugh wildly, without any apparent contagion. At such times he appeared to be responding to purely inner ideas or stimuli. He was out of control, violently hit at the chair or the wall, and threw his body about by his paroxysms of laughter. This behavior appeared frankly psychotic.

Aro would listen intently to the sound of the elevator taking his mother down. As soon as the noise ceased, Aro roamed about the room investigating its contents. He would look, touch and retouch, smell and mouth the objects, and compare their weight. He would both taste and bite them.

He would question the analyst: "What is it?—How long have you had it?—How old is it?—What's it for?—Which is best?" etc. Such questions were repeated over and over again, in a nagging querulous voice. Attempts to answer them were drowned out by Aro's loud vocal tic and his repeating the first few words of the answer. When an answer was finally completed, Aro repeated the answer over and over again, each time with a different tone and inflection so that the answer would range the gamut from a simple statement to puzzled, disbelieving, astonished, angry, scornful affects.

Aro's restitutive attempts to orient himself in the environment were successful with inanimate objects. Because of their stability and constancy, and because he could explore them at his own speed, he was able to make them a part of his own experience and to categorize them as to good or bad. Aro was unable to blend, modulate, or synthesize. There was no grey—only black and white. Cars made by General Motors were good—all others were bad. Aro could not discriminate or grade within either group. There was no difference between a Cadillac and a Chevrolet. They were both General Motors and hence both good. Unlike himself, inanimate objects did not change rapidly in an unpredictable way and thus served as a frame of reference for the child struggling for control in a chaotic world.

Aro's attempt at orientation by means of questioning succeeded less happily. The answers provoked by his questions were not predictable, either in terms of their final form, ultimate meaning, or effect on him. Aro, constantly threatened with loss of self-identity through ego-alien powers gaining ascendancy, had to maintain a dominance and control over the answers his questions provoked. His interruptions, mimicry, etc., served this end. He was careful not to be taken by surprise and not to be emotionally stirred. An emotion which arose unbidden and which took an unpredictable course was experienced by Aro as if it were a foreign body threatening the integrity of his ego. Because he could not synthesize and modulate, Aro had to employ the above-mentioned maneuvers—to "tame," as it were, the answer and thus to achieve mastery over it. He made it his own through a process of alternating ejection and incorporation.

The transition from one situation to another was very difficult for Aro. This was demonstrated by his behavior when he heard the elevator noise, indicating the return of his mother. He would tic violently, run to the door, run back to the center of the room, repeat this several times, and ask repeatedly, "Is it time—is it time?"

Most striking in Aro's relationship to his mother was his endeavor to remain at an optimal distance, spatially and emotionally, from her. He sought to attain an equilibrium between his weakened ego that needed to obtain constant supplies from her and the threat of being engulfed by her and losing his self-identity.

He was unable to go more than a few blocks from home. He screamed in protest when his mother planned to leave the house; and if she persisted, he would gag himself and retch. The father, who, particularly in the preanalytic period, used to baby-sit with Aro, related that shortly after the mother had left the house, Aro stuffed himself with food. He ate an inordinate number of hot dogs and gulped down unbelievable amounts of soda pop. Then, in great distress, he would turn to his father, and through frantic gestures implore help in getting rid of the ingested pain-producing food.

Aro permitted no intimacy. He did not suffer his mother to kiss or get close to him. He was abusive and hostile to her and took a particular delight in uttering obscenities in her presence. He hit her, told her she was ugly, and frequently ordered her to leave the room.

His fear of engulfment and his separation anxiety were dramatically illustrated by a frequent occurrence. Aro would call to his mother in a piteous and pleading whine, "Mommy, Mommy," and start toward her. Then he would stop, but continue to call, entreating her to come to him. When she came to him, he lashed out, hit her, and screamed, "Get away, bitch." If she retired, he called her back. When she finally refused to come to him, he implored her, broke into sobs, stuck his fingers down his throat until he gagged or retched.

It appears that Aro's ambivalent behavior is a result of his inability to create a fused and blended representation of his mother, as well as of his own self. Because of an inner need, it is toward the good mother he moves and it is she whom he so imploringly calls. The mother who comes cannot be reconciled with Aro's idealized mental image of the all-good mother. Aro reacts to the actual mother who comes to him with violent warding off, reminiscent of the primitive ridding mechanism of the baby in the symbiotic phase—the gesture with which that baby tries to expel the introjected painful stimulus.

As Aro undoubtedly entered the oedipal phase (the passive negative aspects of which were prominent in the analytic material), the father somehow became the helping, glorified figure—basically a "good object." On the other hand, Aro's oedipal strivings toward the mother maintained his image of her as mainly bad and threatening. Because of castration anxiety, the "ugly, castrated" mother must not come too close physically or emotionally; i.e., she must sit in the back of the car when he sits in front with his father, etc. Intimacy with the bad mother would result in re-engulfment, in a shattering of Aro's ego organization. The fear of being eaten and castration anxiety receive additional impetus from the boy's terrifying tic seizures. The involuntary movements are a loss of control of a part of the body and a loss of that part of the body from Aro's self representation to an evil and stronger force, the bad mother and perhaps the oedipal father.

In Aro's case, the psychotic mechanisms existed side by side with neurotic ones. By virtue of appersonation of the mother's executive functions as external ego (Spitz, 1951), Aro was still able to function on a regressed and constricted level. Although he had had several frankly psychotic episodes, his break with reality was not final and not complete. The main difference between cases like Aro's, where remissions are predominant, and others, where the loss of reality seems permanent and irreversible, is whether or not representations of outside love objects remain partially cathected or whether cathexis has been completely withdrawn.

Bowlby et al. (1952) described the observation that in the course of actual separation of the small child from his mother, both the good and the bad image of the mother undergo rapid changes. The good mother becomes glorified and the bad mother a hateful image. James Robertson's well-known film, *A Two-Year-Old Goes to Hospital* (1952), clearly documents that when the child is reunited with the mother after having been separated, even the normal two-year-old temporarily has some difficulty in identifying either of his inner images with the real mother. The child shown in the film displayed a fleeting blank response when confronted with the "mother in the flesh." (Significantly, with the father, the girl's reactions even at a second separation within a half year showed practically no lasting adverse effects—unlike the disruptive near-detrimental effect which the second separation had on the mother-child relationship.)

An effect similar to that produced on the normal two-year-old by actual repeated separation from the mother occurs, even without actual separation, with a symbiotic child for whom, through the factors previously enumerated, the prepsychotic stage had been set. A psychotic break may occur in response to any additional trauma, during the relative strain of the process of individuation. Experiences of disappointments in the course of the oral, anal, but particularly the oedipal phases of psychosexual development harbor the threat of castration, which in turn reinforces the threat of oral attack, in those children. The fantasies of being robbed of the contents of the body and finally of being engulfed and eaten up dominate. This latter, we repeat, is the projected counterpart of the avid tendency of these children to suck in, to gulp—good and bad objects alike.

We know, in retrospect, that integration of the good and bad mother images, as well as clear differentiation of representations of the part objects in the outside versus the part images of the self, has been defective in the cases in question. Hence, at the point when fear of re-engulfment, a fear amounting to fear of dissolution of identity, accumulates simultaneously with its apparent opposite, i.e., separation panic—the two overwhelm the ego. This occurs with such intensity that the progressive integration and gradual unlocking of couplings of scattered part-image representations of the self and object are prevented. There is regression to the stage in which unneutralized libido and aggression were vested in the symbiotic system within the child's inner delusional reality. At this point the real mother ceases to exist as a separate entity. The introjected split objects dominate the psychotic child's world. These, then, are the extreme cases of children who do not seem to respond to outside stimuli but who seem to be continuously in communication with the introjected objects, as shown by bizarre posturing, giggling, and stereotyped activities. Very often the introjected objects gain symbolic personification by means of exclusive preoccupation with a piece of cardboard, hallucinated bell, an "adored" extremity, a toy animal, and the like, to which the patients address passionate endearments. If they are told that the psychotic fetish is in danger, or if it is symbolically removed, they fall into an abysmal panic. At this stage the patient may no longer show any signs of missing his real mother. It is at this stage that these children are routinely misdiagnosed primarily autistic infantile psychosis cases.

B.S. AND M.C.

The following, very brief vignettes illustrate the genesis and dynamics of a complete psychotic break with reality.

B.S. was six years old when he was admitted to the Children's Service of the New York State Psychiatric Institute. He was extremely hyperactive and destructive. He not only displayed blind aggression toward other children but mutilated himself by biting and scratching, so that big brown calluses covered his two forearms and his left hand.

His illness began at two years of age. B.S.'s first year of

life was marred by illness, chronic diarrhea. He was so weak and debilitated that his early maturational growth was gravely delayed. He would lie quietly by himself, flat on his back, and make no demands on his mother who attended to his physical needs. He made no response to his brother or father; he did not seem to know them. When he was two years old, his mother developed pleurisy and was hospitalized. The child's reaction to this was not recorded, but when at two and a half he did start to walk, the hitherto overly placid child became hyperactive, banged his head against the crib, tore his hair out in bunches, and displayed increasingly bizarre behavior. He withdrew from people, but used his carriage blanket as his constant companion. He rolled it up and talked to it and appeared to be "in a different world." He continued to be a grave feeding problem and took no food unless his mother spoon fed him. He attacked younger children and, when prevented, bit and scratched himself.

On the ward he talked only to his fetish in a continuous babble, frequently simulating his mother's talking to *him*. In this monologue, the fetish obviously represented himself.

B. S., like Aro, seemed possessed by unneutralized, destructive aggression which manifested itself, at times, in catatonic agitation and violence toward objects and his own body.

The actual break with or withdrawal from reality rarely occurred before our eyes. Such observations as those described by Kubie and Israel (1955) in "Say You're Sorry" are exceptional. In Kubie's case, the little girl's acute psychotic regression was triggered by the loss of the good substitute mother figure, represented by the supportive houseworker concurring with severe corporal punishment by the "good father."

We believe the stable image of a father or of another substitute of the mother, beyond the eighteen-month mark and even earlier, is beneficial and perhaps a necessary prerequisite to neutralize and to counteract the toddler's age-characteristic oversensitivity to the threat of re-engulfment by the mother.

We have mentioned the dread of re-engulfment versus separation panic in the phase of individuation. We tend to think of the father too one-sidedly as the castrating figure, a kind of bad mother image in the preoedipal period. Loewald (1951), to our knowledge, was the first to emphasize that, "Against the threat of the maternal engulfment, the paternal position is not another threat or danger, but a support of powerful force" (p. 15). If there is a relative lack of support on the part of either parent (or the "uncontaminated" mother substitutes[25]), a re-engulfment of the ego into the whirlpool of the primary undifferentiated symbiotic stage becomes a true threat.

The toddler in the second eighteen months of life, whose ego is constitutionally vulnerable, symbiotically fixated, and now during the separation-individuation phase is additionally traumatized, may regress to even earlier archaic stages of personality development. A lapse into the objectless, autistic stage may be the only solution. The child may suddenly or gradually lose his individual identity and his contact with reality.

This happened to five-year-old M.C., whose mother said: "All my children seemed to be the same." Although there are no detailed data of the symbiotic stage of M.C.'s development, from the mother's actual behavior at the time of M.C.'s hospitalization when he was five and a half years old, we can readily reconstruct it. At this time he was still exclusively on bottle feedings. The mother had made no attempt to foster the growth of independence in other areas either. M. C. was never permitted or encouraged to dress himself or to develop any spontaneity.

Shortly after M.C.'s birth, the father began to indulge in

[25] As Ernst Kris called it when he discussed the paper by Mahler and Gosliner (1955) at the New York Psychoanalytic Society in 1954.

alcohol, at first only moderately, but gradually to an ever-increasing degree. During the earlier phase, well beyond M.C.'s second birthday, the father remained a moderately devoted father, caring for the infant and tending to his needs. In time, however, the father's behavior became more and more unpredictable. When intoxicated, he was frequently physically abusive toward the mother. This eventually culminated in a particular episode when the patient was four and a half years old. The father's behavior was so threatening toward the mother that she called the police, who then proceeded to arrest the father. M. C., who had witnessed the entire episode, was extremely disturbed, not only about the father's physical abuse of the mother, but particularly about the rough treatment which the father received at the hands of the policemen. When the father was subsequently removed by the police, M. C.'s agitation and distress were very great. He cried repeatedly, "Where are they taking my Daddy?" The mother was obliged to take M. C. to the police station and there obtain her husband's release. It was following this experience that M. C. gradually regressed: his speech, which had been age adequate, eventually became limited to two words. He reverted to urinating wherever the urge overpowered him, and defecated in closets. An earlier phase of father-child communication was used as stereotyped patterned behavior. The father's throwing the child, half angrily, half playfully, to the bed or ground became a pattern of behavior in which M. C. would slump to the floor and lie there quietly and unresponsively with a vacuous stare. This was only one evidence of his withdrawal from reality into his self-created inner world.

We have seen that Aro functioned (to a great extent) on the level of the symbiotic infant and toddler between eighteen and thirty-six months. He used his mother as his external ego. He also warded her off with autistic defenses for fear of complete dissolution of his individual entity. Aro's case as well as the complete autistic withdrawal into a self-sufficient autistic inner world in the cases of B.S. and M.C., we feel, show that autism, this psychotic form of negativism, is an attempt at reactive restitution. When the good images in the outside world are insufficient or unusable to counteract the menace of demoniacal inner powers that harass, attack, and almost annihilate the ego from within, as in the case of tiqueurs; or if both parental images become completely deflated and useless against castration threat (Jacobson, 1953); if, against consuming introjected bad objects and the hostile world (police, dangerous psychotherapist, death of grandfather, etc.), no object image in the outside world can be depended upon—then the break with reality and withdrawal into an inner world serve the function of survival. We designated this per se regressive psychotic defense, this secondary autism, a reactive restitution, because the ego thus restores, albeit regressively, the blissful oceanic feeling, the oneness with "the object," which seems the delusional substitute for that child whose ego is unable to endure the second hatching process: separation from the good object.

CHAPTER V

Prototypes of Mother-Child Interaction

This chapter will be devoted to some considerations of the complex dovetailing of the psychopathology of mothers and that of their individual psychotic children.

As I stated in Chapter II, it is difficult to assess which part intrinsic and which part environmental factors play in the etiology of infantile psychosis. In our first report about the autistic syndrome, we emphasized Kanner's finding of the environmental condition, the "frigidaire" atmosphere of these children's homes. In our subsequent experience, however, we became more and more aware of the variations in the types of parents and home atmospheres, which ranged from the "average expectable" (Hartmann, 1939) to the frankly "frigidaire" atmosphere and the psychotically violent. We cannot confirm the high incidence of either depressed or highly narcissistic parental personalities reported by Rank (1955).

In a number of cases, we have been able to throw light on the complex interaction between pathological mothering and the development of the psychosis. In many other cases, especially where the mother appeared to be less disturbed, a pathogenic interaction between mother and child is not so clearly discernible.

Children who are suffering from infantile psychoses are not to be thought of as normal children in whom a psychotic process is induced by an emotionally disturbed mother. These children are constitutionally vulnerable or they may be predisposed toward the development of a psychosis. It is often the very existence of a constitutional ego defect in the child that helps create the vicious circle of the pathogenic mother-child relationship by stimulating the mother to react to the child in ways that are deleterious to his attempts to separate and individuate (cf. Goldfarb et al., 1959; and Goldstein, 1959).

It is obvious that such accidental factors as early and prolonged illnesses or pain interfere with the fusion and blending of good and bad images of both objects and self. Instead, fused and confused faulty couplings of part images of self and object occur, and these hinder reality orientation. In constitutionally oversensitive and vulnerable infants, the pathogenic effects of these intrapsychic events (which are the result of interaction between the predisposition, accidental events, and the mother-child relationship) are enhanced. A prepsychotic stage may be set, especially if fixation to the symbiotic phase is reinforced during the individuation process.

The pathogenic effect of the attitude of the symbiotically overanxious mother is particularly increased if that same mother's hitherto doting attitude changes abruptly at the advent of the separation-individuation phase. Coleman, Kris, and Provence (1953) have drawn attention to the important fact that the attitude of the mother toward the same child may, in different phases of his development, undergo radical changes. A complementary pathogenic factor is the well-known parasitic, infantilizing mother, who for her own reasons needs to continue her overprotection beyond the stage when it is no longer beneficial. This attitude becomes a threat of engulfment and, for that reason, detrimental to the child's normal disengagement and individuation from his second year of life on. Another type of symbiotic parasitic mother, unable to endure watching the loss of her hitherto vegetative appendage take place, must, emotionally at least, slough him off abruptly.

TYPES OF INTERACTION

Communicative Mismatching

In the course of our "therapeutic action research" (in which the psychotic child's mother has always been included) we have been struck by an apparent discrepancy: the psychotic child's mother is often most adept and useful in observing and explaining the meaning of some of the child's—to the therapist's at first entirely enigmatic—behavior.

Yet we have also found, during the course of our therapeutic action research, that this understanding of the child's behavior was not at all matched by appropriate responses on the part of the mother. This discrepancy was puzzling and could not be simply brushed off by labeling it "intellectualization."

In general, there are two major types of cues manifested by the psychotic child: symbiotic and secondary autistic patterns. The understanding of some mothers seems to be geared to the autistic patterns: they either exclude the "symbiotic cues" by denial, or else some mothers of symbiotic psychotic children, even though they seem to acknowledge the symbiotic cues as well, seem to be unable to respond to them. We cannot help but surmise that the lack of appropriate response to symbiotic cues on the part of these mothers comes about because these cues carry with them the psychotic child's intense demand for symbiosis made upon the "perplexed" mother (Goldfarb et al., 1958, 1959). Thus, just as mothers flee therapy at the stage where in therapy the child's symbiotic demands become more intense, so they also flee from understanding or responding to the cues that are the carriers of these demands. This is but one example of the phenomenon that we have called "communicative mismatching" between mother and child (see also Goldfarb et al., 1956; Lidz, 1963; Lidz et al., 1965).

Autistic Equilibrium

It should be remembered that once the psychosis takes over the personality of the child and dominates almost all of his functioning, an adaptation to that fact is required of all mothers, of whatever type. This adaptation almost always means the mother's giving up of her normal mothering function. In many instances, especially when secondary autistic patterns are predominant, a withdrawal similar to that on the part of her child can be observed with varying degrees of bewilderment, perplexity, and hostility. There are variations between this extreme and the opposite, in which the mother fits herself so completely to the cues that serve the child's delusion of magic omnipotence that the observer gets the uncanny feeling that there is really no separation between mother and child. We wish to make it clear that the variations and adaptations of the mother do not necessarily mean severe pathology on her part or that in all instances her reactions to her child are created by the mother's need for "parasitic symbiosis." It is our experience that these equilibria between mother and child tend to support a static state of psychosis in the child, a state that therapy must disrupt if progressive change is to take place.[1]

Complementary Series and Prognosis

When the syndromes of infantile psychosis were first delineated and a sharp distinction was made between autistic and symbiotic psychosis, the prognosis of the symbiotic psychotic child was felt to be better than that of cases of early

---

[1] This very important thought was formulated by my former co-worker, Dr. David L. Mayer.

infantile autism. Our further experience, as will be described in Chapter VI, has led to a revision of this opinion concerning the types of clinical syndromes and also of the prognosis. Our emphasis would now be put upon the constitutional as opposed to the experiential factors in the etiology of psychosis (both autistic and symbiotic), though these are often difficult to determine. Our recent experience has been that one is hard put to make a reliable prognosis without prolonged observation and trial treatment.

As noted, what clinically appear to be autistic children may emerge rather rapidly from this withdrawal (secondary autism), whereas certain symbiotic psychotic children, especially those with severe self-destructive impulses, may be relatively intractable to treatment. Furthermore, we have also noted in the course of treatment that what may appear to be autistic withdrawal is sometimes in the service of self-healing and is temporary and reversible. Other children who seem to have more symbiotic features and who suffer without relief during treatment unfortunately do not progress beyond this level of "psychotic preobject relationship."

The following cases of child psychosis are prototypical. The children suffered from the sequelae of the failure of the mother-infant symbiosis. Neither child could use the mother as a beacon of orientation, as the external ego (Spitz, 1957). In the case of Violet, secondary autism dominated the clinical picture, whereas in the case of Benny delusional symbiotic mechanisms prevailed. In the third case, that of Steve, the mother's psychosis prevented the entire process of individuation-separation.[2]

[2] I believed initially that in the early stages the two types of infantile psychosis—the *autistic* versus the *symbiotic*—can in many cases be clearly differentiated. Later the pictures tend to overlap. Differential diagnosis in retrospect may be attempted by reconstruction and appraisal of the earliest mother-infant relationship. The specific factor in differential diagnosis is the mother's role as reflected in the baby's nursing behavior during the process of individuation, during the period when the infant's body ego and representation of the self should emerge from the primal somatopsychic symbiotic stage and the fused representation (Jacobson, 1954). As described

CASE REPORTS

Violet

The case of Violet and her mother illustrates with unusual clarity the history of a primarily autistic mother-child interaction.

Violet's parents were both very young, both of them in fact rather infantile, when she was born. The mother, who had grown up friendless and alone in the house of her brutally sadistic grandmother, felt profoundly abandoned by both parents. In addition to the grandmother, there had been a crippled maternal uncle; he had died shortly after Violet's parents had married. The uncle's death had caused Mrs. V. recurrent nightmares in which he would emerge from his coffin, neither alive nor dead, and fold up upon himself like a fetus. In struggling to distract herself from these dreams, it had occurred to Mrs. V. that a child might completely preoccupy her; it would be something all her own!

In relating this fantasy, Mrs. V.'s immediate association was that her father had given her a doll when she was three years old. She had kept this doll all her life; she still had it in a trunk. The little girl born to this twenty-year-old mother obviously represented in her emotional economy another, this time an animated, living doll (Kestenberg, 1956).

Seven weeks after Violet was born, Mrs. V. became deeply depressed; this coincided with the death of her father. From that time on, the mother's relationship to the baby changed

---

above, the autistic baby behaves quite differently during the nursing period than either the normal infant or the symbiotic baby. We stated that the primarily symbiotic child often cannot be detected before awareness of separateness from the mother image throws these infants into a state of panicky separation anxiety. When we meet cases of child psychosis at a later stage, it seems that pure cases of autistic child psychosis as well as pure cases of symbiotic-parasitic psychosis are rather rare, whereas mixed cases are frequent; by this time, symbiotic mechanisms have been superimposed on basic autistic structures and vice versa.

abruptly. According to her own statement, her care of Violet was limited to breast feeding her, the closeness of which she felt was her sole reason for hanging on to life itself. In between, the "live doll" was carted away; she was never played with, talked to, or smiled at; no interest of any sort was shown in her. There was thus an alternation of extremes—on the one hand, the very intense relationship of the breast feeding; on the other, the mother's complete withdrawal between feedings.

Mrs. V. was unable to gratify Violet's overall symbiotic needs except in this incongruent, in fact, contradictory, way. Not even a fully structuralized ego—let alone the rudimentary ego of an infant—could possibly have synthesized and integrated such a compartmentalized pattern, with its sharply contrasting feeling tones. Whether the infant's constitutional "sending power" was normal or underdeveloped we do not know, but it certainly went unheeded, and by one year of age it had petered out.

During the first nine months, the infant cried a great deal, expressing her need tension quite vociferously. Mrs. V. frequently responded to this with rage, at times even with physically aggressive acts. We do not know how far this baby was able to find solace in her own, fitfully libidinized body through autoerotic means such as sucking, stroking herself, etc. We do know, however, that at eight or nine months of age Violet made an attempt to smear her feces, and that when her mother discovered this, she flew into a violent rage and beat up the infant, with the result that Violet allegedly never smeared again.

At least during the first months, Violet seems to have engaged the mother with her eyes during feeding, and smiled at her; she vocalized at around eight or nine months. All these signs of "social contact-seeking" stopped or slowly disappeared by the age of fifteen months. Although there were no events such as might have provided evidence of a massive regression, at about one year of age something seems to have gone wrong. Violet did not respond to people, did not "smile much," did not appear to have fun, etc. The parents were told by the pediatrician when Violet was fifteen months old that there was something "strange."

The description of Violet's daytime routine at the time of intake, at two years seven months, indicated the same kind of almost bizarre handling that must have prevailed during the first year of the child's life. Violet's parents were both musicians, and for many hours she was "locked out" while the parents practiced their instruments, even though Violet protested and usually had a temper tantrum. "If the mother had time, she might take time to bribe Violet in various ways. But the chances were that she would put Violet in the hall and leave her there to bang her head on the floor and thrash her arms and legs about while the mother resumed her practicing. She believed that Violet would stop when she heard her mother starting to play, and "realize that she just wasn't going to get anywhere with her tantrums."

When Violet made her first appearance with us, she was mute; she had an absolutely blank and unanimated facial expression, and she focused on nothing and nobody. She had no verbal language. The child's movements, large and small alike, seemed to be well coordinated; she moved with that well-known elflike grace that some psychotic girl patients display. Her straight blond hair was frequently unkempt. While her features were delicate and pixielike, they were congealed, as it were, into a flat and spiritless expression. She showed no response to people and acted as though she did not hear their voices. Psychological testing (at twenty-three months) placed Violet in a superior classification on the performance scale; her neurological examination was completely negative; EEG was mildly and diffusely abnormal.

The chief complaints of the mother were the child's destructiveness and unmanageability and her sleep and feeding disturbance. She was concerned that Violet was not toilet trained, that she threw frequent temper tantrums, and that she did not speak.

From the time she was able to crawl, upon being left alone, Violet would tear books and chew music records and strew these around until the room was a shambles. This usually happened when the parents were practicing and Violet, with great skill, was able to get hold of those scores and records. (Mrs. V. felt that it had been natural for her to leave Violet so much alone, because she herself had always been so much alone.)

We made some noteworthy observations of Mrs. V.'s interaction with Violet, when she brought Violet to us for diagnosis at intake. Mrs. V. appeared to be a somewhat tense, slender woman in her early twenties, who smiled a sphinx-like, enigmatic smile. She appeared to be easily irritated in her relations with the child and generally quite tentative in her contacts with her. She would frequently offer a half-formed direction to the child, but at the first sign of withdrawal on the child's part (a typical reaction), the mother would also withdraw. The mother was observed through many a long session during which she did not utter a single word to the child.

During intake, while the mother and the psychiatrist were talking in the playroom for about fifty-five minutes, the child occupied herself with wandering about the room, examining and momentarily playing with small toys, the phonograph, and the light she reached by climbing on a chair. On one occasion she went exploring down the hall; she had to be recovered by the psychiatrist, because the mother made no effort to follow her out of the room. During the time of intake observation, the child did not attempt to engage the mother's attention and only occasionally approached the doctor. When she did, she avoided eye engagement; instead, she would glance at the doctor very briefly, and then turn her eyes away.

The only communication involving sound between mother

and child, the only situation that elicited smiles from the child in relation to the mother, pivoted around the piano. In fact, the child displayed phenomenal musical gifts, an unusual ear, and an incredible ability to reproduce on the piano almost any music she heard, even if she heard it only in passing. If her father, in practicing, failed to produce music precisely as she had repeatedly heard it on a record by a great master, she would have a temper tantrum.

In Violet's case we have a schizoid mother who is warding off her own murderous impulses by detachment and isolation.[3]

Benny

In Benny's case, we meet, by contrast, an intrusive, smothering, managerial, overwhelmingly affectionate and physically overstimulating mother, who pushed her son to individuate at a rapid pace, and without really giving him the chance to disengage himself gradually from what was a mutually parasitic symbiosis.

Benny, on the occasion of his first visits to the Center, was essentially dragged or carried into the building and into the room. He exhibited extreme distress and diffuse panic. He clung to and pulled at his mother, but as soon as the latter actively attempted to soothe him by taking him into her arms, he would try violently to extricate himself, pushing against her and arching backward.

When he was first seen by us, he was in what one would have to describe as an acute catatonic state. He clung to his mother, emitting shrieks of distress, alternately arching his body into an extreme opisthotonus or melting into her body. When standing alone, he was up on his toes, with an extreme tension in all his muscles, to the point where one could not help believing that this was very painful. On the other hand,

---

[3] For details of our therapeutic endeavors with Violet, see Chapter VI.

he showed some degree of waxy flexibility, and could be directed up the stairs by the tip of one's finger.

The child gave the impression of a classical symbiotic-psychotic syndrome in a three-and-a-half-year-old. Benny's speech was mostly in fragments, which the mother related to TV commercials that he had heard many months before. However, at intake we immediately felt that there were occasionally brief, but directed verbal communications. He said "hello" when he was introduced to the doctor and made small appropriate remarks from time to time.

A great deal of the child's energy seemed to be directed toward eluding the mother, who was astoundingly ever-present. He did occasionally follow her directions with some pleasure, even though the mother was often physically and directly overwhelming, kneeling over him, blotting out the sky from him, tickling him. The mother's entire array of comforting behavior was displayed; she talked to Benny, even lied to him, almost incessantly, and at the level of the most primitive reality, "causes and consequences." For example, if she wanted to keep him in the room, she would tell him that the door was broken or jammed; when she wanted to distract him from play, she said that his fingers would get stuck. She could be observed constantly hovering over Benny, "teaching" him, offering endless directions to his play.

In spite of careful consideration, during Benny's and his mother's lengthy treatment, the mother could not come up with any evidence of deviation during the first year of his life; he had been an attractive and responsive infant.[4] In his second year, too, the mother was pleased with him, thinking this firstborn son of hers to be a gifted child (the correction, she hoped, for her own denigrated self image). At this time, the child performed, to the amazement of everyone, such feats as reading the totals on the cash register and reciting

---

[4] Scrutiny of recently viewed "home movie pictures" revealed Benny, at eight months of age, looking without focus upon the outside world, his facial expression indicative of some disturbance.

memorized songs and rhymes that he had heard both from his mother and on TV.

When he was sixteen months old, he became very anxious; this was at the beginning of toilet training. During the next half year, there was a fairly rapid development of the symbiotic-psychotic clinical picture. He developed severe tantrums and very severe anxiety upon being separated from his parents, even for the shortest time. He alternately clung to the mother and pushed her away, gradually developing a continuous state of extreme distress that lasted throughout the day and night. He slept only little. He would implore the mother with gestures to help, moaning pitifully; but as soon as the mother took him into her arms, he would ward her off, arching his back in a stiff opisthotonus. There was a very apparent avoidance of meaningful interchange with any human being through facial expression or bodily contact.

During treatment, this boy made a considerable advance in the direction of awareness of, and communicative involvement with, other human beings, including the beginnings of speech. However, with each new step in development, in individuation, there was a regression to the state of acute panic, expressed in alternate clinging and pushing away such as we saw at first. It should be mentioned that, as time went on, despite the panic, the extent of withdrawal from human contact in these states seemed to decrease.

Steve

This case illustrates a possible connection between mechanical mothering and the psychotic fetish.

It seems that contact-perceptual and kinesthetic experiences are essential for the development of the body image in its central and peripheral parts (Greenacre, 1953) as well as for the formation of a concept of the self (Jacobson, 1954), whereas distance perceptions seem to facilitate separation from the mother's body and demarcation of the own body image from the environment. We assume that formation of structure (ego) (Hartmann et al., 1946) is dependent upon both of these processes—upon the contact- and distance-perceptual experiences. Progressive libidinization of the rind of the body ego (the *Pcpt.-Cs.* system) and ego development involve a circular process. In this circular process the mothering partner is an indispensable catalyst. We know from the work of Greenacre (1953), in particular, about the vicissitudes of the mother-infant relationship and distortion of the body image in the fetishist. Greenacre has shown that in the prefetishist child increase of visual overstimulation at the expense of tactile experiences has caused distortions. In some of our cases the opposite seems to have occurred. The mothers in these cases would walk or pace back and forth holding the baby tightly clutched in their arms with the intent to keep him quiet or, preferably, somnolent. Hence the crucial disproportion concerned overstimulation of contact and kinesthetic perceptions, with frustration, even almost total elimination of distance-perceptual (particularly visual) experiences. This kind of "mothering" predominated in one of our cases (briefly described by Mahler, Ross, and De Fries, 1949).

Steve's mother, a psychotic woman who was desperate over having a boy child for fear he would become a ne'er-do-well like her brother, could not stand the baby's wakeful state. She thought that if the baby would just sleep for long periods of time, the chances for his vegetative thriving would be better. Hence she would walk up and down with Steve clutched in her arms, until: "My arms were numb and I did not know where I ended and the baby began." No wonder that, when we met Steve at the age of eight, his main symptom was a complete lack of identity, uncertainty, and perplexity about his body image, particularly its boundaries. He would walk up to each and everyone asking the question: "Are these my hands, are those your hands? Can these hands kill? I am many people!" Steve sought another mode of compensation through histrionics and addiction to TV and movies, mirroring all the actors. That is to say, he tried to compensate for the deficit concerning the visual part of his body-image demarcation by his voyeurism and by attempts at mirroring identification (Elkisch, 1957).

The anxiously coercive mechanical mothering which kept this infant in such close bodily contact with the mother in infancy prevailed throughout Steve's childhood. Distance-perceptual, visual, and auditory orientation, experimentation toward exploration of the world beyond the mother-infant symbiotic unit, in Steve's case (as also in the case of Stanley [see Chapter IV]), was thwarted. The mother discouraged any sign of individual autonomy of the toddler. Increased auto-erotic manifestations, the increased need for which was created by the mother's overstimulation through tight and prolonged closeness, were met with scathing impatience and punitive hostility. A symbiotic parasitism with hypochondriacal self-observation was nurtured, and progress from primary to secondary identification was thus impaired.

From the point of view of the separation-individuation process, what occurred in this case, as in similar cases, was that during the symbiotic phase there was no choice or possibility for experimentation which ordinarily prepared the infant for gradual separation, gradual and partial identification with the object (mother). Hence in some cases in which during the symbiotic phase experimentation with separation fails to pave the way to gradual separation-individuation, separation panic becomes so great that partial introjection, gradual identification with the mother does not abolish the fear of annihilation. Total introjection is employed to counteract separation panic with the symptomatology of psychosis following this fateful occurrence (see Chapter I).

When the mother is totally introjected, this very defense mechanism removes her as the beacon of reality orientation, and concomitantly the peripheral parts of the body image (the *Pcpt.-Cs.* system) seem to become proportionately depleted of libidinal cathexis. The mechanism of total intro-jection thus creates a regressed situation similar to that of primary identification. Object choice and object finding remain in the realm of the own self, with impairment of perceptual awareness of the nonself. The result is loss of the ego's ability to integrate external and internal stimuli. In other words: if the representation of the human partner as the beacon of orientation in external reality is missing (because totally introjected and bare of object libido), the ego loses its perceptual integrative capacity.

SUMMARY

It is my belief that the cases presented in this chapter indicate that the core of child psychosis must be sought in one or the other of the described distortions of the symbiotic phase. In the first case, what lay at the heart of the psychotic disturbance was the marked emotional unavailability of the mother, which alternated with a purely physical extreme closeness during the breast-feeding situation, and particularly with the destructiveness of the mother's unpredictable rage attacks. The contrasting experiences drove the child to the autistic warding off of any human contact and the de-animation of the world of reality. Constitutional factors could not, in this case, be evaluated with any degree of accuracy.

In the second case, it was, by contrast, the mother's omnipresence that created an unendurable intrusion upon and interference with the structuralization of the budding ego, which constitutionally and perhaps predispositionally may have been very vulnerable. This made it impossible for the infant to experience the normal alternation of the gratification-frustration sequences at his own pace; it also made the process of individuation in the separation-individuation period one which was beset with abysmal panic.

In the third case, the mother's psychosis prevented the entire process of separation-individuation. The child developed only part object representations and his body image remained fragmented. These were, moreover, coupled in a faulty manner.

In all three instances, we can see that it was primarily in the severe distortions of the normal symbiosis that the child psychosis had its roots.

CHAPTER VI

Therapy

ASSESSMENT AS GUIDELINE TO THERAPY

In the initial assessment of the psychotic child of preschool age, many factors must be taken into account for the purpose of dynamic diagnosis and prognosis as well as to determine at what point, along the line of object relationship, the therapeutic approach should start.

To begin at the "autistic" end of the spectrum of psychotic phenomenology, there are children who avoid the external world completely. They are occupied only with sensations within their own bodies; they may relate to some hallucinated object that they "clutch" in their hands. Attempts to impinge upon their isolation generally result in severe panic tantrums.

There are also children who show some relationship, essentially a ritualistic one, to an inanimate object or part object. This relationship draws all the available cathexis upon it, but its meaning is at first quite enigmatic and puzzling to the observer. Whatever interest these children may have in anything outside their bodies seems to be directed toward such objects as a baby bottle, a jar, a piece of cloth, or the edges of furniture, boxes, a revolving fan, etc. They may voice no words at all; if they do, it is in imitation and with no apparent intention of communicating. They show a great deal of random movement, which we have learned to recognize as their reaction to physical discomfort or pain, however slight, and which seems to be a direct motor discharge in response to the internal stimulus, with little organization.

In hospitals, we have also seen more deeply regressed children whose entire waking day is spent in continuous auto-aggressive or kinesthetic self-stimulating activity, such as whirling about or head banging, with no relationship at all to either external objects or inanimate ones.

Some children form a fleeting contact with the human object—revealed, for example, in an alteration of their facial expression when the eyes of such a child meet those of the observer. Speech may be present, but it is in the form of echolalia, although among more disturbed children this echolalic repetition is likely to be of words or short sentences that they have heard from nonanimate sources, such as television or records.

Among the less severely disturbed children, there seems to be some interposition of thought or fantasy between, for example, bodily distress and its external manifestations. In Malcolm's case, for example, the hallmark of distress was a kind of back-and-forth movement of the hand; later, he held a toy (a train car) at such times. In our observation this movement seemed to represent an awareness of the downward movement of feces. Later we learned that he feared the expulsion of feces and that he had connected the word "broken" with it.

The conceptualization of these phenomena in terms of ego development and psychic structure can be only speculative. What we observe at the outset can be explained by disordered development, very deep drive and ego regression, or lack of development, in combination with a very primitive defense organization.

Some of the phenomena suggest primitive levels of ego-id functioning—for example, what appears to be immediate motor discharge in the entire body of any slight internal discomfort, or what would appear to be a somewhat more organized attempt to combat this discomfort by the quasi-deliberate production of other sensations, as seen in the whirling and head banging phenomena. It is difficult to find any thought content in these activities, although subsequently, when the child's ego development in general seems to be more advanced, these movements and activities become organized in such symptoms as tics or play activity, the psychic content of which we are better able to understand.

Another striking feature of the disease is that very frequently neither the mother nor any other observer can predict whether the child, when he approaches her (or, let us say, another child) is in a mood of affection or of aggression: e.g., whether he will bite or kiss when he presses his lips against the face, which he does without any of the puckering or sucking that is usually involved in a kiss. The observer's inability to understand the child's intentions is probably due to the fact that the child has regressed to or is fixated at a stage *at which the drives lack differentiation.* Moreover, while one feels somehow unable at such times to empathize with the distress that the child appears to be suffering, at a later period of treatment both the mother and the therapist do have the feeling that, when the child cries, he is indeed pathetic and in need of them; they also become quite sure of his intentions when he approaches them. These changes, which definitely are changes in the child rather than in the observer, are among the most heartening events for the mothers.

The psychotic child suffers from extreme panic and anxiety, and at first cannot in any way be comforted. The source of this anxiety is not always clear, although the frequency of such self-stimulating and body-defining activities as rubbing the body with sand, or head banging, as well as the wild aggressive outbursts, have led us, among many others (e.g., Elkisch), to speculate that this behavior has to do with the child's fear of loss of body boundaries and with his lack of capacity for binding aggression.

The most prominant defensive maneuvers are withdrawal from reality, especially from the animate, human external world: *deanimation* (Mahler, 1958). Any awareness of or involvement with a human object that is separate from the self seems to be quite beyond the capacity of the most severely disturbed children, and can be sustained, if at all, for only short intervals. When a more sustained involvement with an external human object occurs, it appears to take the form of a primitive identification, in the sense of an omnipotent mother-child fusion.

There are many indicators of what would seem to be an incomplete separation of self from object: the echolalia; the use of the other person, especially parts of that person's body, as extensions of himself; the expectation of the other person's omniscience and omnipotence in response to the most minimal cues; and, as has been described here and by Furer (1964), and Searles (1960), the imitation of inanimate objects. As said at the outset, one might not find any meaning, in the sense of communication, in the repetitive phrases or actions. However, the echolalic speech later begins to be used in an appropriate context; for example, "good-by, Chet, and good-by, Dave," imitating the parting words of newscasters of a TV newscast, is used at the time of leaving. Later on in the treatment, such phrases are integrated into more complex communications of feelings and thoughts. Many other examples can be found in the case reports in this book, e.g., Betty (Chapter II) and Lotta (Chapter IV).

Although investment of actual human objects is, in the most severe cases, almost completely withdrawn, in the children with better prognosis some cathexis of the mental representations of objects, merged with self representations, does seem to be maintained. This is shown by their investment—often an intense investment—of an inanimate object, the "psychotic fetish." In our experience, children who are brought for treatment with such a stereotyped, yet outward-directed and focused activity have a better prognosis. Other, more regressed children must first develop some awareness of the therapist and the mother before such an organization and focusing of behavior take place; when this happens, the first indications are usually the child's involvement with inanimate objects. During the course of treatment, the child will make both destructive and loving gestures toward such objects; even more important, there will often be long periods during which the child plays a game of throwing the object away, with the expectation that the therapist will return it. Such activities are indicative of the child's growing differentiation between self and object and his attempt to master the fear of object loss. Still later, when the invest-ment turns to the mother and separation anxiety appears, this object can substitute for her, just as one sees in normal development.

EARLY PRINCIPLES OF TREATMENT

Of relevance to the evolution of our principles of the treat-ment of the psychotic small and preschool child is our pre-vious work, from which has emerged the hypothesis that children pass through a normal autistic, a symbiotic, and a separation-individuation phase of development. We postulate that in the normal autistic phase, the infant is not yet aware of anything beyond his own body, whereas in the symbiotic phase he seems to have become vaguely aware that need satisfaction comes from the outside. The mother is still, however, a part of his own self representation: the infant's mental image is fused with that of his mother. In the third phase (the period of separation-individuation), the infant gradually becomes aware of his separateness: first, the sepa-rateness of his body, then gradually the entity and identity of his self, as he establishes its core and boundaries.

In another nine-year research project, we have been engaged in studying the separation-individuation process as it takes place from about five to thirty-six months.[1] As we have already indicated, in earlier chapters of this volume, in the group of psychotic small children who are seemingly what Kanner has described as primarily autistic, the child appears never to have developed even a symbiotic attachment to the mother or to any other living being—that is to say, he has not developed beyond the autistic phase. The symbiotic psychotic small child, on the other hand, has regressed, as a result of the challenge of separate functioning at the onset or during the course of the separation-individuation phase, into a symbiotic panic-ridden state.

However, as somatic and physiological maturation takes its course, there is no conceivable environment in which the primarily autistic child could maintain his shell against the demands of the outside world, and especially against the challenge of having to respond to the social-human environment. His autistic self-isolation and omnipotent delusional contentment are automatically disturbed and threatened by the maturational process and by drive development per se. Thus, nothing is more panic-creating for the autistic child than the intrusion of the human contact of the symbiotic stage, which follows the autistic stage, and in which the fact that need satisfaction comes from an outside mothering agent must be recognized.

In our opinion, human development cannot possibly proceed without showing vestiges of the symbiotic phase. Indeed, the prerequisite for personality development, and therefore the first requirement for treatment of the autistic child, is contact with a human love object. Thus the autistic child must be lured gradually into a quasi-accidental, tangential (not "head on") contact with the human object. If this step does occur forcefully and head on, then reactions that

[1] The results of this developmental study will be dealt with in detail in the second volume of this book.

resemble symbiotic panic may ensue. With our present careful method of treatment, attacks of this sort can be minimized or even avoided altogether.

On the other hand, children who begin with a symbiotic psychosis respond to any realization of separateness with panic and abysmal separation reactions, as well as with dread of the loss of self through symbiotic parasitic fusion. There are certain rare cases of symbiotic psychotic small children whom the clinician sees in protracted states of panic. Since states of panic are unbearable for any organism, however, most cases appear to regress further and to attempt to escape the symbiotic state of panic by turning to autism secondarily, in a desperate effort to ward off the fear of losing whatever minimal individual entity and "sameness" they may have succeeded in achieving, either through development or through treatment, and attempting, by way of the opposite psychotic mechanism of autism, to preserve that entity and identity.[2] Thus we often see children whose psychosis had at the start the characteristics of a symbiotic disturbance, but who then turned to autism in an effort to ward off the threat of regression into symbiotic fusion and to maintain their individual entity, distinct from that of either mother or father.

Our first therapeutic endeavor, in both types of infantile psychosis, is therefore to involve the child in a "corrective symbiotic experience."[3] This most essential step requires a long period of time to achieve and to consolidate; a still longer interval elapses before the higher levels of personality development, starting with the separation-individuation phase, are attained.

[2] Cf. the beautiful paper by Anna Freud on negativism and emotional surrender (1952a).

[3] "Corrective" is not used here to indicate a manipulative kind of intervention. By re-experiencing earlier stages of development, the child should be enabled to reach a higher level of object relationship. We arrived at calling this approach "corrective symbiotic experience" by comparing it with Augusta Alpert's research on "corrective object relationships" (1959).

It is helpful for therapy to determine whether the syndrome is a primarily autistic or primarily symbiotic disturbance because, depending on which is the case, the initial therapeutic approach must follow correspondingly different lines. In both types, as well as in the mixed type of early childhood psychosis, it is essential to keep in mind the extreme brittleness of the ego.

As we mentioned above, the autistic child is most intolerant of direct human contact. Hence he must be lured out of his autistic shell with all sorts of devices, such as music, rhythmic activities, and pleasurable stimulation of his sense organs. Such children must be approached gradually with the help of inanimate objects, always keeping in mind that gross bodily contact, touching, cuddling—which one might have expected to reassure a deeply disturbed child—is of no avail, and often a deterrent, with these autistic children. Time and again we see that cases of the autistic type, if they are forced too rapidly into social contact and into facing the demands of the social environment, are thrown into a catatonic state and then into as fulminant a psychotic process as we see in some cases of symbiotic child psychosis.

In the symbiotic type, on the other hand, it is important to let the child test reality very gradually and at his own pace. As he cautiously begins this testing of himself as a separate entity, he needs constantly to feel the support of an understanding adult, preferably the mother or the therapist as mother substitute. Such continual infusions of borrowed ego strength may have to be continued for a lifetime.[4] In other words, separation as an individual entity can be promoted only very cautiously in the case of the symbiotic psychotic child.

Even with cautious, prolonged, and consistent therapy, the prognosis for arresting the psychotic process and con-

[4] This opinion was shared by the late Paul Hoch, who stressed the necessity of possible lifetime substitution therapy in certain cases of adult psychotics.

solidating the ego is only moderately favorable. In cases of symbiotic infantile psychosis, the achievement of individuation has been missed when it was essential—that is to say, at a time when basic faculties of the ego are usually acquired within the somatopsychic matrix of the primal mother-infant unity. In our experience, if differentiation within this matrix, which is highly specific for promoting sound individuation, has not been achieved, the ego may remain irreparably warped, narcissistically vulnerable, unstructured, or fragmented.

In the autistic type of infantile psychosis, the deficiency is even more severe because the specific matrix itself did not exist, and therefore the growth that it fosters could not take place. Establishment of contact and substitution therapy over a long period of time may sometimes lead to spurts in development and what appear to be impressive and gratifying results. But they may be followed by a plateau of intractably arrested progress, which usually taxes the patience and frustrates the renewed hopes of the parents. Impatient reactions and pressures then may enter the picture and progress is forced. As we said before, however, if the autistic child is forced too rapidly into social contact, and particularly if the newly formed symbiotic relationship causes frustrations, he is often thrown into a catatonic state and then into as fulminant a psychotic process as we see in some of the symbiotic child psychosis cases, when separation panic causes the brittle ego structure to break into fragments. If such catastrophic reactions cannot be avoided, such autistic infants may be better off if they are allowed to remain in their autistic shell, even though, in a "daze of restricted orientation," they may drift into only a very limited degree of reality adjustment. Their "original condition," of course, in that case usually escapes proper diagnosis; they are thrown instead into the category of the feebleminded.

Any pressure in the direction of sudden separate functioning must be cautiously avoided in the symbiotic psychotic child. If the ego of the symbiotic type is overrated and thus overtaxed, if it is expected to be able to cope with reality without continual ego infusion from the therapist, who substitutes for the mother, then the ensuing panic reactions and acute hallucinations may cause regressions and withdrawal into stuporously autistic states or hebephrenic deterioration. Therefore, simultaneous supportive treatment of the mother, if at all possible, seems to constitute the optimal and, perhaps, even a *sine qua non* approach to the problem.[5]

Treatment of the psychotic child aims at (1) the restoration or establishment of greater body-image integrity, which should convey a better sense of entity and identity; (2) the simultaneous development of object relationships; and (3) the restoration of missing or distorted maturational and developmental ego functions.

In achieving this, the child must progress through the previously missed or unsatisfactory phases of development (presymbiotic, symbiotic, and separation-individuation), with the therapist serving a substitute function by providing a more readily utilizable auxiliary ego. It is quite common, for example, for psychotic children to have been toilet trained before they have reached the anal phase of psychosexual development. As a result, they not only fail to experience the libidinal gratification that is associated with the normal erotization of the anal area, but they have also been deprived of the feeling of control and mastery that accompanies toilet training when it is achieved *after* the myelinization of the central nervous system pathways, a requisite of conscious control from the second half of the second year. Libidinal gratification not only balances and neutralizes the aggressive drives that are generated in abundance from the inevitable frustrations and overstimulations which may be experienced by any child during the anal phase; libidinal gratification is also important for a more adequate development of the body

[5] Compare also the opinion of Beata Rank and Macnaughton (1950), as well as the work of Melitta Sperling (1951), Elkisch (1953), and others.

image. The deficiency of the body image is due to the lack of libidinal cathexis of certain important areas of the body periphery, especially the erotogenic zones.

The therapist will then (at the appropriate time) encourage a "living through" of this phase of development, providing suitable substitutive expressive means for the beginning sublimation of the anal preoccupations—offering the child, for example, clay or finger paints—and at the same time permitting and even encouraging a temporary regression to actual soiling or defecation in the treatment situation, if this be the child's need. In so doing, the therapist usually places himself in opposition to the mother. If symbiotic fusion with the mother is still the only way of adaptation that the child knows or can accept, the psychotic child, even more than the neurotic child in a similar situation, will perceive the therapist as "the devil's advocate," and panic may ensue. Extreme caution, therefore, is necessary, particularly if the child is being treated as an outpatient while continuing to live with mother.

Barbara, age six, was diagnosed as suffering from a symbiotic type of childhood psychosis and was treated in a residential institution. Prior to placement, she manifested acutely psychotic behavior: she had no specific relationship to anyone; she ate ravenously with her fingers, in an animallike way; she stayed up most of the night for several nights, wandering aimlessly about the house, while singing and talking to herself; she repeatedly took off all her clothes, and either attempted to climb into the toilet bowl or ran down the street in the nude, entering any door of any house.

Barbara's mother had been diagnosed as an ambulatory schizophrenic. The history revealed generally severe emotional deprivation and a particularly harsh and much too early toilet training. As an example of this child's early experience, it was reported that much of her first two years of life was spent in the crib, which was completely covered by a blanket except for one small corner through which the child could peer out at her surroundings.

In treatment with a woman therapist, Barbara's first activity consisted of soiling herself, defecating in the corner of the playroom, and playing with her feces. This behavior was repeated almost daily over a period of several weeks. The therapist was accepting of this behavior, offering no rebuke or criticism while continuing to reach out emotionally to the child. Finally, having been permitted to have this experience, Barbara stopped the actual defecation and smearing of feces, and turned to the use of clay as substitute means of expression. She continued to live through and work through this phase of development for a good many months thereafter. This and similar remedial experiences made Barbara slowly and gradually ready for object relationship, by helping her to feel and accept her own body as a separate entity and particularly her femininity, first on the body-image basis and later on the basis of the idea of being a girl.

We found that in several instances the recognition, enjoyment and acceptance of the own stool coincided with giving up the pronominal reversal, as if the recognition of the cybalum which had been within and actively pressed out helped to establish body-self identity. This is "I"; I made this, but it is not me. More observation and research, however, are necessary in order to establish this connection.

James was first seen at the age of three and a half. The outstanding presenting symptoms were failure to develop intelligible language, failure of adequate relationship to other people, and a general hypertonicity, a muscular tension, which caused awkwardness in movement. The history revealed that preverbal communication had developed in a seemingly normal fashion until the age of fourteen months. At that time, his father went into the service and the family life was disrupted. The mother, who prior to this time had been living with her own mother, was forced to move all the way across the country to a strange city. She was very up-set by this and stated frankly that her own anxieties and needs claimed all her attention. Simultaneously, James developed a very severe case of diarrhea, which persisted for several months, causing him great bowel distress and considerable pain and irritation of the anal area, and producing in the mother an even greater amount of anxiety. Another part of the history was the fact that James experienced a sudden weaning from the bottle at age nine months. The mother, a generally insecure person, did this upon the advice of a friend. James reacted to the weaning by becoming a thumb sucker, immediately and avidly. Observation of James showed that, in his attempts at speech, his tongue was curled concavely, in the position of the tongue of a sucking infant.[6]

In treatment, the therapist provided candy for James to suck on and demonstrated that sucking was all right, by sucking candy himself. He also encouraged thumb sucking. Initially James refused the offer of candy. Again, we see that the maternal taboo was operative in this child, whose ego was so rudimentary and psychotically fragmented. This evidence of conflict (probably with the mother) should serve as a warning to the therapist to use caution in permitting, no less encouraging, this necessary reliving of missed infantile experiences, without adequately preparing the mother and also the child for it.

Sy, an autistic child, at five showed a readiness to relive some of his missed or hurriedly passed libidinal experiences. His asking for his fetish pillow was taken as an indication that he would be ready to relive the oral phase and thereby to overcome some of his oral frustration. However, the mother's unconscious fear of regression and the boy's by that time strong symbiotic need for the mother made him com-

[6] Compare Augusta Bonnard (1958).

pletely refuse the bottle of milk that was unobtrusively made available to him. He withdrew from the analyst for a while and became quite suspicious.

Hence, in Sy's case, the therapist felt that introducing the milk bottle caused even more anxiety about loss of, and/or fusion with, mother. Gradually, as Sy permitted himself oral gratification and as he became very active and eager in this process, improvement in speech and clearer enunciation became evident.

In addition to permitting and aiding the living through and working through of early developmental phases, the therapist provides particularly those ego functions that are lacking in the child but are necessary to the development of a concept of self. The therapist may have to serve as a substitute stimulus barrier, protecting the child against excessive stimulation from the environment. At the same time, the therapist draws the child's attention away from the threatening inner stimuli by engaging him in their common pursuits, as elaborated later in this chapter.

Because of such ego deficiencies as faulty reality testing, primary process type of thinking, and poor orientation as to time, place, and person, the communications of the psychotic child are often so obscure as to be incomprehensible. Accordingly, the therapist must be able to delve into the primary process type of symbolic behavior of the patient with great empathy and without anxiety (cf. Sechehaye, 1947, 1956a). At the same time, he must be able to translate the patient's primary process material, which leads eventually to assimilation, integration, and synthesis. This type of activity on the part of the therapist aids in the gradual establishment of the boundaries between the self and the rest of the world, and accordingly allows for reality testing in distinguishing between the inner and outer environments. In time, the patient's ego becomes better structured and differentiated, and he can begin to take over these functions for himself.

Another seemingly contradictory task of the therapist is to set limits, particularly to the child's overwhelming self-destructive and aggressive impulses, so as to protect both the child and himself from harm and to prevent unnecessary or panic-creating destruction of the physical environment. The therapist must try to establish sufficient contact with psychotic children to be able to convey to them that he cannot let them harm themselves and others, and that he will protect them against their rage reactions. In general, there has to be a firm definition of limits and boundaries in both the play situation and the interpersonal relationship. The therapist needs to function in such a way as to reflect adequate responses back to the child's soundings, thus helping the child to explore and to gain some judgmental ability concerning himself and his environment. It may be necessary to help the child maintain coherence in his play, which is all too inclined to become scattered and altogether impossible to read. The therapeutic endeavor ever so often, if not always, is and has to be started by way of the *cognitive function,* since emotional adjustment can be attempted only after a measure of control—often purely intellectual or conscious habitual control—has been established.[7]

The case of Danny, age four, illustrates the need for this type of substitutive ego function by the therapist. Danny was brought to the child psychiatry clinic with two major complaints: (1) he was an extremely fearful child, laden with what, at first glance, appeared to be phobias—for example, fear of the dark, fear of wild animals, fear of witches, fear of dogs; and (2) he was a management problem, tending to become wild and uncontrollable; various forms of parental threat and physical discipline either had no effect or else provided only a temporary control. It was learned that both parents were quite anxious and quite immature people. The

---

[7] This is in marked contrast to the correct psychoanalytic approach to neurotic patients.

mother had had a stillborn child prior to her pregnancy with Danny, and this had greatly increased her already existing feelings of inadequacy and inferiority as a woman. When Danny was born, he had a congenital atresia of the bowel, which required surgery on the second day of his life and resulted in a colostomy. The colostomy was surgically closed at age four months. At eight months of age Danny had a surgical repair of bilateral inguinal hernia under general anesthesia. Two months later he was again taken to surgery for circumcision. The mother recalled that Danny seemed to suffer a good deal in each of these experiences; she felt that he had a "conscious reaction" to the circumcision and to the separation from her at age ten months.

In a play situation, Danny would characteristically begin to play in a seemingly reasonable fashion, and with fairly good rapport with the therapist. Shortly thereafter, however, the therapist would perceive that Danny's fantasies were increasingly overstimulating him. He would have the therapist make witches or wolves out of clay and then use them in fantasies in which people were threatened by them. Very soon Danny began to run about the playroom screaming wildly, or he ran in and out of the playroom and generally threw play materials about the room. The same sort of sequence occurred when he chose to paint: what would begin as a fairly orderly process of applying paint to paper ended up with an impulsive dumping of the paint jar on the floor. In the meantime, Danny would be alert to every new sound or stimulus in the environment. If a door slammed, a dog barked outside, the steam radiator hissed, Danny stopped his play, listened attentively, and insisted that the noise be identified and explained. Whereas with a neurotic child we would try to learn about the fantasies connected with this preoccupation with noises, and work on the probability of frightening primal scene observations to which this frightened fascination perhaps referred back, in this case the need to strengthen the ego meant facilitating controlled regression rather than attempting to undo it.

The therapist not only tried to reduce outside stimuli to a minimum, but gradually insisted that Danny not divert himself from his play to identify every extraneous noise. When Danny began to get excited in his fantasy play, the therapist actively intervened and quietly but firmly stopped the play for the time being. At the same time the therapist stated in simple terms that Danny was, in effect, scaring himself with these play stories. As the pattern of these play stories became established and their meaning could be understood, the therapist verbalized that meaning in terms of Danny's fears not only of what might happen to him but also of what he feared his anger would or could do to others. Eventually, witches and wolves were translated into Danny's fears about his mother and himself. As all of these various things were accomplished in therapy, Danny began to develop a feeling of control over his fantasies and his impulses. Simultaneously with the work with Danny, his mother was treated, in order to relieve her of her feeling guilty about somehow being responsible for Danny's "defectiveness" and to enable her to be firm with him in the setting of limits.

Because of the primary process character and therefore incomprehensibility of the psychotic child's behavior and communications, it is absolutely essential to have a close and effective informative alliance with the mother if the child lives at home, or with a substitute parent figure if the child is in an institution. The communication of the psychotic child can often be understood only if the therapist has prior knowledge concerning those events in the child's life that took place during the twenty-four or more hours preceding the therapy session. This is even more important than with a neurotic child, since the cause-and-effect relationship between stimulus, conflict, and behavior needs to be almost immediate or at least current in the psychotic child's experience in order for the therapist to be able to perceive and to understand it.

The psychotic child often needs considerable verbal reassurance as to his basic worth and his basic integrity as an organismic whole. There is usually much distortion and defect in the body-image concept, these being reflected in the fear of body disintegration, mutilation, and castration anxiety, all of which culminate in panic reactions.

At one stage in treatment, Barbara (who was mentioned earlier) was working out her concern and her questions about her female self. She began by putting her slacks on backward, calling attention to the seam which was now over her genital area. Similarly, she approached this subject by putting her jacket on backward, then viewing herself in the mirror from the rear (the jacket had a seam which normally ran down the middle of the back). Later, she exposed her genital area and examined it in front of the mirror. As she did so, she asked questions of the therapist concerning the difference between boys and girls. It became obvious that Barbara felt that her mother had taken her "little boy genital" away from her. The therapist reassured Barbara with the explanation that little girls were born to be as they were and that there was nothing wrong with her. Eventually this led to a discussion and explanation concerning the female function of bearing children.

At another time, Barbara was engaging in play in which she had clearly established a large girl doll as a representation of herself. She had the doll engage in some "naughty" behavior and then proceeded to beat the doll mercilessly. The therapist intervened, preventing Barbara from beating the doll (herself), and insisting that we would not allow her doll-child to be harmed. For a while, Barbara persisted in her attempts to beat the doll, but when she saw that the therapist really would not permit this, she gave up and instead became very tender to the doll. The therapist then began to explore with Barbara the meaning of the play.

Although this was important, it was equally important, in terms of Barbara's developing identity and self-esteem, to prevent the "beatings" from going still further to the actual destruction of the "Barbara-doll."

With psychotic children, it is often necessary for the therapist to serve an educational type of function—for example, to teach the child about relationships in time, about the functioning of the body, and about the realities of various social relationships, at a time when the child is ready for such knowledge. Because of their early and pervasive ego disorganization, most psychotic children fail to acquire these important and basic concepts at the appropriate age. The problem differs from that with neurotic children in that it is not a matter of distortion out of neurotic need, but rather distortion as a result of failure of structuralization.

When Danny first came for treatment, he had no conception whatsoever of the sequence of the days of the week. Some vague awareness of this time relationship began to emerge around the regularity of his visits to the therapist on Monday, Wednesday, and Friday. When Danny showed a desire to anticipate or to predict the visits, the therapist attempted to concretize the time concept by representing days of the week in pieces of clay. After he did this, the pieces that represented Monday, Wednesday, and Friday were arranged in a row separate from the row that represented the seven days of the week as a whole. Danny then repeated this activity on his own, and within two weeks he was able to state correctly the sequence of the days of the week, and indicate particular days, past, present, and future.

While she was engaging in fantasy play, Barbara had a herd of cows go out into the pasture and defecate before they ate their feed. When the therapist expressed interest in this, Barbara disclosed her fantasy that the cows would die if they ate food without first moving their bowels. This fantasy, of course, had a good deal of meaning in terms of Barbara's psychopathology. On the other hand, it was felt to be important that Barbara have a clear understanding of what happens to food in the body and of the relationship between ingestion and elimination (cf. Paula Elkisch, 1956). Actually, upon further exploration of the fantasy, and after a realistic explanation of the eating and eliminating functions, Barbara revealed that she had previously visualized the abdomen as an empty sac. This had to do with her conception of the baby in the mother's body, which in turn led to another fantasy: that she must somehow have harmed her mother; otherwise her mother could not have been so "rejecting" of her.

Thus far we have been discussing treatment technique as it applies to psychotic children in general. There are specific differences, however, between the treatment approach to the primarily autistic psychotic child and that to the primarily symbiotic psychotic child.

It seems apparent that, at the outset, individual psychotherapy is best suited for the autistic child, since he needs the one-to-one relationship to lure him from his withdrawn state. He cannot profit fully from the specialized educational techniques and the other forms of environmental supplementation of special residential schools until he has begun to accept the symbiotic type of relationship. On the other hand, the primarily symbiotic psychotic child is able to profit from the special environment as soon as his panic reactions subside, since what he needs is diversified substitute relationships in place of his unspecific, yet parasitic state of fusion with the mother. Such children must be gradually approached with the help of inanimate objects.

Bobby, from the age of six years on, was treated in a residential institution. At home he was seen as a quiet, reserved child, who seemed content to play by himself and to make few demands upon the rest of the family. They did not recognize that he had a problem, therefore, until he went to school. Here he was found to be completely unable to learn, because he made no attempt to relate to the teacher or to the other children in his class. Upon being studied diagnostically, he was found to be quite uncommunicative; nevertheless, there was evidence in his isolated play behavior that he had a good intelligence potential. He was quite skilled in making complicated objects out of clay. He showed a great deal of interest in the record player and would watch it for hours, apparently fascinated as much by the mechanical repetitious movement—the spinning of the disk—as by its sound. As long as he was left to his own devices, he was relatively contented; but as soon as demands were made upon him, he became irritable. Ultimately, he would have violent "temper tantrums," in which he would bite himself on the hand, slap himself in the face, and hit his head against the floor or wall (cf. Geleerd, 1945).

In the beginning period of treatment, Bobby was quite happy to go to the playroom and engage in an active and persistent way in activity of a seemingly creative sort. He particularly enjoyed making miniature record players out of clay, and also building castles out of blocks, which he would then knock down with great glee. In all this activity, the therapist was either ignored altogether or treated as an inanimate part of the environment. There was no attempt on Bobby's part at communication of experience. Instead, he used the therapist as an extension of himself—for example, to get to an object that was on a shelf out of his reach. Any attempt by the therapist to establish either verbal or physical contact with Bobby was warded off. If the therapist persisted in trying to get Bobby's attention, for example, by turning Bobby's face to the therapist and holding it there, Bobby seemed annoyed; he then looked as if he was going to cry, although he never shed any tears; he became red in the face, seemingly with rage, and finally he screamed out and bit himself repeatedly on the back of the hand. The same type of behavior occurred if the therapist frustrated Bobby's "omnipotent" gesturing for help, by failing to function as a "lever" for the securing of a particular play object.

Very gradually, over a period of many months, during which the therapist did not force himself upon Bobby, he increasingly began to pay genuine attention to the therapist. He would be waiting for his appointments and would become upset when they were not kept promptly. He asked for things verbally and seemed quite well related, particularly during the routine of "going to the store for candy." The relationship continued to be quite tenuous, however, and Bobby was always withdrawn and autistic again after interruptions due to illness or vacation.

In the secondarily autistic type of a primarily symbiotic psychotic child, one needs to evaluate carefully the child's ability to relate, by considering each child, to begin with, as an individual case. The initial approach is much the same as with the primarily autistic child. The fact that the autism is a defense against a previously established symbiotic relationship makes the defense no less intense. Once the symbiotic relationship has been re-established, however, progress tends to be comparable to that of the primarily symbiotic psychotic child, and the prognosis, therefore, is better than with the primarily autistic child.

In contrast, the initial approach to the primarily symbiotic type of psychosis must be "played by ear"; it is important to let the child test reality very gradually and at his own pace. As he cautiously begins this testing of himself as a separate entity, he needs constantly to feel supported by the emotionally "uncontaminated" (Ernst Kris's expression) auxiliary egos of a team of adults, who represent diversified subst᷎᷎ tes for the pathological symbiotic object, thus diluting the impact of the pull to merge and the dread of fusion. Continual infusions of borrowed ego strength may have to be given for a long, long time.

Early in the treatment situation, Barbara acted out her symbiotic defense by relating immediately and quite unselectively to almost any adult in her environment, particularly women. Barbara had great verbal facility which she used to establish contact and to take possession of the adult, indiscriminately, and for as long a time as was possible. She asked a great many questions, and was apparently able to keep some degree of control over her inner impulses and fantasies by actively directing her attention toward tangible objects in the environment. Once she realized, however, that she had established a steady and more discriminating relationship with the therapist, she came directly and immediately to the therapist's office when she was brought to the treatment building. For a long time she burst right into the office, opening the closed door, quite unable to understand that she had to wait until her appointment time. She would not leave the office except in the company of the therapist; it was even necessary for the therapist to go with her to the car when she was returned to her own building. When she went to the toilet, she would leave the bathroom door open, partly because of her lack of awareness of social convention, but primarily in order to avoid having a closed door between her and the substitute symbiotic partner.

It was felt to be definite evidence of progress in her individuation when Barbara began to wait for her appointment, or when she actually made the therapist wait for her. Ultimately, she gave up her unselective clinging attachment to people and began to show a more judicious and normally reticent way of relating. Needless to say, these changes occurred only after a good deal of treatment, during which the therapist was functioning much of the time as a synthesizing and integrating agent, structuring Barbara's ego functions and her concept of herself as an individual.

A fundamental principle of this mode of treatment is that the therapist works toward becoming a substitute mother figure. He offers himself as a symbiotic partner, and allows and aids the child to relive—re-experience—in a way, more normally, yet more age-adequately, the early phases of psychic life that are so important to separation-individuation and independent functioning.

It is apparent that, by contrast with the less severely disturbed child, the psychotic child is, from the beginning of treatment, and continues afterward to be, more dependent upon his mother or a mother substitute. During the treatment, there may be times when the child needs to be physically separated from the mother because institutional care is indicated.[8] Even in the case of physical separation, a substitute for the mother—in a one-to-one relationship—must be regarded as an essential part of the treatment program at all times. Even though the child may be able to function on a higher level, he will still continue to require a certain degree of anaclitic relationship and infusion of ego strength, perhaps throughout the rest of his life. It is vital, consequently, that the actual mother, or the person who will substitute for her, be simultaneously guided as to the special needs of the psychotic child, or if necessary, simultaneously receive treatment herself. The goal is to re-establish a relationship that offers the only real promise for the child's growth and development.

THE TRIPARTITE THERAPEUTIC DESIGN: MOTHER-CHILD-THERAPIST

In our efforts to achieve our therapeutic goal of "corrective symbiotic experience," we have had at our disposal, and at first could not help but use, the existing methods of approach to the treatment of psychotic children within conventional institutions, all of which routinely entail exposure of the

[8] Cf. Mahler's contribution to the discussion *Residential Treatment of a Schizophrenic Child* at the Hawthorne-Cedar Knolls (see Gavrin, 1952).

preschool psychotic child to group situations. Our experience with these facilities, however, convinced us of the harmfulness of premature efforts to expose such children to group situations, which interfered with or diluted the corrective symbiotic experience, even in the most carefully planned therapeutic nursery, by subjecting the child to one or another kind of social situation. Not only was progress impeded thereby; in many instances, there were also detrimental traumatic effects.

Sy, for example, who was referred for private treatment at the age of four and a half as a case of infantile psychosis, promptly developed a symbiotic attachment to the therapist. Prior to referral, Sy had been given a thorough preliminary examination in an academic center. During the psychological testing, it was readily observed that he responded best to bodily affection. In fact, during the course of treatment, his need for bodily contact, which he could provide for himself either only very passively and surreptitiously, or else eruptively and violently, was continually in evidence. Before referral, the psychologist noted: "It may be of interest that Sy's highest level of success occurred when he was being caressed by patting or stroking on the head and shoulders; he was given this demonstration of affection because he seemed to be entirely impervious to vocal expressions of praise and encouragement." His selective awareness of emotional situations was demonstrated by his correctly noting in one picture of the test that a child who was depicted with his mother was crying.

Sy responded rather unspecifically but very well to any exclusive relationship with an adult. In fact, he loved to have two or more adults concentrating on him at the same time. However, he clearly showed anger or proneness to tantrums if any of the adults excluded him by talking with each other. When his mother talked on the telephone, for example, he deliberately took apart one of his toys and yelled, "Fix it, fix it!" He seemed to be fascinated by his baby cousin to the point of imitating the baby talk—which showed us the way he himself wanted to be treated.

His mother was, unfortunately, a very rigid and proper lady. Although she loved her child very much in her own way and was consciously ready to make any sacrifice for him, she could not provide the warmth he needed. (The child's father had abandoned them on Sy's first birthday.) The mother could not tolerate her child's bizarre behavior, particularly in public. She talked with him almost exclusively on a rather adult level, despite her awareness that what she said had very limited meaning for him. She did not give him any tender physical affection; she was probably incapable of it. Gravely deficient as she was in adequate self-esteem herself, the child was for her a conspicuous proof of her worthlessness and social inacceptability.

After a few months of treatment, it became apparent that four hours of weekly therapy in the office was not adequate either for the child or for the mother. The concentrated, partly symbiotic-parasitic, partly autistic atmosphere of an exclusive living arrangement of mother and child in a small furnished room needed to be counterbalanced; furthermore, the mother felt keenly that some more formal learning situation with other children needed to be provided for her child. We succeeded in having Sy accepted in a small nursery school. He behaved there as we had expected—not as a participant in the group, but as a tangential appendage to it. Even this was possible only because his mother remained passively close by and because the school staff was most patient and helpfully understanding. He did not profit either socially or intellectually during the months when he was patiently tolerated there, despite the fact that in the therapeutic relationship he made definite progress.

At the end of the school year, the teacher's report stated: "Sy does not participate in most of the activities of the class. He seldom talks to children or adults, but frequently communicates by sound and action rather than words. When he does talk, and this is when *one* teacher has time to be with him, he shows particular interest in trains and book illustrations, etc."

Sy grew to be especially tall for his age, and since it was impossible to keep him in the nursery, he was transferred to a kindergarten when he was five and a half years old. In kindergarten, his panic and tantrums instantly recurred. He had catastrophic reactions to the situation, especially since his mother was not permitted to remain with him. Within a few days, she was asked to withdraw him. This failure upset her more than all the signs and proofs that should previously have made her aware of the gravity of the child's mental illness.

A few weeks later, special tutoring was provided for Sy. Once again, in this exclusive one-to-one relationship, he made progress in a characteristic, peculiarly unspecific symbiotic experience, just as he had done in the therapeutic relationship. With the help of the tutor and of the therapist, his tendency to autistic withdrawal diminished. His courage to test reality increased, as did his vocabulary and his perception of the outside world. For the first time in his life, he displayed a fondness for such soft, transitional objects as pillows and toy animals. These now served—as they had not before—to allay his anxieties and tensions. He surrounded himself with these transitional objects, particularly at night, and thus relived early stages of babyhood in a more normal way.

Again we made the mistake, however, of enrolling him in a group, this time in our pilot project, in what we thought was a particularly sheltered learning situation in a special therapeutic nursery group. Sy was bewildered, but made what we thought to be an initial adaptation because he shared the teacher with only one other child. His distress soon became apparent, however, when a few more children joined the group. We were still inclined to attribute a rapid regression in his speech, and in other areas of his functioning, to measles, which he had contracted near the end of the school year. But when, after a fairly good summer at the seashore, he rejoined the group, his ego threatened rapidly to disintegrate. In uncontrollable panic and rage, he violently attacked his mother and teachers. His speech became unintelligible, and he seemed to hallucinate.

This much of Sy's case has been presented in order tô demonstrate that, in all situations, he desperately craved and violently demanded exclusive attention, symbiotic complementation by one adult, and sheltering by such an adult from social situations involving groups. He repeatedly retreated, following severe tantrums, into lethargic states of hallucinatory withdrawal, if he could not be given the exclusive attention of an adult to the extent that his fragmented ego craved and needed.

The last of numerous experiences of the same sort that led us to abandon the therapeutic nursery design for psychotic preschool children was the case of a four-year-old psychotic child, who had been placed in a smoothly functioning group of five disturbed but not psychotic children, with two teachers. When Peggy arrived at the therapeutic nursery school, she appeared to be a serenely beautiful child. She quickly became extremely restless, however, and sought constantly to find her mother, roaming through the building followed by the teacher, who had to leave the other children and go after her. The teacher learned that, by rocking her and by other devices, she could induce Peggy to remain in the room with the other children, to whom Peggy paid absolutely no attention. In her relationship to the adult, Peggy seemed to have only two alternatives: either, in a phase of autistic withdrawal, she used the teacher as an extension of her own body, in order to control the environment by way of this executive part object; or else she showed a clinging, burrowing type of behavior, during which the teacher had to focus her attention completely on Peggy lest she have a panic tantrum. It became apparent that, in order to keep the child at this higher level of relationship, the teacher would have to abandon her duties to the other children. Peggy's behavior called for an exclusive relationship with the teacher; any demand for the teacher's attention by other members of the group was increasingly deleterious to her.

For a while we continued to believe that the deleterious effect of the group on Peggy was due primarily to the fact that she was a case of early infantile autism, who became particularly vulnerable when she began to attain a symbiotic relationship. When we saw the same process occurring with still another child—a symbiotic psychotic one—we realized that a revised "therapeutic action research" had to be designed for cases of early infantile psychosis. Our hypotheses about psychosis, as elaborated in the previous chapters, had already indicated this from a theoretical point of view.

That there was a conflict in Peggy's mind between her growing attachment to the teacher and her relationship to her mother was apparent, for example, whenever she was hurt. She would run to and from the door leading to where her mother was, and then back again to the teacher, until finally she rubbed the injured part against the teacher's body. It was most amazing to observe that, as the child's conflict mounted and she ran to seek her mother, the mother became increasingly difficult to find in the building. The mother was, in fact, almost consciously trying to avoid her child, as the child became more demanding and expressive. These changes in Peggy made the mother so anxious, in fact, that she became angry with the child's therapist.

From these cases we recognized the imperative necessity for revising therapy and research in early infantile psychosis. The revised design would not involve the child with other children in a group situation until he was ready for it. The two cases described, and many others like them, made it clear that provision for the psychotic child's need for protection within the corrective symbiotic experience must be the basis for treatment. The child's development from autistic withdrawal toward primitive, unspecific clinging to the therapist, as well as to the mother, gave us another significant clue for the revision of our research design. We had often observed that the presence of the mother within the therapeutic situation was not only very well tolerated, but that it was a sign of progress for a mother to be sought by her psychotic child. The mother's presence proved, furthermore, to be most helpful to our understanding of the child's "signal communications" in most of the earlier phases of treatment.[9] In our experience, even though the mothers were unable to fulfill the needs of these children, to a surprising degree they were able to understand their own child's nonverbal communications.

It was evident that these considerations not only were of theoretical importance but also indicated the direction that had to be taken for the immediate treatment and for optimal future planning for the psychotic child's mental health. We evolved from this a method of research in which the mother, the child, and the worker are present in the room during the sessions, which extend from two to three hours, mother and therapist joining in the rehabilitation of the psychotic child.[10]

The advantages of this design are manifold. Our initial understanding of the child comes not only through observations, but also through information and explanations given by the mother. With this method, there can be mutual exchanges of information and understanding between the child's therapist, the supervising psychiatrist, and the mother, while the child's behavior is being observed by all three.

[9] See "Stages during Treatment" below.

[10] While with respect to theory, my hypotheses and those of Bettelheim (1956, 1967) are rather akin, we differ diametrically in the conclusions we draw with regard to therapy. Bettelheim does not believe in restituting the original mother-child symbiotic relationship, but recommends separation of the child from his family and the introduction of a residential milieu.

The mother is first gratified by our interest, and then heartened by the feeling, which she gradually acquires, that there is someone who believes that her child can be helped. There also appears to be a great sense of relief produced by the understanding, initially intellectual, that the mother gains. She may, and often does, use that understanding defensively, but it gives her the feeling that some control can be exercised over what had previously seemed to her to be a desperate, hopeless, and insurmountable problem.

The information that the mother gives us enables the therapist to institute those procedures that seem to foster the development of the need-satisfying symbiotic relationship between the child and the worker. In the beginning, for example, a signal type of communication has to be fostered between the child and the therapist; this can later be used by the therapist in a corrective manner.

A four-year-old boy, Malcolm, frequently rolled a toy car to and fro. The mother explained to us that this indicated that he had to urinate. We discovered from our observations that he also meant by this action that there was something wrong with the car, that it was broken. We learned, finally, that this activity, which we took to be a signal of his bodily need, occurred after many hours of withholding his urine, to the point where he was in pain and probably afraid that he could no longer withhold. We then understood these signals to mean that he was afraid of being overwhelmed by these inner bodily stimuli. Our therapeutic procedure has been to respond to this signal as a mother would to an infant—that is, as an auxiliary ego, which we hope the child can add to his own ego, thereby overcoming otherwise overwhelming anxieties. Instead, therefore, of interpreting the displacement and anxiety, the therapist tells the boy that he will feel very good when he goes to the toilet and that she will help him. She takes him with her to the toilet, encouraging him to urinate, and expressing her pleasure and approval when he does. In this way, we believe, we have begun to liberate the child from the feeling of being the passive victim of bodily discomforts and discharges; with this help, he may go on to independently active functioning.

In general, the new design allows for the development of a more and more specific relationship with the therapist, without interference from other children. The development of the child's relationship to the therapist, which always brings with it changes in the relationship with the mother, can be observed directly, and the frequently defeatist attitudes of the family counteracted (cf. Mahler, 1955). With the emergence from autism, and the achievement of a higher level of behavior, the patience of the families of these children is often greatly taxed. The repetitive banging of doors, throwing of objects, switching on and off of lights often generate uncontrollable hostility within the family, and sometimes lead to an ill-considered placement of the child away from home.

After Malcolm became better able to comply upon being encouraged to urinate, he began to spit in an uncontrollable way. He first spat at his therapist, and soon at his mother. When his mother reprimanded him for it, he withdrew into his autistic shell. We had learned previously that the disturbance in the child's urinary functioning had occurred as a consequence of the mother's disgust at finding that he urinated into the bathtub instead of the toilet. Had the spitting happened at home, as an extension of the child's behavior in the therapeutic situation, this mother might well have reacted, as had Peggy's mother, with hostility. But Malcolm's mother had been made a member of the "therapeutic alliance," and the simple explanation that she was given of the beneficial value of Malcolm's transient regressive behavior made sense to her. She had, in fact, previously reported, during the course of the therapy, that Malcolm had begun at home to invite her to exchange babbling and cooing sounds with him. The mother spontaneously expressed her opinion that he seemed belatedly to be permitting himself indulgences of babyhood that—in contrast to his brothers—he had missed completely. Observing the way in which the therapist handled the situation gave the mother a sense of security, a way of understanding, a model for helping her child.

Such experiences with the example and help of the child's therapist, the supervising psychiatrist, and the social worker become assimilated in time—provided the mother herself is capable of learning, and of providing the additional and essential corrective symbiotic experience for the child. The reason why the spitting developed in the case of Malcolm could be explained directly to the boy's mother by the child's therapist, and subsequently gone into more fully by the social worker. Whatever deeper fears and defenses may be involved in her initial reaction, the mother's immediate response to the child—and this is always partly dictated by unconscious forces—is thereafter opposed by her conscious determination, which is aided by her understanding and by the example given to her by the team. This kind of therapeutic help for the mother of the psychotic child is consistent with our theory that the treatment of the child must extend over many years of the child's life, and that his development must be re-experienced and relived, not only with the therapist but with the primary love object. The mother must therefore be trained to assume and maintain the corrective symbiotic experience she has seen being developed by the therapist. This emotional-intellectual learning is stabilized by the mother's individual sessions with the supervising psychiatrist and the social worker.

In this method we have evolved a mother-child-therapist unit, supervised by a child psychiatrist, which can lead to the development of the child's personality, instead of fixation at the stage of the psychosis. It is interesting—and somewhat disquieting—that it took us so many years to arrive at these inevitable conclusions and to apply their logical implications in therapeutic research. They were inherent from the start in our theoretical hypotheses of autistic and symbiotic psychosis. Gradually, tardily, and retrospectively we came to these conclusions by way of clinical data, which abundantly demonstrated that failures ensued whenever the corrective symbiotic relationship was threatened by disruption—as it too frequently was when we were adhering to traditional methods.

The crucial therapeutic problem in psychosis remains the same: the psychotic child must be kept from retreating into the autistic defensive position. He must be enticed into, and encouraged to relive, a more fully gratifying—albeit regressive—exclusively symbiotic-parasitic relationship with a substitute mother. This relationship is liberally made available to the child, for whom it becomes a buffer in the process of dissolving the vicious cycle of the distorted relationship with the mother. Gradually and cautiously, the child is then helped to develop some autonomous substitutes for the pathological primitive regressive demands that he has been helped to exact from the reactively defensive mother. In this manner, the child is led to discover the boundaries of his self, and to experience a sense of himself as a separate entity in his environment.

In the treatment of young psychotic children, a contradiction sometimes confuses workers in the field. Although these infants seem insatiable in their need for the passively available symbiotic partner, their symbiotic claim is at first not at all specific. Several adults are well tolerated and often simultaneously enjoyed. But at first, and for a long time thereafter, these children are utterly intolerant of any type of group relationship involving other children, even those that are established by the most carefully devised methods. Only the most important symbiotic partner, who seals herself off from the rest of the world as completely as possible with the child, can form for him an insulating layer against those give-and-take aspects of social group situations for which he has no capacity or tolerance during the period referred to. It is only after a prolonged period of corrective symbiotic experience that the psychotic child should be given carefully gradated doses of rhythmic play within a group— preferably to the accompaniment of soothing music—during which the symbiotic partner is right at the side of the child. During the course of the therapeutic research, we carefully observe the preferences of these children, as they slowly evolve interest and reach out for association with the other children being treated at the Center. They show us un- mistakably just when they are ready for such social learn- ing, as well as how much of it they can "take."

STAGES DURING TREATMENT

There are two stages through which the treatment process passes in the tripartite setting of mother, psychotic child, and therapist: an introductory stage and a stage of treat- ment proper.[11]

The Introductory Stage

The therapist's task, to begin with, is to establish some form of contact, some form of primitive communication with the symbiotic psychotic child, who is unable at that point either to establish or to experience any direct relationship to another person (secondary autism). The therapist's task can be conceived as being that of somehow making her presence felt, allowing the child to experience it as something positive without any need to acknowledge the existence of the thera- pist as a person.

[11] Many of the conceptual formulations in this section derive from the work of Anni Bergman and M. Ben-Aaron, M.S., senior therapists.

This entails the creation of a nonintrusive, attentive presence, which, instead of increasing the child's anxiety (as any other sort of presence would), slowly follows the child's lead, thereby making it possible for him gradually to come to accept the therapist's presence as a soothing phenomenon, with which he finds himself more comfortable than he has been without it. At this point we conceive of the therapist as a part object, which the child begins to use as an extension of himself—e.g., in making use of the therapist's arm as a tool with which to obtain objects that are out of his reach, or by leaning against the therapist as a supportive surface, or falling into her arms as a soft and sustaining platform, all the time taking for granted that she is always there to be used in those ways. Gradually the therapist is allowed to meet the child's needs more actively—for instance, in feeding. The child accepts parallel playlike activity, which later becomes the beginning of an interchange between himself and the therapist, as, for example, in their alternately drumming on the table or humming a song. At the start, even visual contact may be warded off by the child, so that an approach to him with sound can be made only so long as it is not within his visual field. This limitation was clearly illustrated in the case of one child, who had a panic tantrum upon observing the therapist in the mirror, even though she could not see her directly.

In Chapter V we have described Violet and the type of interaction she had established with her mother when she first came to our attention at the Center. As mentioned, she was mute and severely autistic. She played busily with toys and totally ignored all the people around her. Here I wish to focus on the course of Violet's treatment. The therapist tried to establish contact, cautiously and indirectly. She never approached Violet from within her visual field, but rather from behind—for example, by offering her body as a cushion. She also allowed the child to use her arms as extensions of the child's own. She used her voice sparingly at first, deliberately with a neutral singsong quality, devoid of any emotional appeal so as not to intrude upon the child by seeming to demand a response. After a while, the child, while playing, would more obviously lean against the therapist. Gradually she could be fed in an unlimited fashion by the therapist.

At home, Violet had been fed simply by having the food put before her on a plate, to be eaten or not, without the mother's participation. Illustrative of the mother's attitude in the feeding situation was her belief that, if the child was not given sweets, she would not know about them and thus never crave them. It is also interesting that the mother took food from Violet's plate clandestinely while she was being fed by the therapist. Only in subsequent periods of treatment, and only after the mother had been offered a meal along with her child, and after other symbolic forms of love had been supplied both to her and to her child—only then could the mother herself be "giving" to her child.

Physical contact—which the therapist initiated and the child acknowledged—was first made through the intermediary of soap bubbles. Added stimulation could also be introduced through water play. During one of these games, Violet lifted up her shirt and allowed the therapist to blow the soap bubbles onto her naked stomach; she seemed to derive great pleasure from the sensation.

The therapist then started to accompany the child's activities by singing simple, familiar tunes. Soon song and activity became associated, an association that offered the possibility of pleasure as well as of the recognition of repetition, and provided a beginning structure—a language, as it were—which slowly became more and more meaningful and varied. There was a song for playing with trains, a song for playing with pegs, a song for playing together.[12]

[12] We wish to express our gratitude to Mrs. Miriam Ben-Aaron, who was Violet's first therapist, and made valuable contributions to this and other treatment cases. Mrs. Ben-Aaron is now head of a treatment center in Israel.

In attempting to conceptualize how the symbiotic psychotic child experiences the therapist at this first stage of treatment, it was formulated that the therapist represents a "mothering principle": at this point she cannot yet represent a distinct and separate human object. The place of the "mothering principle" in the child with a predominantly autistic defense organization may perhaps be comparable with that stage of the normal symbiotic phase at which the baby dimly recognizes that ministrations that re-establish homeostasis are coming. from a good outside environmental source.

Part of the functioning of this "principle" with regard to the child—its providing an experience of comfort rather than one of intense discomfort—is that it acts as a buffer between him and his environment. We believe that, while the child perceives such discrete attributes of the therapist as voice or feeling tone or nearness, he does not seem to realize clearly where they come from. We liken this experience to what has been called the "transitional phenomenon" (Winnicott, 1953b). Slowly the child comes to take for granted the soothing atmosphere emanating from the therapist. He then seeks out this comfort and gradually recognizes its source in the person of the therapist, who, however, is not yet a whole separate human object to him. It is this atmosphere, emanating from and created by a human object, the therapist, that becomes the source of this comfort and acts as a protection against the environment, as well as against the child's inner discomfort and distress.

It is likely that the therapist's comforting presence helps to diminish some of the child's intense aggression and destructiveness (self- and outward-directed), thereby reducing his level of anxiety and making his functioning more comfortable.

During Violet's tantrums, when no other physical means could yet be used to maintain contact with the child, a singsong commentary, in a low and soothing voice, seemed to lessen some of the intensity of the self-destructiveness and thereby lessen the intensity of the tantrum. This commentary contained a verbalization of the child's sensations and emotions, and at the same time emphasized the libidinal atmosphere created by the therapist and the mother. "Oh, it hurts!" "Don't hurt Violet. She's a nice girl." "You are angry with Violet, but we don't want you to hurt yourself because we love you."

In the second portion of the introductory phase, after the therapist has accomplished these initial changes—that is, after the child has begun to accept her as a mothering principle—the therapist leads the mother into the same kind of relationship with her child. The therapist is always cognizant of the fact that the goal of the tripartite design is, from the very beginning, the re-establishment of a symbioticlike tie to the original object, the mother—a stage that was either missed or gravely disturbed in the psychotic child, yet without which no further improvement (no measure of individuation) can occur. The rediscovery of the mother is cautiously but continuously fostered by the therapist, who functions as the catalyst of this process.

In this phase, the therapist's intuitive perception of nascent feelings in both mother and child and her timing in bringing them together are of vital importance. Opportunities for the emergence of short-lived but genuine emotional interchange between them often occur when the mother and the therapist discuss events in the child's life. At those times, the child will add to the discussion from his memory and in his own primary process fashion, which is often understood first by the mother.

At the beginning of treatment, Violet's mother was almost as unresponsive as Violet herself. She would sit in total silence, rigid and stony-faced. She interpreted Violet's unresponsiveness to the therapist as well as to her as rejection of herself, and could only react in kind. In order to draw the mother into a relationship with both therapist and child, it was necessary first to feed her, both figuratively and literally, in an effort to compensate in some small measure for the emotional starvation of her own childhood. Food was of great importance to the mother, for which reason it was necessary to provide meals for her as well as for the child, taking the clue from the fact that she had been observed secretly to snatch bits of food from her child's plate. The therapist, the therapeutic institution itself, had to become a mothering principle to the mother. When she was angry, she was fed; when she was tired, she was given a place to nap. Furthermore, the therapist showed the mother a practical way of dealing better with the child—for example, handling Violet's temper tantrums. The mother was extraordinarily sensitive to anything that could possibly be interpreted as adverse criticism of her. Years later, she revealed that, following a remark from the social worker that she had interpreted in that way, she had actually attempted suicide. Slowly the mother became able to identify with the therapist and at times even to be more gratifying to her child. This dawning relationship remained extremely fragile, however, and would give way at any setback or renewed frustration.

After the initial stage of establishing contact with both mother and child, and creating a more benign environment for both, the therapist drew the mother into the treatment process in a more active way, by asking her to talk during the treatment sessions about their life at home. This was difficult at first, because life at home was less idyllic than the mother liked to admit. The therapeutic situation provided a haven, and both mother and child were reluctant to have this haven invaded by the difficulties that persisted at home. However, once the mother could accept including their homelife in the therapeutic process, her talking about it drew both her and the child into a more active participation in the treatment and into a closer relationship with each other.

Because of her unusual musical talent and her innate sensitivity, Violet was able to indicate her participation by way of music. For example, one day when the mother said that Violet had been upset that morning, Violet started to play a Mozart sonata on the piano; to this the mother reacted by saying, "This morning Violet's father played a record of this sonata, to quiet Violet when she was upset." Or, later in treatment, on a day when the mother was very angry with Violet and had relapsed into her old hostile silence, Violet played a song on the xylophone. The mother recognized the song, saying, "That is a song I sing to Violet at night. The words to it are 'I love you, my dear.'" This was one example of the child's astonishing capacity, which later developed in the treatment process to the point where it was able to bring about a reconciliation with the mother and to draw her into a more positive and active relationship at times when she was giving clear evidence of withdrawal and rage.

As the child's feelings now come to be directed toward more differentiated human objects—namely, the therapist and the mother—we often find that he tends to focus the positive aspects of his response on one of these newly found part objects, and the negative aspects on the other. This split in emotional response, which may go along with a defensive split into good and bad object images, is something we also observe in the behavior of the mothers. Generally the positive feeling is maintained toward the therapist and the supervising child psychiatrist, whereas the anger and disappointment are focused on the mother's relationship with her social worker.[13]

It has been our experience that many of the severely disturbed children who begin treatment with us appear at first to be almost totally disorganized. Their behavior is aimless and impossible to understand, and even their needs seem to

[13] In our treatment design, the mother is seen once a week by the supervising psychiatrist, to gather information, and also by the social worker, who focuses more on problems arising in the mother's own life, both during the treatment process and in the rest of her life.

go unrecognized or to be discharged in diffuse motor reactions, without meaningful communication to anyone around.
During the first several months with us, we often observe
a rapidly increasing organization of the child's behavior, so
that we can begin to recognize such reactions as hunger and
pain. The child also makes some of his wishes known to us,
even though in the private gesture language that has already
been described in psychotic children. Most important from
our point of view, there takes place a flowering of symptoms
that are often related to ritualistic demands for sameness,
but include, in addition, a focusing upon cherished objects
(the "psychotic fetish"). At first the cathexes may shift rapidly from one inanimate object (or collection of objects, or
aspect of an object) to another, but they soon seem to settle
on a relatively few. Then the picture, or the pile of buttons,
etc., must at all times either be in the child's hand or else
placed somewhere in the room where he can always find it
with his eyes. At the same time, the child's involvement with
the psychotic fetish—an inanimate object, such as the piano,
edges, numbers, fans, jars, bottles, tops, etc.—comes to include a primitive relationship to the therapist. We believe
that these are transitional objects, in that they represent
both the child's own distorted image and also the image
of the therapeutically created part love object. We observe
many instances of the child's love, hate, and anxiety about
the loss of this object, the psychotic fetish—instances derived
from past experiences with the mother. Through his growing
understanding of what the fetish represents, he comes to
further awareness of the reality of his environment, as well
as of the memories and conflicts to which he is giving expression in his behavior with the fetish.

This is well illustrated in the case of Johnny, whose psychotic fetish was a particular kind of baby-food jar with the
picture of a baby on it. After this preoccupation developed,
Johnny showed a variety of behaviors involving the baby
jar. Sometimes he held it very fondly and caressingly against

his face; at other times he sought desperately to find a way of throwing it out the window or down the stairs. Eventually a repetitive game took shape, in which he did throw it away from him, and the therapist repeatedly brought it back. In the process he gradually began to show anxiety when he threw it away, and relief when it was returned. The mother was able to tell us that Johnny himself sometimes tried to jump out the window, and that he also tried to throw his baby brother out the window, which brought out violent reactions in the mother. Gradually, Johnny could be made aware of his ambivalent reactions to his brother and mother. As his conscious awareness of his feelings toward the inanimate object became available to him, there developed an increased awareness of the therapist and the mother during the therapeutic sessions.

With this new accessibility of his needs and the availability of an actual love object to gratify them, the child turns toward mother and therapist with intense symbiotic needs and demands—demands that can be so overwhelming to the mother that some have actually attempted to hide from, and finally to rid themselves of, their children. It is at this point that the mother's identification with the therapist is of primary concern to us, for that is what makes it possible to prevent the panic and bewilderment we had previously observed in mothers when their children began to turn toward them for gratification in a manner that had been precluded by the previous state of the psychosis (secondary autism). The mother is further helped by keeping her positive feelings directed mainly toward the therapist, while focusing her negative feelings on the social worker who sees her without the child.

The Phase of Treatment Proper

In the second phase, the therapist both leads the child and follows his development from the mother of part-object relationship to an investment of the more differentiated whole human object. Whereas the first phase has been concerned with the re-establishment of the beginnings of object relationship, this phase is concerned with the child's reliving and understanding of the traumatic experiences that have hampered his development. The therapist here forms the bridge between the psychotic preoccupations and the reinvestment of the mother. The understanding and gradual recovery of the derivation of the meaning of the psychotic fetish is a prerequisite for the stable investment of the mother.

The piano was Violet's psychotic fetish; it played a major role both in her life and in her therapy. Violet's connection with the piano had started in her earliest infancy. While still an infant in the cradle, Violet had been placed near the piano when the parents were practicing. The child, being endowed with an unusual and sensitive ear, seems to have enjoyed these early experiences. Later, however, when she became a toddler, the piano seems to have become her greatest competitor. She was no longer content to allow the parents to practice; instead, she showed her anger by attacking the piano furiously, by biting and scratching, and by attacking and tearing up the parents' music sheets. The parents, both of whom were young and ambitious musicians, could not bear to have their practicing interfered with, and they resorted to locking Violet into her room while they went on with their work. In her room Violet would have severe temper tantrums, kicking with her feet against the closed door. Thus, the piano came to be both loved and hated: it produced a lifeline of sound between her world of isolation and the world of her parents, at the same time that it was the cause of her isolation.

Early in her therapy, Violet explored the insides of the piano in a way that made one feel that the piano represented the mother's body: it was reminiscent of the way in which an infant of about ten months will carefully examine and inspect the mother's face and her body, in his attempts to differentiate himself after his emergence from the symbiotic phase. It was through music that Violet expressed her first dawning awareness of people outside herself. She did this by playing the piano in different ways, in imitation of either her mother or her father. She improvised music as she looked at pictures and listened to stories that her therapist told about them. Later, her playing became more complicated and extensive. She would sometimes spend hours of her therapy at the piano, playing pieces she had heard her parents play, and improvising in many different moods and styles. At certain times, her playing could be tender or ecstatic; at other times she would bang at the piano mercilessly and would even try to jump on it. (Years later, when Violet had progressed to a much higher stage of object relations and ego functions, she still expressed her anger by banging or jumping on the piano.)

During the second stage of therapy, Violet communicated through the piano in many subtle ways. Through her particular primary process mode of behavior via music, and through her behavior at the piano, she now expressed more complex intrapsychic conflicts. For instance, one day, before a Christmas vacation, Violet chose to play a Clementi sonata on the piano. She took all the repeats over and over again, and thus did not bring the piece to an ending. The interpretation was made to Violet that she did not want the piece to come to an end, just as she did not want her time with the therapist to come to an end. Violet's crying and tantrum indicated that this interpretation was correct. After recuperating from the tantrum, she leaned affectionately against her therapist and played her favorite Christmas carol, "Jingle Bells," but this time transposed to a minor key, which expressed her libidinal longing and tender parting feelings.

Somewhat later Violet began to play duets with both mother and the therapist. She indicated the song to be played as well as the key in which to play it. When the therapist had difficulty following the child's elaborate modulations, Violet stopped and patiently showed her how to do it. By contrast with her previous imitation of other people as she played the piano, it appeared that now there was a sense of a self and a love object that were separate from each other. While on the one hand Violet used the piano for these communications, particularly in the duet playing, on the other hand she treated the piano as if it were alive. At times she would lie on it, hugging it; at other times she would beat on it or bite it.

When Violet's first therapist took leave of her—following one year of therapy, and after the autistic balance had been altered and a measure of object relations established—she gave Violet as a good-by present a stuffed dog, which she called "happy dog." Violet too said "happy dog," and for a long time to come this was one of the few words in her vocabulary. The first therapist had occasionally also called Violet "happy girl." Violet used that phrase when she felt happy, but also when she felt unhappy; by saying these words she could express the wish to feel happy, to feel better when she felt bad. "Happy dog" became Violet's first cherished possession. It definitely carried the image of the lost love object—the therapist. Her feelings toward "happy dog" were less ambivalent than her feelings toward the psychotic fetish, the piano, and did not carry the burden of the unneutralized aggression. "Happy dog" continued to be of importance to Violet in her second year of therapy with her new therapist. Another cherished possession was added by Violet's mother when, after a day of great difficulty, she gave Violet a present of a stuffed cat, named "kitty cat"— another word that remained in Violet's vocabulary.

After the second year of therapy, Violet's new therapist went on vacation. Violet showed great sadness at the time of parting; during the therapist's absence and in the absence of the haven provided by the therapeutic institution to both mother and child, the relationship between Violet and her mother became a difficult one, regressing in many ways to the level at which it had been earlier. It is no wonder that during that summer Violet lost both "happy dog" and "kitty cat," her two cherished possessions.

In the next year of therapy, early traumatic incidents between mother and child were re-experienced and re-enacted with the help of the piano. One of these had to do with Violet's having been locked out of the room (as described earlier) while the parents practiced. Violet now tried to master this situation more actively by putting the therapist into one corner of the room and demanding imperiously that she stay there while she, Violet, practiced the piano in the manner of her parents. Another one had to do with early traumatic incidents that had occurred between Violet and her mother in connection with Violet's bowel movements. Once, when Violet was about nine months old, she had smeared her feces while she was alone in the crib. On seeing this, the mother had attacked Violet with great rage. Violet never smeared again, but she never looked at her bowel movement again and refused to have a bowel movement unless she wore either a diaper or panties. In therapy, it became possible to create awareness in Violet of both the need to defecate and her bowel movement after she had had it. Instead of hiding in a corner, she started to have her bowel movement near the piano. She also started to respond to a signal played by the mother on the piano to indicate when she thought that Violet had to have a bowel movement. This signal was a descending major third. Violet would sometimes play it herself. One day, when she was playing a Brahms waltz, the therapist recognized after a while that it was built on the descending major third. She could then interpret it to Violet as a song she had invented, based on the mother's signal, to play when she needed to have a bowel movement.

During the third year of therapy, although there was progress, there was also a great deal of renewed difficulty in the relationship between Violet and her mother. The strain on the mother became too great and Violet had to be brought to her therapy sessions by various "babysitters." Violet's rage and disappointment were taken upon herself by the therapist, who told Violet that she could understand her anger since she, the therapist, was always encouraging Violet to trust and love people, only to have these same people time and again disappoint her. They developed a game in which the therapist would play the recorder, while Violet would interrupt her playing with violent banging on the piano. When Violet stopped banging, the therapist continued to play, and then explained to Violet that bad things could happen but that their relationship, once established, could not be destroyed. Violet responded to this interpretation by accompanying the recorder playing instead of interrupting it by banging.

Following this, Violet gained courage to re-enact her own vengeful destruction of the piano, which she had attempted very early in her life by continuously attacking either the parents' piano or their music. At that point in the therapy situation, there were two pianos—an old one, which Violet was permitted to use in any way she chose, and a newer one, which she used to play. One day she started methodically to take out the insides of the old piano. This was interpreted not only as a reliving of old conflicts around the piano, but also as a direct attack on the mother. The therapist talked to Violet about the repeated disappointments that she was experiencing from her love objects. While thus attacking the mother symbolically by destruction of the piano, Violet at the same time showed increasing ability to bring about a reconciliation when her mother was angry with her. For instance, she once went to the front door as if to leave the house. She opened the door and went out, but then she came back, remaining on the threshold. The mother reacted to this by saying that Violet had acted more maturely than she herself had, her rages toward the child at that time being so completely violent and destructive. As soon as she realized this, she was able to forgive the child and take up a more positive relationship once again.

The mother's ability to accept Violet remained very precarious, however, and with a new summer vacation at hand it was decided that it was not safe for mother and child to be together without the presence of the therapist. It was considered less dangerous to place Violet for the summer in a special school for disturbed children, a small place with a particularly warm and tolerant atmosphere. Several events of great importance took place during this period of Violet's separation from all her loved objects. Just as, the summer before, she had lost "happy dog" and "kitty cat," she now gave up the piano; even though a piano was available to her, she never touched it during the entire summer; nor did she play for many months after her return. Violet also gave up her bottle, to which she had been extremely attached. The mother had tried very hard during the preceding year to bring this about, but without success. Violet's early oral history had been a happy one: the period of breast feeding had been the happiest time between mother and child. One has to wonder whether the bottle carried some vague memory of the happier time at mother's breast. During the summer Violet also became toilet trained; this apparently happened rather naturally as she watched the other children. But Violet also gave up the few words that she had said earlier. When she returned from the summer vacation, she was once again mute, much more removed and unrelated than she had been earlier.

During the second part of the treatment proper phase we see greater differentiation between self and object, a greater awareness of the surroundings, and the investment of the objects that form the most important part of it. We also see more evidence of ego control, such as secondary process thinking, and the acquisition of speech. These changes lead to the ability to differentiate between the thing, such as the toy or fetish, and the word symbol. The course of language development proceeds from parroting of phrases heard in such inanimate situations as television commercials, to the imitation of the human object's language, and then to the use of language as an expression of the child's own thoughts.

In many cases, other modes of communication, especially singing and music, reach a high level of development before words are used for that purpose. For instance, Amy used songs in a very elaborate, communicative pattern. She was brought out of withdrawal and muteness by familiar nursery songs, to which she first rocked herself and which she later hummed. Eventually she conveyed her thoughts by evoking familiar songs, either through pantomime or through humming, communicating her meaning by means of their words while actually remaining mute. For example, she hummed the tune of "Oh, take a little girl and tap her on the shoulder, oh Johnny, I'm tired" in order to complete the therapist's account of an outing that the latter was narrating to the mother, by inserting in it something the therapist had left out—namely, that Amy had become very tired during the walk and that the therapist had had to carry her. Verbalizations accompanying the songs at a later time were either gibberish or neologisms. The meanings seemed to be conveyed through the tune rather than through words, and the humming was often accompanied by the appropriate affect, as reflected in her facial expression.

In Violet's case this stage of treatment was ushered in by the apparent relapse into autism that followed her separation from both mother and therapist during the summer months. While her facial expression seemed serene, she was unable to invest interest in any activity. She ignored the therapist and often dashed rapidly and abruptly from one activity to another. The sand table was the only thing that occupied her for any length of time. Both she and her mother seemed unapproachable to any interpretation about the effect of the recent separation. The mother maintained that she felt guilty, not for having sent the child away, but for having brought her back, rationalizing this by saying that Violet had seemed so much happier at camp. Violet would not respond to anything said to her about it. She showed her disappointment with the therapist by ignoring her, rejecting the former close affectionate relationship. Neither the presence nor the absence of the mother from the sessions seemed to make any difference.

At this point Violet's sessions were in the later afternoon, following school. (Violet had started school that fall. She was by then six years of age, and the mother could no longer cope with her alone on an all-day basis.) One day Mrs. V. went shopping. When it became quite dark and she still did not arrive to take Violet home with her, Violet became visibly uneasy, showing her uneasiness by dashing from one place to another. The therapist suddenly realized that she, too, was beginning to feel uneasy, out of the fear—though it did not seem possible—that Mrs. V. might abandon Violet in this unconventional way. After this experience it became possible to talk to Violet about how she must have felt at camp when it became dark and her mother did not return. Slowly a new relationship to the therapist was established, different from the former, a symbioticlike tie. Clearly, the therapist and the mother had become her love objects, as Violet showed by her great anxiety to please her mother. She also became attached to a doll, with which she acted out scenes from her life. The doll would have temper tantrums, for example, and be sent out of the room. With a nursery teacher who came to visit at home, Violet acted out separations from her doll by throwing it out of the window and retrieving it. This capacity for symbolic play appeared in Violet for the first time at that point, and seemed to mark a very important step forward. In the therapy sessions she played for hours with many small dolls, acting out with them in great detail situations she was experiencing in school. In these games there was always one doll that represented her: this doll was always given large quantities of food, its plate heaped high.

At this time Violet also began to draw. When she drew pictures of herself, a little girl labeled with her name, she depicted herself licking ice-cream cones, lollipops or holding a bottle. Her drawings and paintings became increasingly more detailed and expressive, and she was able to use drawings to console herself over unavoidable frustrations. For example, when Violet arrived one day in an upset mood, her mother explained that Violet had wanted her to take gasoline from the red pump, red at that time being Violet's favorite color. This had not been possible, however, and Violet, still angry, went to the easel and started to paint. She painted a bright red pump and then a green one, defiantly painting the hose from the red tank filling the gasoline tank in the car. But then she also painted a hose from the green tank to the car. In this way she showed, in her painting, that if only she could have her way first, mother could have her way also. The important thing, however, seemed to be that the symbolic satisfaction of her wish by painting was able to function as a substitute for the real thing.

Violet's language development seemed to proceed in pace with her developing body image, as well as with exploration of the mother's and the therapist's face.

Violet had first become aware of the sexual differences at the age of four and a half. This was at a time when the rapport between her and her mother was particularly good. Following a visit to a friend's house at which there had been a little boy, Violet's mother observed Violet in the bathtub putting bubbles between her legs. The choice of bubbles was interesting in that, during the first year of therapy, bubbles had been used to give Violet her first body sensations. About a year later, Violet became interested in her father's body, wanting to touch and grab his penis. At the same time she would not allow her mother to undress and would be upset when the mother wanted to take a bath, probably in an effort to deny the fact that mother and she did not have a penis. Again, about a year later, Violet became interested in small hurts and started to put Band-aids all over herself.

Some of Violet's first words were directed to her body and to the gratification of her oral needs. They were "belly-button," "ice-cream cone," and "lollipop." During this period she played in her therapy sessions with the doll, and would put sand into the doll's pants, possibly representing either the bowel movement or the penis, or both. The mother reported that at home Violet had tried to urinate through a pipe. There also was some evidence that the child was passing through an initial phallic-oedipal phase—that is, pretending to be a boy and wooing the mother—which expressed itself in a wish to sleep with the mother and exclude the father. In her drawings she clearly showed her wish for the penis by drawing figures with many protrusions and penises. During one therapy session she produced a dramatic series of drawings depicting first a little girl with the penis and then a little girl wearing beautifully patterned stockings, such as her therapist and nursery teacher often wore, and a hat with a long tassel. Later Violet insisted on having her hair put into ponytails.

During the following summer, when Violet was once again sent away to the same camp, she was able to give active signs of missing her mother, being sad when her mother left, and eager to return home at the end of the summer. This time she did not react with withdrawal or loss of speech upon her return. On the contrary, her speech developed quite rapidly, progressing beyond words having to do with her own body and oral gratification. Her next two words were "no" and "mommy." She took delight in saying these words as if they were a great discovery, and she always used them appropriately. A little later she also started to say her own name, "daddy," and the names of people she liked; in general, she began to imitate words and, later on, whole phrases and sentences. Further evidence of the stability of the self and object representations was seen in a further development of her ability to play—namely, the ability not only to play with dolls and assign roles to them, but also to take roles herself. Sometimes she would say that she was not Violet, but Bobby, a little boy; at other times she would be "mommy," and ask her mother to be Violet.

The mother's rages and withdrawal, when these occurred, now no longer seemed to threaten the child's existence. Instead, Violet developed the ability to show that her feelings had been hurt, to be sensitive, to cry, and even to approach the mother in a spontaneous demonstration of affection, hugging and kissing her.

GENERAL PRINCIPLES

In general, we have found during the course of treatment that several of the children with secondary autistic mechanisms are able, to some degree, to give up their autistic withdrawal and to enter into a symbiotic relationship with the therapist, within an extraordinarily short time. We have also found that, during the course of treatment, we must allow for periods of rest, in which the child may withdraw into his secondary autism; this, however, now seems to have a more daydreaming, libidinizing quality rather than a rigidly isolating one.

Furthermore, we have found that the development of a predominantly symbiotic relationship to the mother and the therapist may be accompanied by remarkable developmental spurts in ego functions, such as the appearance of communicative speech. This second finding has also confirmed our impression that the autistic withdrawal in these primarily symbiotic children is a secondary mechanism.

Another phenomenon that regularly occurred during our therapeutic action research was the appearance of an intense resentment on the part of the mothers about assuming the necessary restitutive symbiotic role. This resentment is more or less acute, and if it is not dealt with skillfully and as a primary consideration of the tripartite treatment, it may find expression in the abrupt removal of the child from treatment. This seems to be part of the pathological equilibrium between a mother and her psychotic child. One determinant of this balance is the degree of abandonment by the mother of her maternal commitment to the greater or lesser symbiotic demands of the child, whereas the secondary autistic defense described above is the child's contribution to this equilibrium (personal communication from Dr. David L. Mayer).

Special attention must be directed toward the aggressive manifestations in these children. They are at first directed against the bodily self and usually are not accompanied by any expression that suggests either pain or anxiety, although the quality of the autoaggression does seem to be violent, hurtful, and destructive. This phenomenon of seeming absence of pain is only partly explained by the fact of greatly diminished pain sensitivity in these children. It should be kept in mind that the autoaggression is not simply a discharge phenomenon. It is probably directed at an already formed self and object representation that, for various reasons, may be connected in the child's mind with a particular part of the body. The autoaggressive activity, like some autoerotic activities, is probably also an attempt on the child's part at defining the body-self boundaries, an attempt to feel alive,[14] even if at the price of enduring pain. This experience seems preferable to the child to not feeling alive at all, even though the price of self-injury has to be faced. The initial period of autoaggression is followed by a phase in which manifestations of self-aggression diminish. Previously completely autoaggressive patterns may to some extent be

[14] This thought was first suggested to the author by Lucie Jessner and confirmed by our research results.

directed outward, with a concomitant diminution of the destructive quality of the original autoaggression.

The change in direction and quality of the aggression comes about through the therapist's efforts: she acts as a buffer by physically shielding the child from hurting himself; she interprets his feelings and makes it clear to the child that she cannot let him hurt himself, that his body is to be cared for and loved and not to be harmed. Her "soothing presence" results in a neutralization of the child's aggression, while her libidinal input helps the child to invest his own libido in his body, a mechanism very similar to the nursing mother's libidinization of her baby's body (Hoffer, 1950a). This change is aided by other therapeutic interventions, especially those that are aimed at establishing some measure of orientation of inside and outside and of body-ego boundaries. The fact that, in the therapeutic situation, outward aggression can occur without punishment or with the relatively greater pain that accompanies autoaggression can perhaps be considered as contributory, but certainly not as the central factor in the change.

It is an interesting speculation that the splitting into good and bad object images is represented by the fetish object as the good object, and the part of the body against which the self-aggressive behavior is directed as the bad object. One might then say that in therapy, the libidinally available human object, as quasi-"transitional phenomenon" (Winnicott, 1953b), brings about an increase in the libidinization and the cathexis of the fetish object, and a diminished cathexis and especially a deaggressivization of the bad internalized object.

Clinical examples of self-aggressive behavior are numerous. Among them are temper tantrums and denudification tendencies, in which the child frantically tries to rid himself of his clothing as if to rid himself of parts of his body. There are continual attacks against a specific body part, e.g., the skin, through smashing, biting, falling. The temper tantrums are at first self-destructive, directed in a murderous intent toward the "bad" body part; later they become more diffuse and appear more akin to ordinary temper tantrums, although in the symbiotic psychotic child they acquire a paranoid, unappeasable character (Geleerd, 1945, 1958).

Some of these clinical manifestations differ markedly from others in their motivation. For instance, they may aim more toward hurt or more toward an attempt to cause body sensation. Later in treatment, one can observe that the amount of effort on the child's part to discharge aggression may vary with the aggression in the parents at that time. For instance, we can see increased aggressive manifestations, especially self-aggressive manifestations, when the parents' aggressiveness is expressed in an openly hostile and intrusive attitude. The development of the ego may make other reactions available to the child, as, for example, Violet's leaving the mother but also waiting at the threshold.

It should be pointed out that the therapist does not allow or encourage the child to be aggressive toward her or toward other objects. When some behavior on the part of the therapist tends to stimulate an aggressive act toward an inanimate toy, the child may respond with great anxiety (cf. Barbara's case). Despite the fact that the instinctual differentiation is not yet complete and that libidinal and aggressive elements are thus not distinguished from each other, we conceive of this anxiety as resulting from the fear of object loss as the consequence of the aggressive investment.

Another problem is the role played by aggression in the development of object relationships. The beginning organization of the instinctual investments results in a split into good and bad part objects, with the bad part object externalized in the mother, and the good part object externalized in the therapist. Clinical material supports this by showing that when the child begins to invest libido in love objects, aggressive behavior toward the mother appears more readily than toward the therapist. It is important to keep in mind that any aggressive display is accompanied by considerable anxiety. Some of the apparent aggression may be linked with the child's attempt to establish a separate self from the mother, which is reminiscent of similar behavior in six- to eight-month-old infants, who push against the mother's body within a setting of progressing separation-individuation from her, which makes it imperative for them to extricate themselves even physically from the symbiotic union. The shift from self-aggression to externally directed aggression occurs within the context of a general shift from autistic withdrawal to an interest in the external world. The shift in direction of interest and of aggression is probably parallel rather than causally related.

In the transition from autoaggression to outwardly directed aggression, the child is helped by the libidinal, soothing, buffering atmosphere provided by the therapist, which decreases the child's anxiety and establishes boundaries. His capacity to respond to and integrate various stimuli increases, and he is able to accept larger segments of the external world without anxiety. Often this is conveyed by the descriptive statement of the therapist: "The child dares to look around."

Another observation that might be useful in explaining what happens during the therapeutic process is the retention by many of these small children of certain capacities which become part of their stereotyped isolated activity during the psychosis. When the situation is altered, and when the intensity of the tension and of the self-destructive activity is diminished, these capacities can function to aid maturation and development. For example, Violet retained the capacity to play the piano and another child retained the capacity to draw human figures creatively despite the depth of their psychoses. At first these activities were wholly self-contained, but as therapy progressed, they became the vehicle for communication with a separate love object (the mother and the therapist) as a result of individuation.

CHAPTER VII

Conclusions

My concepts of the normal autistic, the normal symbiotic, and the separation-individuation phases of personality development are genetic constructions, which refer primarily to the development of object relationship. They are complementary to the concepts of the oral, anal, and phallic phases, constructions referring to the genetic theory of drive development, with its patterning effect on ego development and object relationship.

There is a multiform and complex circular interaction between the shifting and progressive drive development, the maturing ego, and the separation-individuation process, whose result is the differentiation of self and object representations. The maturation of the perceptual-conscious system, the core of the ego, paves the way for the emergence of the infant from the "normal autistic" phase of the first weeks of life—Freud's "primary narcissistic," and Spitz's "objectless" stage—toward the symbiotic phase, a twilight stage of still primary narcissism, which I postulated in 1949.[1] The danger situation in the autistic phase is loss of physiological homeostasis; there are essentially only physiological maintenance mechanisms available for the survival of the organism.

The symbiotic phase coincides in time with what Anna Freud (1953) has called "the need-satisfying object relationship." Anna Freud (1965) and Spitz (1965) speak of this

[1] See Mahler, Ross, and De Fries (1949, p. 295, n. 2).

phase as a "preobject" and "part-object" phase. It seems that at first a dim sensory impression (Gestalt perception) of the symbiotic object—the object that brought relief from tension by way of ministrations—sets up engrams of some "good mothering principle" or agent within the fused self-object representations. This gives rise to "confident expectation" of forthcoming relief within the omnipotent mother-infant fused and undifferentiated common orbit. In the symbiotic phase the *need* becomes a *wish* (Schur, 1966), or, as I have described in my paper "On Sadness and Grief" (Mahler, 1961), the affect of *longing* replaces the objectless tension state with the feeling of "craving," which already has psychological meaning.

The danger situation in the symbiotic phase is loss of the symbiotic object, which amounts, at that stage, to loss of an integral part of the ego itself, and thus constitutes a threat of self-annihilation.

The peak of the symbiotic phase, the third quarter of the first year, coincides with the beginning of differentiation of the self from the symbiotic object, and thus marks the onset of the separation-individuation phase. The separation-individuation process, which takes place over approximately two years (from six to thirty months), has maturational and developmental, autonomous and conflictual, intrapsychic and environmental components. The normal separation-individuation process takes place within the setting of the child's developmental readiness for, and pleasure in, independent (separate) functioning. The concept of separation, in this sense, means differentiation of the self from the symbiotic object as an *intrapsychic* process. It takes place in the physical—and, for optimal development, with optimal *emotional*—availability of the mother.

During the course of the normal separation-individuation process, the predominance of pleasure in separate functioning, in an atmosphere in which the mother is emotionally available, enables the child to overcome that measure of separation anxiety that makes its appearance at that point of the separation-individuation phase at which a differentiated object representation, separate from the self, gradually enters conscious awareness. Small amounts of separation anxiety are probably evoked with each new step of separate functioning, and may be necessary requirement for progressive personality development (H. Roiphe).

The separation-individuation process implies two distinct, albeit interdependent, kinds of development. One line is the toddler's rapidly progressing individuation, which is brought about by the evolution and expansion of the autonomous ego functions. These center around the child's developing self-concept. The parallel line of development is the child's growing awareness of his functioning independently of, and separately from, the hitherto symbiotically fused external part of his ego—the mother. This line centers, perhaps, more around the child's developing object representations.

At the stage of object relationship referred to as separation-individuation, the particular danger situation is that of *object loss*. I would hesitate to speak of this anxiety, during the process of achieving separateness, as "separation anxiety" per se,[2] but would instead retain that term to refer to anxieties

[2] By "separation anxiety" we do not mean the behavioral sequelae and reactions to *physical* separation from the love object, as John Bowlby has used the term, but rather the gradual yet inevitable *intrapsychic* sensing of a danger signal anxiety on the part of a small child during the normal separation-individuation process.

It must remain for the second volume of this book to deal with the important, but highly controversial papers of Bowlby (1958, 1960a, 1960b). Yet I would like here to quote a few very pertinent sentences from Anna Freud's (1960) discussion of Bowlby's (1960a) paper. "The object—to use an expression introduced by W. Hoffer—is drawn wholly into the internal narcissistic milieu and treated as part of it to the extent that self and object merge into one." (This corresponds to what I name the symbiotic dual-unity stage of primary narcissism.)

Anna Freud then goes on to say: "There is no other point where the clash between metapsychological and descriptive thinking becomes as obvious as it is here. It leads to the apparently paradoxical result that what in terms of the libido theory is the apex of infantile narcissism, appears in Dr. Bowlby's descriptive terms as the height of 'attachment behavior'" (p. 56).

In Volume II of this book I shall deal with the ontogenesis of depressive

of a later stage, after the beginning of object constancy has been achieved (third and fourth years). By object constancy we mean that the maternal image has become intrapsychically available to the child in the same way as the actual mother had been libidinally available—for sustenance, comfort, and love. The specific danger situation toward the end of the separation-individuation phase, as object constancy is approached, is akin to the danger of *loss of the love of the libidinal object*, although there may still remain some fear of object loss as well.

The dangers of loss of love and of object loss are very much aggravated by the accumulation of aggressive impulses during the oral-sadistic and anal-sadistic phases, in which the child must struggle to preserve the object in the face of his own great ambivalence. By the end of the second and the beginning of the third year, the fear of loss of love is compounded by castration anxiety. When the child reacts to the anatomical sex difference, usually at the height of toilet training, and complicated by anal fears, the ambivalence toward the mother, especially in girls, is contaminated with anger at the mother for not having given them a penis.

It is the mother's love of the toddler and her acceptance of his ambivalence that enable the toddler to cathect his self representation with neutralized energy. Where there is a great actual or fantasied lack of acceptance by the mother, there is a deficit in self-esteem and a consequent narcissistic vulnerability, which is also dependent on other factors, such as the drive distribution, the relative stability of self and object representations, and the course of subsequent development.

The culmination of the separation-individuation phase is

reactions on the part of the small child to the inevitable (maturational) *intrapsychic* separation process during the course of the differentiation of his self representations from the libidinal object representation; I shall also discuss the views of authors other than Bowlby, both similar to and different from his views (Mahler 1961, 1966a, 1966b; Spitz, 1960; Schur, 1960a; Loewald, 1962a; Rochlin, 1953, 1959; Pollock, 1964).

the establishment of object constancy, which we feel should be regarded as a stage in the development of object relationship and not as an ego function. The term "object constancy" was originally proposed by Hartmann (1952), who contrasted it with the stage of need satisfaction (A. Freud, 1953). In the latter phase, the object image is conceived of as being cathected intrapsychically when a need arises (that is, when an urge is present), and the cathexis as being diminished, if not indeed absent, when the need is satisfied. The stage of object constancy develops gradually and may be regarded as having been attained when, by contrast with the previous stage, a firmly established object image is available, the cathexis of which persists regardless of the stage of instinctual need (A. Freud, 1965; Mahler and McDevitt, 1968).

There are three aspects of the stage of object constancy that I would like to emphasize. I propose that these elements of development should be regarded as implying transitions from the stage of need satisfaction to that of object constancy. *First*, I believe that, in the course of development to the stage of object constancy, the maternal image becomes intrapsychically available, just as the actual maternal object was available as a part of external reality during the need-satisfying stage. This process is closely related to the development of "confident expectation" (Benedek, 1938) or "basic trust" (Erikson, 1950), which can be thought of as the beginning of the transfer of the external availability of the object from the actual object to the intrapsychic representation (mental image) of the mother. Once this process of internalization has begun, the child can, in the absence of the mother, accept someone else, or a quasi-symbol for the mother (such as the chair on which the mother sat), for a short while, without any longer requiring the constant presence of the mother herself. This person- or attribute-symbol for the mother is not a substitute, as it was during the earlier need-satisfaction phase; it is now sustained by virtue of a degree of availability of the *internal* image of the love object. The carrying power of the internal image of the mother, by contrast with the situation in the stage of stranger anxiety, affords the child the capacity to utilize a symbol, plus the internal image of the mother, until the actual "mother in the flesh" returns.[3]

Second, during the course of this development of object constancy, the object image is increasingly invested with predominantly libidinal and neutralized energy, although not necessarily postambivalent. From the standpoint of infantile psychosis, I want to emphasize that it is the predominantly aggressive investment of the object and self representations that seems to account for the relative propensity for regression from object constancy to the previous symbiotic phase.

Third, I believe that the stage of object constancy can be said to have been reached when one particular defense—the splitting of the object images—is no longer readily available to the ego. By "splitting" I mean the clinically observable phenomenon that, when both longing and anger occur at the same time (our definition of ambivalence), the child, in order to preserve the good object image, will (during the mother's absence) separate the longed-for image of the love object from the hated image of it. The longing is directed toward the actually absent "good mother," while the anger may be directed toward the other person present at the time in the environment. On the mother's return, the ambivalence (both love and anger) is seen to be once again directed toward her —the representations no longer being split and projected (Mahler and McDevitt, 1968).

In infantile psychosis, unmitigated rage and ambitendency may dominate the picture.

It is clear that I take into account Hartmann's suggestion that object constancy requires a certain degree of neutraliza-

---

[3] Dr. John McDevitt and I jointly arrived at these conceptualizations concerning the development of object constancy during the course of our study of the normal separation-individuation process.

tion, especially of aggression, and that there is also a greater specificity of the object image, which corresponds to the actual qualities of the mother (objectivization). According to Hartmann (personal communication), the stage of object constancy can be present in different degrees. In other words, that stage evolves gradually out of the phase of need satisfactions; it is firmly present only when the proclivity to regression is greatly diminished.

I believe that particular danger situations can be more or less correlated with these levels of object relationship: the loss of the object (fear of abandonment) in the symbiotic and beginning separation-individuation phases; the loss of love in the later separation-individuation subphases and on the way to object constancy. Just as the oral, anal, and phallic phases are not altogether sharply demarcated, neither are these phases of object relationships. Not only does one phase continue into the next, but under certain conditions—such as the stage of need tension—a normally allowable degree of regression must be anticipated.

In reference to the achievement of the stage of object constancy, clinical experience indicates that the greater the ambivalence and the longer its duration, the longer is the full accomplishment of this stage delayed, the greater is the proclivity to regression, and the greater is the tendency to utilize such defenses as splitting the object image under the stress of anxiety.

The most extreme separation reactions, as has been noted, seem to occur *not* in those children who have experienced actual physical separations, but in those in whom the symbiotic relationship was too exclusive and too parasitic, or in whom the mother did not accept the child's individuation and separation. Their reactions may be somewhat reminiscent, clinically, of the annihilation dread of adult psychotics.

This must be re-emphasized because of the misconception that our hypothesis of separation as part of the intrapsychic separation-individuation process implies actual physical separation. This misconception leads in some instances to the idea that the normal painful reactions to physical separation —such as clinging, protestations, coercions, and the like—are the sole behavioral criteria for the intrapsychic separation-individuation process. Such behavior, like the behavior of the psychotic child, may reflect intrapsychic vicissitudes of the symbiotic and separation-individuation phases, but these vicissitudes are not the sole or predominant feature of the behavior from which we hypothesize evidence for conflicts of a symbiotic psychotic nature.

During the separation-individuation process, disturbances in the developing object relations may result in an impoverishment of the neutralized energy available to the ego. There results a deficit in pleasure in independent functioning, a diminished capacity for sublimation, and a surplus of unneutralized aggression, which is vested at first in the fused self and object images and then, in varying vicissitudes, may be directed at the more separate self and object representations, with an eventual outcome in various psychopathological syndromes.

From the clinical picture of the child with the symbiotic psychotic syndrome, one can infer that restitutive attempts are made in an effort to attain, once again, a quasi-symbiotic dual unity; the child behaves as though he has magical control of the object, which he does not distinguish from himself. Clinging and manifest goal-directed separation reactions, such as one sees in normal two-year-olds during a certain phase of separation-individuation, do not represent a prominent or distinguishing clinical feature of symbiotic child psychosis. Instead, it is such symptoms as extreme negativism, or combined desperate clinging to and pushing away of the love object, that are typical of the latter illness. From this we infer an intrapsychic conflict, a fantasy which consists both of a wish for fusion with the object and a dread of "re-engulfment by the object."

In this restitutive defense formation, the psychotic child

does not cling to an adequately perceived whole person. Instead, the psychotic child clings to a greatly reduced, "burned-out," often deanimated pattern-symbol, a representation of the part object. It is not the mother he clings to, therefore, but a psychotically hypercathected, yet at the same time devitalized and deanimated, concrete symbol that he substitutes for her—a psychotic transitional object to which he constantly resorts in an endlessly stereotyped fashion. To distinguish these processes from their normal counterparts I have spoken of "maintenance mechanisms," which in the psychotic child substitute for "object relations" and "defense mechanisms."

This stereotyped gesture or object does not, as transitional phenomena or objects do, facilitate the development of object constancy. They serve instead as a "psychotic fetish," drawing all, or almost all, available libido and aggression upon themselves, as if the psychotic child's life and death depended upon them (Furer, 1964).

In the pathological processes of infantile psychosis, there are two factors that highlight the difference between the pathological regression and the normal phases of development, as we see them.

First, in the psychotic regression, there is a defusion of the drives and a predominance of aggression in a primitive form. The quantity and quality of aggression and its degree of deneutralization greatly influence the nature of the psychotic symptomatology—for example, almost purely self-destructive behavior, such as a child's diving onto the floor head first. This is in contrast with apparently more autoerotically tinged autoaggressive actions, such as scratching and biting the body. These latter stereotyped actions, we believe, serve to define body boundaries; they also serve libidinization of the body-ego boundaries.

Second, by the time the psychosis takes over the personality of the child, certain structural changes in the psyche have already taken place, as a result of maturation and development, and may have caused fundamental distortions in the basic structures themselves. The regression of the ego structure and of the ego and object representations consists of the fragmentation of these elements into parts, plus refusion of part-self and part-object representations into various combinations, which I had described as "faulty couplings." (They were described by Furer as "the psychotic fetish.") These are made up of part representations of the object as well as of the self, not clearly differentiated from one another, and varying, at different times, in the quality of their instinctual investment.

In other words, the pathological regression in psychosis involves a return to the earliest levels of preobject and part-object relationships, which is why I have given similar names to the predominant defensive organization in psychosis and to the very early phases of preobject and part-object relationships.

However, it should be emphatically stated that, in infantile psychosis, as in the general theory of psychosis, it is the distortion, the *depth, and the permanence* (irreversibility) *of the ego and drive regression* that distinguish these syndromes from simple regressions to the normal autistic or symbiotic preobject, part-object, primary narcissistic, or need-satisfying object relationship stage.

In my earliest studies I developed the theory of a prezonal splanchnic libido position, in which the undifferentiated drive energy is vested in the splanchnic visceral organs, and does not yet fully cathect the periphery of the body. In the psychotic child, autistic and symbiotic alike, there seems to be a failure to perceive the symbiotic partner's need-satisfying ministrations, primarily as the result of failure of cathexis of the periphery of the body. This prevents distinction between inside and outside, and thus does not afford any opportunity for perceptual-integrative organization of the self and object world (Jacobson, 1964).

In reference to the theory of etiology, therefore, I would

include such innate defects as the ego's incapacity to neutralize the drives; defects in the primary perceptual capacities of the ego; and, in addition, the disorganizing effects of the states of infantile organismic panic upon an ego that is lacking in organizing and synthetic functions. This view is similar to that of Hartmann (1953), who postulated a defect in the ego's capacity to neutralize the drives; this defect then interferes with the development of other ego functions and object relations. These, in a dialectical interaction, thereafter continually distort the processes of maturation and development. My theory places special emphasis, however, on the interaction of both these factors with the circular processes between infant and mother, in which the mother serves as a beacon of orientation and living buffer for the infant, in reference to both external reality and his internal milieu. In early life, the infant must be thought of, not as an individual, but as only one part of a nurturing unit, from which he gradually differentiates, as an individual, with the mothering partner serving as a catalyst and a living buffer.

If, for intrinsic or extreme environmental reasons, the mothering partner cannot be utilized, the organism is exposed to repeated instinctual drive inundations, as well as to traumatic overstimulation from the external world. Stimuli from the human elements in the external world are more dangerous than stimuli from those elements in it that are inanimate. The ever-changing and, for the psychotic child, unpredictable social stimuli involve drive activity to a much greater degree. The psychotic defense of deanimation, which I also used to call devitalization, aims at rendering those "unpredictable" stimuli less threatening to the fragile ego of the prepsychotic and psychotic child.

The consequences of organismic distress in the normal infant, and of psychotic panic in the infantile psychotic syndrome, may be vaguely similar, in that maturational and developmental acquisitions in both—as, for example, the awareness of body boundaries—may be *temporarily lost* in the junior toddler, even after the stage of being "hatched," but are more *permanently disordered* in the prepsychotic and psychotic child.[4] The temporary lapses of awareness of the state of separateness, on the part of the normal infant and junior toddler, are of short duration and highly reversible. On the other hand, a similar experience in the vulnerable ego of the psychotic child may result in sustained and irreversible loss of these acquisitions. I believe that annihilation panic is the result of the sense of helplessness vis-à-vis the overwhelming power of the instinctual drives, particularly of aggression, acting upon an ego with little capacity to deal with them and without the expectation of a relieving external agent. The other side of the psychotic conflict that results in panic entails the threat to personal entity and identity, as well as danger to the sense of separateness, and the threat of the dissolution of body-ego boundaries.

It should not be forgotten that the development of object relations occurs concomitantly with the maturation of the id (Schur, 1958). It is necessarily interrelated with the changing nature of the drives. The anal-sadistic phase, for example, by adding its increment to the load of aggression of the ambivalence, can be thought of as a maturational factor that delays the full achievement of object constancy. It is at this, the anal-sadistic, stage that we see a prevalent use of the splitting mechanism. Since the ambivalently cathected maternal image, even under slight stress, does not have at first the "carrying power" that it will have later on, we consider splitting at that time to be a normal defense, an indication of the child's mounting need tension and his inability to bear it without this defense. Another sign of the increased ambivalent investment and of the lack of "carrying power" of the maternal image is the incessant coercion to which some children subject their mothers during the third year and beyond. In instances of pathology, this continues and increases dur-

---

[4] The second volume will deal in detail with these processes in the normal development.

ing the latency period. One of the characteristic features that I have noted in the psychotic child is the extreme coercion, *as well as* repulsion, of the love object, in "ambitendent" rapid alternation (see Aro's case in Chapter IV).

In the psychotic child, these defenses may use up the entire instinctual reservoir and derange the entire personality. In borderline and less severe pathology, there is serious interference with the maturation of ego functions, and especially with the establishment of stable self and object representations, but without a break with reality and the predominance of psychotic defenses (Geleerd, 1958; A. Weil, 1953a, 1953b, 1956).

In terms of the interrelationship between ego development and object relationship, the satisfaction from the outside has made energy available for the investment of various ego functions and has promoted their optimal maturation ("refueling"). On the other hand, severe frustration from the outside may have created unrelieved tension, which interferes with ego development. One must again point to the contrast between normal development and psychosis, in that the mother, as a beacon of orientation and a buffer to the normally developing child, is the *sine qua non* for successful attainment of object constancy during the early stages of object relationship. In the psychotic child, on the other hand, a vicious circle is established. There seems to be a limitation to his inner capacity to utilize the mother, as a result of which he does not obtain the gratification and relief of tension that are preconditions for progressive development.

The situation of the psychotic child does not involve a regression to any known normal phase of development. The concepts of a normal autistic, normal symbiotic, and subsequent normal separation-individuation phase of development were derived in part from genetic reconstructions that had been made during the course of the study of symptom pictures presented by children with psychoses. Their behavior indicated that the delusion of the psychotic child was primarily one of being part of an omnipotent mother-child unit. It also indicated an autistic withdrawal from, and a de-animation, devitalization of the psychotic child's human object world. Inferences from these pathological situations led me to the reconstruction of normal phases of object relationship, with progressive investment of the mental representation of the human love object. The psychotic process was defined by lack of cathexis of the mothering functions and of the mothering object, as well as by confusion of inside and outside—that is to say, that stage of the "mothering principle" that may be designated as the normally autistic phase, and the mother-child dual-unity stage, characterized by lack of differentiation of and from the maternal object—the stage of normal symbiosis.

Although one could say offhand that, in certain phases of infantile psychosis, there is a regression to the stage of object relationship involving the mother-child dual unity, that feature as such would not be sufficient to define the situation that prevails in the symbiotic psychotic syndrome. In order to define symbiotic psychosis properly, one must contrast the normal infant's relationship to the need-satisfying object during the stage of normal symbiosis with the situation that is true of infantile psychosis. In the former, the mother is utilized as a beacon of orientation and of integration; she is the organizer and living buffer in reference to the external and internal milieu, and this results in the structuralization of the infant's ego and his differentiation of inner and outer world. By contrast, in the psychotic syndrome, the mother's ministrations are not perceived as a "mothering principle" of this kind—that is, as coming from the outside to relieve the child's inner tension; much less is she perceived as an increasingly differentiated object that can supply the needed external ego. Instead, in that condition the mother is delusionally drawn into the internal milieu. Hence, the psychotic child more or less lacks the faculties for differentiation and for individuation from the object (from the "external ego"—Spitz).

Due to the inability of the utterly brittle, vulnerable ego structure that the symbiotic psychotic organization entails, the problems of coping with the inundation of unneutralized instinctual drive from within, as well as with complex traumatic overstimulation from without, continually threaten the child's ego to the breaking (fragmentation) point. Kanner's (1944) concept of the need for the preservation of sameness, and Weiland's (1966) concept of the fear of change and of unfamiliarity in child psychosis, both seem to be relevant to these dangers. The secondary "restitutive mechanism" that is employed to cope with change and unfamiliarity is the defense of "deanimation," along with other mechanisms of dedifferentiation (Mahler, 1960).

Not only is the psychotic child unable to utilize the mother's ministrations as such—that is, the "mothering principle"; there is also a generalized fear of the human object, and a constant attempt to ward it off—that is, to ward off the "mother in the flesh"—because of the destructive investment in the previously described combined psychotic mental representations. There is a constant threat of panic, derived from the equally impelling, even overwhelming craving for fusion within this, for the most part destructively invested, relationship in the symbiotic psychotic syndrome, which leads to this projection of destructive impulses and fears of attack. When these projective and introjective defensive mechanisms fail, however, and there is a build-up of primitive aggression within, what follows is a dread of the complete dissolution of boundaries and of annihilation. In reference to the quality of the panic and its overwhelming nature, the same consideration applies: it is because of the absence of any possibility of a relieving, comforting "mothering principle" that the child is left in an extreme state of helplessness vis-à-vis the instinctual danger from within and from without.

In consequence, as we have earlier pointed out (see also Mahler and Furer, 1966), we would not use the term "separation anxiety" to refer to the anxieties in infantile psychosis, specifically because of the stage of object relationship postulated. Rather, we would think that the term "separation anxiety" should be limited to a phase in development in which there is, in our terms, an "intrapsychic availability" of a mother image that can bring gratification and assuage pain. The absence of the mother then exposes the normal infant, if he is in a certain state of need or drive tension, to the danger of helplessness and longing, with consequent anxiety. In fact, in observing psychotic children with predominantly autistic mechanisms, we have discovered that the mother's actual physical leaving of the child does not lead to anxiety until, as the result of treatment, much intrapsychic development has taken place toward separation-individuation. The appearance of the true "separation anxiety" is thus to be taken as an indication of improvement. Prior to that, as the autistic withdrawal is lessened, we usually observe temper tantrums and destructive behavior—if there is any reaction at all to the mother's leaving.

In this regard, we feel that it is important to point out that one should make a distinction between "separation reactions" and "separation anxiety." Only confusion is generated if one calls all manifestations in a child that result from separation from the mother "separation anxiety." One simple example is the whimpering of the child when the mother has gone, which is a complex phenomenon—one of the ingredients of which is surely mental pain; but, depending on internal and external circumstances, there are, of course, other affective responses, such as anger and sadness, as a response to separation.

In reference to the onset of acute psychosis during the second, third and fourth year of life, it is worth restating that the anxiety experienced by a psychotic child is not limited to the psychotic panic states just mentioned. In the anal, phallic, and oedipal phases, the ordinary anxieties of loss of love and castration often act, as they do in other children, as a final blow to the vulnerable and brittle ego. This brittleness and vulnerability have been created by both constitutional and experiential factors, among which the difficulty of separate functioning and the lack of adequate development of object relationship in the separation-individuation phase have been the most important, but not the only factors. This is another illustration of the disastrous consequences that can occur when psychological development lags too far behind the biologically predetermined maturation.

We feel that these formulations and concepts, if properly understood, are useful as well in the understanding of severe neurotic and borderline psychotic conditions in adults. In many borderline psychotic adults, we find the same attempt to maintain a fantasy of infantile magical omnipotence, partly based on a similar regression to a self-and-object dual unity. In addition, because of the similar aggressive investment of these representations and yet the simultaneously existing even greater capacity for a more integrated defensive organization, these patients are able to maintain a safe distance from the object—neither total fusion nor total insulation. However, in the transference they often show forms of behavior that are similar to those of psychotic children, such as overinvolvement followed by pushing away, ridding themselves by autistic withdrawal from the love object—in this case, the analyst. Threats to their defensive regression to infantile omnipotence on account of separation from and frustration by the object, and/or the inability to control the object, make such patients unable, like the psychotic child, to deny their helplessness delusionally or to control the overwhelming aggressive sadistic fantasies that may annihilate both the object and the self representation. In the face of this panic, as noted, there may be further retreat from reality, and overt psychosis may appear (cf. Stone, 1967).

In essence, with these adult patients, as with the children, it is the object and self representations that seem particularly vulnerable to distortion and obliteration. The frustration of libidinal gratification and perhaps, in these cases, even a similar inability to utilize the maternal object—"good mother" —as a source for gratification have not only interfered with development; in later life, they have also intensified the ambivalence and the subsequent defensive maneuver toward merging with or devouring the love object. Adult patients as well are then exposed to the experience of panic, and often their only recourse is to similar primitive defenses, such as denial, deanimation, and autistic withdrawal.

Bibliography

ABBATE, G., DUNAEFF, D., & FENICHEL, C. (1957), A Pilot Study of Schizophrenic Children in a Nonresidential School. *Amer. J. Orthopsychiat.*, 27:107-116.

ALPERT, A. (1959), Reversibility of Pathological Fixations Associated with Maternal Deprivation in Infancy. *The Psychoanalytic Study of the Child*, 14:169-185.*

———— & BERNSTEIN, I. (1964), Dynamic Determinants in Oral Fixation. *The Psychoanalytic Study of the Child*, 19:170-195.

———— & KROWN, S. (1953), Treatment of a Child with Severe Ego Restrictions in a Therapeutic Nursery. *The Psychoanalytic Study of the Child*, 8:333-354.

ANGEL, K. (1967), On Symbiosis and Pseudosymbiosis. *J. Amer. Psychoanal. Assn.*, 15:294-316.

ANTHONY, E. J. & BENEDEK, T., eds. (1968), *Psychology and Psychopathology of Parenthood*. Boston: Little, Brown (in press).

ARLOW, J. A. & BRENNER, C. (1964), *Psychoanalytic Concepts and the Structural Theory*. New York: International Universities Press.

BAK, R. (1939), Regression of Ego Orientation and Libido in Schizophrenia. *Int. J. Psycho-Anal.*, 20:64-71.

———— (1954), The Schizophrenic Defense against Aggression. *Int. J. Psycho-Anal.*, 35:129-134.

BALINT, A. (1954), *The Early Years of Life*. New York: Basic Books.

BELLAK, L. (1948), *Dementia Praecox, the Past Decade's Work and Present Status: A Review and Evaluation*. New York: Grune & Stratton.

BENDER, L. (1942), Childhood Schizophrenia. *Nerv. Child*, 1:138-140.

———— (1947), Childhood Schizophrenia: Clinical Study of 100 Schizophrenic Children. *Amer. J. Orthopsychiat.*, 17:40-56.

* *The Psychoanalytic Study of the Child*, ed. R. S. Eissler, A. Freud, H. Hartmann, & M. Kris; currently 22 Volumes. New York: International Universities Press, 1945-1967.

———— (1953), Childhood Schizophrenia. *Psychiat. Quart.*, 27:663-681.

———— & FREEDMAN, A. M. (1952), A Study of the First Three Years in the Maturation of Schizophrenic Children. *Quart. J. Child Behav.*, 4:245-272.

———— & RABINOVITCH, R. D. (1948), Child Psychiatry. In: *Progress in Neurology and Psychiatry*, ed. E. A. Spiegel, 3:469-482. New York: Grune & Stratton.

———— & ———— (1949), Child Psychiatry. In: *Progress in Neurology and Psychiatry*, ed. E. A. Spiegel, 4:441-454. New York: Grune & Stratton.

———— & SILVER, A. (1948), Body Image Problems of the Brain-Damaged Child. *J. Soc. Issues*, 4(4):84-89.

BENEDEK, T. (1938), Adaptation to Reality in Early Infancy. *Psychoanal. Quart.*, 7:200-214.

———— (1949), The Psychosomatic Implications of the Primary-Unit: Mother-Child. *Amer. J. Orthopsychiat.*, 19:642-654.

———— (1952), *Psychosexual Functions in Women.* New York: Ronald Press.

———— (1959), Parenthood as a Developmental Phase: A Contribution to the Libido Theory. *J. Amer. Psychoanal. Assn.*, 7:389-417.

———— (1960), The Organization of the Reproductive Drive. *Int. J. Psycho-Anal.*, 41:1-15.

BENJAMIN, J. D. (1961), The Innate and the Experiential in Child Development. In: *Lectures on Experimental Psychiatry*, ed. H. Brosin. Pittsburgh: University of Pittsburgh Press, pp. 19-42.

BERES, D. (1956), Ego Deviations and the Concept of Schizophrenia. *The Psychoanalytic Study of the Child*, 11:164-235.

———— (1960), Perception, Imagination, and Reality. *Int. J. Psycho-Anal.*, 41:327-334.

BERGMAN, P. & ESCALONA, S. K. (1949), Unusual Sensitivities in Very Young Children. *The Psychoanalytic Study of the Child*, 3/4:333-352.

BERGMANN, M. (1963), The Place of Paul Federn's Ego Psychology in Psychoanalytic Metapsychology. *J. Amer. Psychoanal. Assn.*, 11:97-116.

BERNFELD, S. (1928), Über Faszination. *Imago*, 14:76-87.

BETTELHEIM, B. (1956), Schizophrenia as a Reaction to Extreme Situations. *Amer. J. Orthopsychiat.*, 26:507-518.

———— (1959), Joey, A "Mechanical Boy." *Sci. Amer.* 200(3):116-127.

———— (1967), *The Empty Fortress: Infantile Autism and the Birth of the Self.* New York: Free Press.

BIBRING, G. L. (1959), Some Considerations of the Psychological Processes in Pregnancy. *The Psychoanalytic Study of the Child*, 14:113-121.

BLAU, A. (1957), Benign Schizophrenia. *A.M.A. Arch. Neurol. & Psychiat.*, 78:605-611.

——— (1962), The Nature of Childhood Schizophrenia. *J. Amer. Acad. Child Psychiat.*, 1:225-235.

BONNARD, A. (1958), Pre-Body-Ego Types of (Pathological) Mental Functioning. *J. Amer. Psychoanal. Assn.*, 6:581-611.

BOWLBY, J. (1951), *Maternal Care and Mental Health.* Geneva: World Health Organization, Monogr. 2.

——— (1958), The Nature of the Child's Tie to the Mother. *Int. J. Psycho-Anal.*, 39:350-373.

——— (1960a), Grief and Mourning in Infancy and Early Childhood. *The Psychoanalytic Study of the Child*, 15:9-52.

——— (1960b), Separation Anxiety. *Int. J. Psycho-Anal.*, 41:89-113.

——— ROBERTSON, J. & ROSENBLUTH, D. (1952), A Two-Year-Old Goes to Hospital. *The Psychoanalytic Study of the Child*, 7:82-94.

BOYER, L. B. (1956), On Maternal Overstimulation and Ego Defects. *The Psychoanalytic Study of the Child*, 11:236-256.

BRADLEY, C. (1945), Psychoses in Children. In: *Modern Trends in Child Psychiatry*, ed. N. D. C. Lewis & B. L. Pacella. New York: International Universities Press, pp. 135-154.

——— (1947), Early Evidence of Psychoses in Children: With Special Reference to Schizophrenia. *J. Pediat.*, 30:529-540.

——— & BOWEN, M. (1941), Behavior Characteristics of Schizophrenic Children. *Psychiat. Quart.*, 15:296-315.

BRODY, S. & AXELRAD, S. (1966), Anxiety, Socialization, and Ego-Formation in Infancy. *Int. J. Psycho-Anal.*, 47:218-229.

BURLINGHAM, D. (1935), Empathy between Infant and Mother. *J. Amer. Psychoanal. Assn.*, 15:764-780.

BYCHOWSKI, G. (1947), The Preschizophrenic Ego. *Psychoanal. Quart.*, 16:225-233.

——— (1956a), The Ego and the Introjects. *Psychoanal. Quart.*, 25:11-36.

——— (1956b), The Release of Internal Images. *Int. J. Psycho-Anal.*, 37:331-338.

COLEMAN, R. W., KRIS, E., & PROVENCE, S. (1953), The Study of Variations of Early Parental Attitudes: A Preliminary Report. *The Psychoanalytic Study of the Child*, 8:20-47.

DESPERT, J. L. (1938), Schizophrenia in Children. *Psychiat. Quart.*, 12:366-371.

——— (1940), A Comparative Study of Thinking in Schizophrenic Children and in Children of Preschool Age. *Amer. J. Psychiat.*, 97:189-213.

——— (1941), Thinking and Motility Disorder in a Schizophrenic Child. *Psychiat. Quart.*, 15:522-536.

——— (1947a), Psychotherapy in Child Schizophrenia. *Amer. J. Psychiat.*, 104:36-43.

────── (1947b), The Early Recognition of Childhood Schizophrenia. *Med. Clin. N. Amer.* (Pediat.), 680-687.

────── (1948), Delusional and Hallucinatory Experience in Children. *Amer. J. Psychiat.*, 104:528-537.

────── (1952), Diagnostic Criteria of Schizophrenia in Children. *Amer. J. Psychother.*, 6:148-163.

────── (1955), Differential Diagnosis between Obsessive-Compulsive Neurosis and Schizophrenia in Children. In: *Psychopathology of Childhood*, ed. P. H. Hoch & J. Zubin. New York: Grune & Stratton, pp. 240-253.

DEUTSCH, H. (1942), Some Forms of Emotional Disturbances and Their Relationship to Schizophrenia. *Neuroses and Character Types*. New York: International Universities Press, 1965, pp. 262-281.

────── (1945), *The Psychology of Women*, Vol. 2: *Motherhood*. New York: Grune & Stratton.

EISENBERG, L. & KANNER, L. (1956), Early Infantile Autism, 1943-1955. *Amer. J. Orthopsychiat.*, 26:556-566.

EISSLER, K. R. (1953), Notes upon the Emotionality of a Schizophrenic Patient, and Its Relation to Problems of Technique. *The Psychoanalytic Study of the Child*, 8:199-251.

────── (1954), Notes upon Defects of Ego Structure in Schizophrenia. *Int. J. Psycho-Anal.*, 35:141-146.

EKSTEIN, R. (1954), The Space Child's Time Machine: On "Reconstruction" in the Psychotherapeutic Treatment of a Schizophrenic Child. *Amer. J. Orthopsychiat.*, 24:492-506.

────── (1955), Vicissitudes of the "Internal Image" in the Recovery of a Borderline Schizophrenic Adolescent. *Bull. Menninger Clin.*, 19:86-92.

────── & WALLERSTEIN, J. (1954), Observations on the Psychology of Borderline and Psychotic Children: Report from a Current Psychotherapy Project at Southard School. *The Psychoanalytic Study of the Child*, 9:344-369.

────── ────── (1956), Observations on the Psychotherapy of Borderline and Psychotic Children. *The Psychoanalytic Study of the Child*, 11:303-311.

ELKISCH, P. (1952), Significant Relationship between the Human Figure and the Machine in the Drawings of Boys. *Amer. J. Orthopsychiat.*, 22:379-385.

────── (1953), Simultaneous Treatment of a Child and His Mother. *Amer. J. Psychother.*, 7:105-130.

────── (1956), The Struggle for Ego Boundaries in a Psychotic Child. *Amer. J. Psychother.*, 10:578-602.

────── (1957), The Psychological Significance of the Mirror. *J. Amer. Psychoanal. Assn.*, 5:235-244.

────── & MAHLER, M. S. (1959), On Infantile Precursors of the "Influencing Machine" (Tausk). *The Psychoanalytic Study of the Child*, 14:219-235.

ERIKSON, E. H. (1950), *Childhood and Society*. New York: Norton.

ESCALONA, S. K. (1948), Some Considerations Regarding Psychotherapy with Psychotic Children. *Bull. Menninger Clin.*, 12:126-134.

—— (1962), The Study of Individual Differences and the Problem of State. *J. Amer. Acad. Child Psychiat.*, 1:11-37.

—— (1963), Patterns of Infantile Experience and the Developmental Process. *The Psychoanalytic Study of the Child*, 18:197-244.

FABIAN, A. A. (1954), Childhood Schizophrenia [Round Table, 1953]: Some Familial Considerations in Childhood Schizophrenia. *Amer. J. Orthopsychiat.*, 24:513-516.

FEDERN, P. (1943), Psychoanalysis of Psychoses: Parts I-III. *Psychiat. Quart.*, 17:3-19; 246-257; 470-487.

—— (1947), Principles of Psychotherapy in Latent Schizophrenia. *Amer. J. Psychother.*, 1:129-144.

—— (1952), *Ego Psychology and the Psychoses*. New York: Basic Books.

FENICHEL, O. (1945), *The Psychoanalytic Theory of Neurosis*. New York: Norton.

FERENCZI, S. (1913), Stages in the Development of the Sense of Reality. *Sex in Psychoanalysis*. New York: Basic Books, 1950, pp. 213-239.

FISH, B. (1959a), Involvement of the Central Nervous System in Infants with Schizophrenia. *A.M.A. Arch. Neurol.*, 2:115-120.

—— (1959b), The Detection of Schizophrenia in Infancy. *J. Nerv. Ment. Dis.*, 125:1-24.

—— (1960), Involvement of the Central Nervous System in Infants with Schizophrenia. *A.M.A. Arch. Neurol.*, 2:115-121.

—— SHAPIRO, T., HALPERN, F., & WILE, R. (1965), The Prediction of Schizophrenia in Infancy. III: Ten Year Follow-up of Neurological and Psychological Development. *Amer. J. Psychiat.*, 121:768-775.

FISHER, C. (1965), Psychoanalytic Implications of Recent Research on Sleep and Dreaming. *J. Amer. Psychoanal. Assn.*, 13:197-303.

FLIESS, R. (1957), *Erogeneity and Libido: Addenda to the Theory of the Psychosexual Development of the Human*. New York: International Universities Press.

—— (1961), *Ego and Body Ego*. New York: Schulte Publ. Co.

FRANKL, L. (1961), Some Observations on the Development and Disturbances of Integration in Childhood. *The Psychoanalytic Study of the Child*, 16:146-163.

FREUD, A. (1936), *The Ego and the Mechanisms of Defense*. New York: International Universities Press, 2nd ed., 1966.

—— (1949), Notes on Aggression. *Bull. Menninger Clin.*, 13:143-151.

———— (1952a), A Connection between the States of Negativism and of Emotional Surrender (*Hörigkeit*). Abstr. in: *Int. J. Psycho-Anal.*, 33:265.

———— (1952b), The Role of Bodily Illness in the Mental Life of Children. *The Psychoanalytic Study of the Child*, 7:69-81.

———— (1953), Some Remarks on Infant Observation. *The Psychoanalytic Study of the Child*, 8:9-19.

———— (1954a), In: Problems of Infantile Neurosis: A Discussion. *The Psychoanalytic Study of the Child*, 9:25-31; 40-43; 57-62; 68-71.

———— (1954b), The Widening Scope of Indications for Psychoanalysis: Discussion. *J. Amer. Psychoanal. Assn.*, 2:607-620.

———— (1958), Child Observation and Prediction of Development: A Memorial Lecture in Honor of Ernst Kris. *The Psychoanalytic Study of the Child*, 13:92-116.

———— (1960), Discussion of Dr. John Bowlby's Paper (1960a). *The Psychoanalytic Study of the Child*, 15:53-62.

———— (1965), *Normality and Pathology in Childhood: Assessments of Development*. New York: International Universities Press.

———— & BURLINGHAM, D. (1943), *Infants Without Families: The Case for and Against Residential Nurseries*. New York: International Universities Press, 1944.

———— & DANN, S. (1951), An Experiment in Group Upbringing. *The Psychoanalytic Study of the Child*, 6:127-169.

FREUD, S. (1900), The Interpretation of Dreams. *Standard Edition*, 4 & 5.†

———— (1911a), Formulations on the Two Principles of Mental Functioning. *Standard Edition*, 12:213-226.

———— (1911b), Psycho-Analytic Notes on an Autobiographical Account of a Case of Paranoia (Dementia Paranoides). *Standard Edition*, 12:3-82.

———— (1914), On Narcissism: An Introduction. *Standard Edition*, 14:67-102.

———— (1915), Repression. *Standard Edition*, 14:141-158.

———— (1917 [1915]), Mourning and Melancholia. *Standard Edition*, 14:237-260.

———— (1920), Beyond the Pleasure Principle. *Standard Edition*, 18:3-64.

———— (1923), The Ego and the Id. *Standard Edition*, 19:3-66.

———— (1924a [1923]), Neurosis and Psychosis. *Standard Edition*, 19:149-153.

———— (1924b), The Loss of Reality in Neurosis and Psychosis. *Standard Edition*, 19:183-187.

† *The Standard Edition of the Complete Psychological Works of Sigmund Freud*, 24 Volumes, translated and edited by James Strachey. London: Hogarth Press and the Institute of Psycho-Analysis, 1953-

———— (1924c), The Dissolution of the Oedipus Complex. *Standard Edition*, 19:173-179.

———— (1926), Inhibitions, Symptoms and Anxiety. *Standard Edition*, 20:77-175.

———— (1938), Splitting of the Ego in the Process of Defence. *Standard Edition*, 23:271-278.

———— (1940 [1938]), An Outline of Psycho-Analysis. *Standard Edition*, 23:141-207.

FRIEND, M. R. (1956), Report on Panel: On Sleep Disturbances in Children. *J. Amer. Psychoanal. Assn.*, 4:514-525.

FRIES, M. E. (1935), Interrelationship of Physical, Mental and Emotional Life of a Child from Birth to Four Years of Age. *Amer. J. Dis. Child.*, 49:1546-1563.

———— (1937), Factors in Character Development, Neuroses, Psychoses, and Delinquency. *Amer. J. Orthopsychiat.*, 7:142-181.

———— & WOOLF, P. J. (1953), Some Hypotheses on the Role of the Congenital Activity Type in Personality Development. *The Psychoanalytic Study of the Child*, 8:48-62.

FROSCH, J. (1966), A Note on Reality Constancy. In: *Psychoanalysis —A General Psychology: Essays in Honor of Heinz Hartmann*, ed. R. M. Loewenstein, L. M. Newman, M. Schur, & A. J. Solnit. New York: International Universities Press, pp. 349-376.

FURER, M. (1954), Schizophrenic Children Under the Age of Six. Abstr. in: *J. Nerv. Ment. Dis.*, 120:105.

———— (1964), The Development of a Preschool Symbiotic Boy. *The Psychoanalytic Study of the Child*, 19:448-469.

———— GOLDFARB, W., MAHLER, M. S., WARD, R. S., & KOLB, L. C. (1966), Panel Discussion: Childhood Schizophrenia. *Bull. Assn. Psychoanal. Med.*, 5(3):35-42.

FURMAN, E. (1956), An Ego Disturbance in a Young Child. *The Psychoanalytic Study of the Child*, 11:312-335.

GALENSON, E. (1964), Comments on Mr Khan's Paper. *Int. J. Psycho-Anal.*, 45:279.

GARDNER, G. E. (1954), Childhood Schizophrenia [Round Table, 1953]: Discussion. *Amer. J. Orthopsychiat.*, 24:517-521.

GAVRIN, J. H., ed. (1952), *Residential Treatment of a Schizophrenic Child*. New York: Jewish Board of Guardians.

GELEERD, E. R. (1945), Observations on Temper Tantrums in Children. *Amer. J. Orthopsychiat.*, 15:238-246.

———— (1946), A Contribution to the Problem of Psychoses in Childhood. *The Psychoanalytic Study of the Child*, 2:271-291.

———— (1958), Borderline States in Childhood and Adolescence. *The Psychoanalytic Study of the Child*, 13:279-295.

GLOVER, E. (1939), *Psycho-Analysis*. New York: Staples Press.

———— (1956), *On the Early Development of Mind*, Vol. 1. New York: International Universities Press.

GOLDFARB, W. (1945), Psychological Privation in Infancy and Subsequent Adjustment. *Amer. J. Orthopsychiat.*, 15:247-266.

——— (1956), Receptor Preferences in Schizophrenic Children. *A.M.A. Arch. Neurol. & Psychiat.*, 76:643-652.

——— BRAUNSTEIN, P., & LORGE, I. (1956), Childhood Schizophrenia [Symposium, 1955]: 5. A Study of Speech Patterns in a Group of Schizophrenic Children. *Amer. J. Orthopsychiat.*, 26:544-555.

——— ——— & SCHOLL, H. (1959), An Approach to the Investigation of Childhood Schizophrenia: The Speech of Schizophrenic Children and Their Mothers. *Amer. J. Orthopsychiat.*, 29:481-490.

——— & DORSEN, M. M. (1956), *Annotated Bibliography of Childhood Schizophrenia and Related Disorders.* New York: Basic Books.

——— SIBULKIN, L., BEHRENS, M., & JAHODA, H. (1958), Parental Perplexity and Childhood Confusion. In: *New Frontiers in Child Guidance,* ed. A. H. Esman. New York: International Universities Press, pp. 157-170.

GOLDSTEIN, K. (1959), Abnormal Mental Conditions in Infancy. *J. Nerv. Ment. Dis.*, 128:538-557.

GREENACRE, P. (1941), The Predisposition to Anxiety. *Psychoanal. Quart.*, 10:66-95; 610-637.

——— (1944), Infant Reactions to Restraint: Problems in the Fate of Infantile Aggression. *Amer. J. Orthopsychiat.*, 14:204-218.

——— (1945), The Biologic Economy of Birth. *The Psychoanalytic Study of the Child,* 1:31-51.

——— (1952a), Pregenital Patterning. *Int. J. Psycho-Anal.*, 33:410-415.

——— (1952b), Some Factors Producing Different Types of Genital and Pregenital Organization. *Trauma, Growth and Personality.* New York: Norton, pp. 293-302.

——— (1953), Certain Relationships between Fetishism and the Faulty Development of the Body Image. *The Psychoanalytic Study of the Child,* 8:79-98.

——— (1954), In: Problems of Infantile Neurosis: A Discussion. *The Psychoanalytic Study of the Child,* 9:16-71.

——— (1958), Early Physical Determinants in the Development of the Sense of Identity. *J. Amer. Psychoanal. Assn.*, 6:612-627.

——— (1959), On Focal Symbiosis. In: *Dynamic Psychopathology in Childhood,* ed. L. Jessner & E. Pavenstedt. New York: Grune & Stratton, pp. 243-256.

——— (1960), Considerations Regarding the Parent-Infant Relationship. *Int. J. Psycho-Anal.*, 41:571-584.

GREENE, W. A., JR. (1958), Early Object Relations, Somatic, Affective, and Personal: An Inquiry into the Physiology of the Mother-Child Unit. *J. Nerv. Ment. Dis.*, 126:225-253.

GREENSON, R. R. (1958), On Screen Defenses, Screen Hunger and Screen Identity. *J. Amer. Psychoanal. Assn.*, 6:242-262.

——— (1964), On Homosexuality and Gender Identity. *Int. J. Psycho-Anal.*, 45:217-219.

——— (1966), A Transvestite Boy and an Hypothesis. *Int. J. Psycho-Anal.*, 47:396-402.

HARLEY, M. (1951), Analysis of a Severely Disturbed Three-and-a-half-year-old Boy. *The Psychoanalytic Study of the Child*, 6:206-234.

HARTMANN, H. (1939), Ego Psychology and the Problem of Adaptation. New York: International Universities Press, 1958.

——— (1950), Comments on the Psychoanalytic Theory of the Ego. *The Psychoanalytic Study of the Child*, 5:74-96.

——— (1952), The Mutual Influences in the Development of Ego and Id. *The Psychoanalytic Study of the Child*, 7:9-30.

——— (1953), Contribution to the Metapsychology of Schizophrenia. *The Psychoanalytic Study of the Child*, 8:177-198.

——— (1964), *Essays on Ego Psychology: Selected Problems in Psychoanalytic Theory*. New York: International Universities Press.

——— KRIS, E., & LOEWENSTEIN, R. M. (1946), Comments on the Formation of Psychic Structure. *The Psychoanalytic Study of the Child*, 2:11-38.

——— ——— ——— (1949), Notes on the Theory of Aggression. *The Psychoanalytic Study of the Child*, 3/4:9-36.

——— & SCHILDER, P. (1927), Körperinneres und Körperschema. *Z. ges. Neurol. & Psychiat.*, 109:666-675.

HAWKINS, M. O'NEIL (1952), Schizophrenia in Childhood [Round Table B]. *Bull. Amer. Psychoanal. Assn.*, 8:149-170.

HENDRICK, I. (1942), Instinct and the Ego during Infancy. *Psychoanal. Quart.*, 11:33-58.

——— (1951a), Early Development of the Ego: Identification in Infancy. *Psychoanal. Quart.*, 20:44-61.

——— (1951b), The Contributions of Psychoanalysis to the Study of Psychoses. *J. Amer. Med. Assn.*, 113:918-924.

——— (1964), Narcissism and the Prepuberty Ego Ideal. *J. Amer. Psychoanal. Assn.*, 12:522-528.

HERMANN, I. (1934), Vorläufige Mitteilung: Urwahrnehmungen, insbesondere Augenleuchten und Lautwerden des Inneren. *Int. Z. Psychoanal.*, 20:553-555.

——— (1936), Sich-Anklammern, Auf-Suche-Gehen. *Int. Z. Psychoanal.*, 22:349-370.

HERSKOVITZ, H. H. (1954), Childhood Schizophrenia [Round Table, 1953]: Introductory Remarks. *Amer. J. Orthopsychiat.*, 24:484-486.

HIRSCHBERG, J. C. & BRYANT, K. N. (1954), Problems in the Differential Diagnosis of Childhood Schizophrenia. In: *Neurology and*

Psychiatry in Childhood ([Proc.] Res. Publ. Assn. Nerv. Ment. Dis.). Baltimore: Williams & Wilkins, Vol. 34, pp. 454-461.

HOFFER, W. (1949), Mouth, Hand and Ego-Integration. *The Psychoanalytic Study of the Child,* 3/4:49-56.

—— (1950a), Oral Aggressiveness and Ego Development. *Int. J. Psycho-Anal.,* 31:156-160.

—— (1950b), Development of the Body Ego. *The Psychoanalytic Study of the Child,* 5:18-24.

—— (1952), The Mutual Influences in the Development of Ego and Id: Earliest Stages. *The Psychoanalytic Study of the Child,* 7:31-41.

JACOBSON, E. (1953), Contribution to the Metapsychology of Cyclothymic Depression. In: *Affective Disorders,* ed. P. Greenacre. New York: International Universities Press, pp. 49-83.

—— (1954), The Self and the Object World: Vicissitudes of Their Infantile Cathexes and Their Influence on Ideational and Affective Development. *The Psychoanalytic Study of the Child,* 9:75-127.

—— (1957), Denial and Repression. *J. Amer. Psychoanal. Assn.,* 5:61-92.

—— (1964), *The Self and the Object World.* New York: International Universities Press.

JAMES, M. (1960), Premature Ego Development: Some Observations on Disturbances in the First Three Months of Life. *Int. J. Psycho-Anal.,* 41:288-294.

JESSNER, L. & PAVENSTEDT, E., eds. (1959), *Dynamic Psychopathology in Childhood.* New York: Grune & Stratton.

JOFFE, W. G. & SANDLER, J. (1965), Notes on Pain, Depression, and Individuation. *The Psychoanalytic Study of the Child,* 20:394-424.

KANNER, L. (1942a), Co-Editors' Introduction. *Nerv. Child,* 2:216.

—— (1942b), Autistic Disturbances of Affective Contact. *Nerv. Child,* 2:217-250.

—— (1944), Early Infantile Autism. *J. Pediat,* 25:211-217.

—— (1946), Irrelevant and Metaphorical Language in Early Infantile Autism. *Amer. J. Psychiat.,* 103:242-246.

—— (1949), Problems of Nosology and Psychodynamics of Early Infantile Autism. *Amer. J. Orthopsychiat.,* 19:416-426.

—— (1954), Childhood Schizophrenia [Round Table, 1953]: Discussion. *Amer. J. Orthopsychiat.,* 24:526-528.

—— & EISENBERG, L. (1955), Notes on the Follow-up Studies of Autistic Children. In: *Psychopathology of Childhood,* ed. P. H. Hoch & J. Zubin. New York: Grune & Stratton, pp. 227-239.

KAUFMAN, I. C. & ROSENBLUM, L. A. (1967), Depression in Infant Monkeys Separated from Their Mothers. *Science,* 155:1030-1031.

—— —— (1968), The Reaction to Separation in Infant Monkeys: Anaclitic Depression and Conservation-Withdrawal. *Psychosom. Med.,* in press.

KEISER, S. (1958), Disturbances in Abstract Thinking and Body-Image Formation. *J. Amer. Psychoanal. Assn.*, 6:628-652.

KESTENBERG, J. S. (1954), The History of an "Autistic" Child: Clinical Data and Interpretation. *J. Child Psychiat.*, 3:5-52.

——— (1956), On the Development of Maternal Feelings in Early Childhood. *The Psychoanalytic Study of the Child*, 11:257-291.

KHAN, M. M. R. (1960), Clinical Aspects of the Schizoid Personality: Affects and Technique. *Int. J. Psycho-Anal.*, 41:430-437.

——— (1962), The Role of Polymorph-Perverse Body-Experiences and Object-Relations in Ego-Integration. *Brit. J. Med. Psychol.*, 35:245-261.

——— (1963), The Concept of Cumulative Trauma. *The Psychoanalytic Study of the Child*, 18:286-306.

——— (1964), Ego Distortion, Cumulative Trauma, and the Role of Reconstruction in the Analytic Situation. *Int. J. Psycho-Anal.*, 45:272-279.

KLEIN, I. J. (1952), Childhood Schizophrenic States Simulating Retardation and Auditory Impairment. *Nerv. Child*, 10:135-145.

KLEIN, M. (1932), *The Psycho-Analysis of Children.* New York: Norton.

——— HEIMANN, P., ISAACS, S., & RIVIERE, J. (1952), *Developments in Psycho-Analysis.* London: Hogarth Press.

KOHUT, H. (1966), Forms and Transformations of Narcissism. *J. Amer. Psychoanal. Assn.*, 14:243-272.

KRIS, E. (1933), A Psychotic Sculptor of the Eighteenth Century. *Psychoanalytic Explorations in Art.* New York: International Universities Press, 1952, pp. 128-150.

——— (1955), Neutralization and Sublimation: Observations on Young Children. *The Psychoanalytic Study of the Child*, 10:30-46.

KUBIE, L. & ISRAEL, H. A. (1955), "Say You're Sorry." *The Psychoanalytic Study of the Child*, 10:289-299.

LEBOVICI, S. & McDOUGALL, J. (1960), *Un Cas de Psychose Infantile: Etude Psychanalytique.* Paris: Presses Universitaires de France.

LEWIN, B. D. (1950), *The Psychoanalysis of Elation.* New York: Norton.

LICHTENSTEIN, H. (1961), Identity and Sexuality: A Study of Their Interrelationship in Man. *J. Amer. Psychoanal. Assn.*, 9:179-260.

——— (1964), The Role of Narcissism in the Emergence and Maintenance of a Primary Identity. *Int. J. Psycho-Anal.*, 45:49-56.

LIDZ, T. (1963), *The Family and Human Adaptation.* New York: International Universities Press.

——— FLECK, S., & CORNELISON, A. R. (1965), *Schizophrenia and the Family.* New York: International Universities Press.

LINN, L. (1955), Some Developmental Aspects of the Body Image. *Int. J. Psycho-Anal.*, 36:36-42.

LOEWALD, H. W. (1951), Ego and Reality. *Int. J. Psycho-Anal.*, 32:10-18.

———— (1962a), Internalization, Separation, Mourning, and the Superego. *Psychoanal. Quart.*, 31:483-504.

———— (1962b), The Superego and the Ego-Ideal. *Int. J. Psycho-Anal.*, 43:264-271.

LOEWENSTEIN, R. M. (1940), The Vital or Somatic Instincts. *Int. J. Psycho-Anal.*, 21:377-400.

———— (1957), A Contribution to the Psychoanalytic Theory of Masochism. *J. Amer. Psychoanal. Assn.*, 5:197-234.

LOURIE, R. S. (1955), Experience with Therapy of Psychosomatic Problems in Infants. In: *Psychopathology of Childhood*, ed. P. H. Hoch & J. Zubin. New York: Grune & Stratton, pp. 254-266.

———— PACELLA, B. L., & PIOTROWSKI, A. Z. (1943), Studies on the Prognosis in Schizophrenic-like Psychoses in Children. *Amer. J. Psychiat.*, 99:542-552.

LUSTMAN, S. L. (1956), Rudiments of the Ego. *The Psychoanalytic Study of the Child*, 11:89-98.

———— (1957), Psychic Energy and Mechanisms of Defense. *The Psychoanalytic Study of the Child*, 12:151-165.

MAENCHEN, A. (1953), Notes on Early Ego Disturbances. *The Psychoanalytic Study of the Child*, 8:262-270.

MAHLER [SCHOENBERGER], M. (1942), Pseudoimbecility: A Magic Cap of Invisibility. *Psychoanal. Quart.*, 11:149-164.

———— (1944), Tics and Impulsions in Children: A Study of Motility. *Psychoanal. Quart.*, 13:430-444.

———— (1947), Various Clinical Pictures of Psychosis in Children (Schizophrenia-like). Paper read at the Schilder Society, New York.

———— (1948), Contribution to Round-Table Discussion on Aggression. Annual Meeting of the American Psychiatric Association, Washington, D. C.

———— (1949a), A Psychoanalytic Evaluation of Tic in Psychopathology of Children: Symptomatic Tic and Tic Syndrome. *The Psychoanalytic Study of the Child*, 3/4:279-310.

———— (1949b), Remarks on Psychoanalysis with Psychotic Children. *Quart. J. Child Behav.*, 1:18-21.

———— (1949c), Les "Enfants Terribles." In: *Searchlights on Delinquency*, ed. K. R. Eissler. New York: International Universities Press, pp. 77-89.

———— (1950), Discussion of papers by Anna Freud and Ernst Kris, Symposium on "Problems of Child Development," Stockbridge, Mass. (unpublished). (For the Symposium on "Problems of Child Development," see *The Psychoanalytic Study of the Child*, 6:9-60, 1951.)

———— (1952 [1951]), On Child Psychosis and Schizophrenia: Autistic and Symbiotic Infantile Psychoses. *The Psychoanalytic Study of the Child*, 7:286-305.

———— (1953a), Discussion of Greenacre's: Certain Relationships between Fetishism and the Faulty Development of the Body Image. American Psychoanalytic Association, Los Angeles.

———— (1953b), Some Aspects in the Development of Childhood Psychoses. Contribution to a Seminar on Child Psychiatry, Roundtable Discussion: Basic Problems in Early Childhood, Los Angeles.

———— (1954a), Childhood Schizophrenia [Round Table, 1953]: Discussion. *Amer. J. Orthopsychiat.*, 24:523-526.

———— (1954b), In: Problems of Infantile Neurosis. *The Psychoanalytic Study of the Child*, 9:65-66.

———— (1954c), On Normal and Pathological Symbiosis: A Contribution to the Understanding of Psychoses in Children. Read at the Baltimore Psychoanalytic Society.

———— (1955), Discussion [of papers by Kanner & Eisenberg, Despert, Lourie]. In: *Psychopathology of Childhood*, ed. P. H. Hoch & J. Zubin. New York: Grune & Stratton, pp. 285-289.

———— (1957), On Two Crucial Phases of Integration of the Sense of Identity: Separation-Individuation and Bisexual Identity. Abstr. in: Panel on Problems of Identity, rep. D. L. Rubinfine. *J. Amer. Psychoanal. Assn.*, 6:131-142, 1958.

———— (1958), Autism and Symbiosis: Two Extreme Disturbances of Identity. *Int. J. Psycho-Anal.*, 39:77-83.

———— (1960), Symposium on Psychotic Object Relationships: III. Perceptual De-Differentiation and Psychotic 'Object Relationship.' *Int. J. Psycho-Anal.*, 41:548-553.

———— (1961), On Sadness and Grief in Infancy and Childhood: Loss and Restoration of the Symbiotic Love Object. *The Psychoanalytic Study of the Child*, 16:332-351.

———— (1963), Thoughts about Development and Individuation. *The Psychoanalytic Study of the Child*, 18:307-324.

———— (1964), Foreword [to "Project on Childhood Psychosis" issue]. *Reiss-Davis Clin. Bull.*, 1:54-56.

———— (1965a), On Early Infantile Psychosis: The Symbiotic and Autistic Syndromes. *J. Amer. Acad. Child Psychiat.*, 4:554-568.

———— (1965b), On the Significance of the Normal Separation-Individuation Phase: With Reference to Research in Symbiotic Child Psychosis. In: *Drives, Affects, Behavior*, ed. M. Schur. New York: International Universities Press, Vol. 2, pp. 161-169.

———— (1966a), Discussion of Greenacre's: Problems of Overidealization of the Analyst and of Analysis. Abstr. in: *Psychoanal. Quart.*, 36:637, 1967.

———— (1966b), Notes on the Development of Basic Moods: The Depressive Affect. In: *Psychoanalysis—A General Psychology: Essays in Honor of Heinz Hartmann*, ed. R. M. Loewenstein, L. M.

Newman, M. Schur, & A. J. Solnit. New York: International Universities Press, pp. 152-168.

———— (1966c), Some Preliminary Notes on the Development of Basic Moods, Including Depression. *Canad. Psychiat. Assn. J.* (Special Supplement), 2:S250-S258.

———— (1967), Development of "Defense" from Biological and Symbiotic Precursors: Adaptive and Maladaptive Aspects. In: Panel on Development and Metapsychology of the Defense Organization of the Ego, rep. R. S. Wallerstein. *J. Amer. Psychoanal. Assn.*, 15:130-149.

———— (1968), The Self-Limitations of Lauretta Bender's Biological Theory. *Int. J. Psychiat.*, 5:230-233.

———— & ELKISCH, P. (1953), Some Observations on Disturbances of the Ego in a Case of Infantile Psychosis. *The Psychoanalytic Study of the Child*, 8:252-261.

———— & FURER, M. (1960), Observations on Research regarding the "Symbiotic Syndrome" of Infantile Psychosis. *Psychoanal. Quart.*, 29:317-327.

———— ———— (1963a), [Moderators of] Workshop IV: Research in Progress. Annual Meeting of American Psychoanalytic Association, St. Louis.

———— ———— (1963b), Certain Aspects of the Separation-Individuation Phase. *Psychoanal. Quart.*, 32:1-14.

———— ———— (1965), Selected Papers and Monograph. Discussion Group No. 9 at Annual Meeting of American Psychoanalytic Association, New York.

———— ———— (1966), Development of Symbiosis, Symbiotic Psychosis, and the Nature of Separation Anxiety: Remarks on Weiland's Paper. *Int. J. Psycho-Anal.*, 47:559-560.

———— ———— GOLDFARB, W., WARD, R. S., & KOLB, L. C. (moderator) (1966), Panel Discussion: Childhood Schizophrenia. Abstr. in: *Bull. Assn. Psychoanal. Med.*, 5:35-42.

———— ———— & SETTLAGE, C. F. (1959), Severe Emotional Disturbances in Childhood: Psychosis. In: *American Handbook of Psychiatry*, ed. S. Arieti. New York: Basic Books, 1:816-839.

———— & GOSLINER, B. J. (1955), On Symbiotic Child Psychosis: Genetic, Dynamic and Restitutive Aspects. *The Psychoanalytic Study of the Child*, 10:195-212.

———— & GROSS, I. H. (1945), Psychotherapeutic Study of a Typical Case with Tic Syndrome. *Nerv. Child*, 4:358-373.

———— & LA PERRIERE, K. (1965), Mother-Child Interaction during Separation-Individuation. *Psychoanal. Quart.*, 34:483-498.

———— & LUKE, J. A. (1946), Outcome of the Tic Syndrome. *J. Nerv. Ment. Dis.*, 103:433-445.

———— ———— & DALTROFF, W. (1945), Clinical and Follow-up

Study of the Tic Syndrome in Children. *Amer. J. Orthopsychiat.*, 15:631-647.

———— & McDevitt, J. B. (1968), Observations on Adaptation and Defense *in statu nascendi:* Developmental Precursors in the First Two Years of Life. *Psychoanal. Quart.*, 37:1-21.

———— & Rangell, L. (1943), A Psychosomatic Study of Maladie des Tics (Gilles de la Tourette's Disease). *Psychiat. Quart.*, 17: 579-603.

———— Ross, J. R., Jr., & De Fries, Z. (1949), Clinical Studies in Benign and Malignant Cases of Childhood Psychosis (Schizophrenia-like). *Amer. J. Orthopsychiat.*, 19:295-305.

———— & Silberpfennig, I. (1938), Der Rorschach'sche Formdeutversuch als Hilfsmittel zum Verständnis der Psychologie Hirnkranker. *Schweiz. Arch. Neurol. Psychiat.*, 40:302-327.

Modell, A. H. (1956), Some Recent Psychoanalytic Theories of Schizophrenia. *Psychoanal. Rev.*, 43:181-194.

Morrow, T., Jr. & Loomis, E. A., Jr. (1955), Symbiotic Aspects of a Seven-year-old Psychotic. In: *Emotional Problems of Early Childhood*, ed. G. Caplan. New York: Basic Books, pp. 337-361.

Nunberg, H. (1955), *Principles of Psychoanalysis*. New York: International Universities Press.

———— (1965), *Practice and Theory of Psychoanalysis*, 2 Vols. New York: International Universities Press, 2nd ed.

Pacella, B. L. (1944-1945), Physiologic and Differential Diagnostic Considerations of Tic Manifestations in Children. *Nerv. Child*, 4:313-317.

———— (1948), Behavior Problems of Children. *Med. Clin. N. Amer.* (Neurol. Psychiat.), 32:655-667.

Pavenstedt, E. (1955), History of a Child with an Atypical Development, and Some Vicissitudes of His Treatment. In: *Emotional Problems of Early Childhood*, ed. G. Caplan. New York: Basic Books, pp. 379-405.

———— (1956), The Effect of Extreme Passivity Imposed on a Boy in Early Childhood. *The Psychoanalytic Study of the Child*, 11: 396-409.

———— & Anderson, I. N. (1952), Complementary Treatment of Mother and Child with Atypical Development. *Amer. J. Orthopsychiat.*, 22:607-641.

Peto, A. (1959), Body Image and Archaic Thinking. *Int. J. Psycho-Anal.*, 40:223-231.

———— (1967), Dedifferentiations and Fragmentations during Analysis. *J. Amer. Psychoanal. Assn.*, 15:534-550.

Piaget, J. (1923), *The Language and Thought of the Child*. New York: Humanities Press, 1952.

———— (1936), *The Origins of Intelligence in Children*. New York: International Universities Press, 1952.

PINE, F. & FURER, M. (1963), Studies of the Separation-Individuation Phase: A Methodological Overview. *The Psychoanalytic Study of the Child,* 18:325-342.

PIOUS, W. L. (1950), Obsessive-Compulsive Symptoms in an Incipient Schizophrenic. *Psychoanal. Quart.,* 19:327-351.

POLLOCK, G. H. (1964), On Symbiosis and Symbiotic Neurosis. *Int. J. Psycho-Anal.,* 45:1-30.

POTTER, H. W. (1933), Schizophrenia in Children. *Amer. J. Psychiat.,* 12:1253-1270.

PROVENCE, S. & LIPTON, R. C. (1962), *Infants in Institutions.* New York: International Universities Press.

PUTNAM, M. C. (1955), Some Observations on Psychosis in Early Childhood. In: *Emotional Problems of Early Childhood,* ed. G. Caplan. New York: Basic Books, pp. 519-523.

RABINOVITCH, R. D. (1952), Observations on the Differential Study of Severely Disturbed Children [Round Table, 1951]. *Amer. J. Orthopsychiat.,* 22:230-236.

RANK, B. (1949), Adaptation of the Psychoanalytic Technique for the Treatment of Young Children with Atypical Development. *Amer. J. Orthopsychiat.,* 19:130-139.

——— (1955), Intensive Study and Treatment of Preschool Children Who Show Marked Personality Deviations, or "Atypical Development," and Their Parents. In: *Emotional Problems of Early Childhood,* ed. G. Caplan. New York: Basic Books, pp. 491-501.

——— & MACNAUGHTON, D. (1950), A Clinical Contribution to Early Ego Development. *The Psychoanalytic Study of the Child,* 5:53-65.

RAPAPORT, D. (1958), The Theory of Ego Autonomy: A Generalization. *Bull. Menninger Clin.,* 22:13-25.

——— (1959), The Theory of Attention Cathexis: An Economic and Structural Attempt at the Explanation of Cognitive Processes. *The Collected Papers of David Rapaport,* ed. M. M. Gill. New York: Basic Books, 1967, pp. 778-794.

——— (1960), *The Structure of Psychoanalytic Theory* [*Psychological Issues,* Monogr. 6]. New York: International Universities Press.

RIBBLE, M. (1941), Disorganizing Factors of Infant Personality. *Amer. J. Psychiat.,* 98:459-463.

——— (1943), *The Rights of Infants: Early Psychological Needs and Their Satisfaction.* New York: Columbia University Press.

RICHMOND, J. B. & LUSTMAN, S. L. (1955), Autonomic Function in the Neonate: I. Implications for Psychosomatic Theory. *Psychosom. Med.,* 17:269-275.

RITVO, S. (1945), Review of Recent Literature on Tics in Children. *Nerv. Child,* 4:308-312.

———— & PROVENCE, S. (1953), Form Perception and Imitation in Some Autistic Children: Diagnostic Findings and Their Contextual Interpretation. *The Psychoanalytic Study of the Child,* 8:155-161.

———— & SOLNIT, A. J. (1958), Influences of Early Mother-Child Interaction on Identification Processes. *The Psychoanalytic Study of the Child,* 13:64-91.

ROBERTSON, J. (1952), *A Two-Year-Old Goes to Hospital* [film]. London: Tavistock Clinic.

ROCHLIN, G. (1953), Loss and Restitution. *The Psychoanalytic Study of the Child,* 8:288-309.

———— (1959), The Loss Complex: A Contribution to the Etiology of Depression. *J. Amer. Psychoanal. Assn.,* 7:299-316.

ROFFWARG, H. P., MUZIO, J. N., & DEMENT, W. C. (1966), Ontogenetic Development of the Human Sleep-Dream Cycle. *Science,* 152:604-619.

ROLLMAN-BRANCH, H. S. (1960), On the Question of Primary Object Need: Ethological and Psychoanalytic Considerations. *J. Amer. Psychoanal. Assn.,* 8:686-702.

ROSE, G. J. (1964), Creative Imagination in Terms of Ego "Core" and Boundaries. *Int. J. Psycho-Anal.,* 45:75-84.

———— (1966), Body Ego and Reality. *Int. J. Psycho-Anal.,* 47:502-509.

ROSEN, V. H. (1953), On Mathematical Illumination and the Mathematical Thought Process. *The Psychoanalytic Study of the Child,* 8:127-154.

———— (1955), Strephosymbolia: An Intrasystemic Disturbance of the Synthetic Function of the Ego. *The Psychoanalytic Study of the Child,* 10:83-99.

———— (1958), Abstract Thinking and Object Relations. *J. Amer. Psychoanal. Assn.,* 4:653-671.

ROSS, N. (1967), The "As If" Concept. *J. Amer. Psychoanal. Assn.,* 15:59-82.

RUBINFINE, D. L. (1958), Report of Panel: Problems of Identity. *J. Amer. Psychoanal. Assn.,* 6:131-142.

———— (1961), Perception, Reality Testing, and Symbolism. *The Psychoanalytic Study of the Child,* 16:73-89.

———— (1962), Maternal Stimulation, Psychic Structure, and Early Object Relations. *The Psychoanalytic Study of the Child,* 17:265-282.

SACHS, H. (1933), The Delay of the Machine Age. *The Creative Unconscious.* Cambridge, Mass.: Sci-Art Publishers, 1951, pp. 100-131.

SACHS, L. J. (1957), On Changes in Identification from Machine to Cripple. *The Psychoanalytic Study of the Child,* 12:356-375.

SCHILDER, P. (1923), *The Image and Appearance of the Human Body: Studies in the Constructive Energies of the Psyche.* New York: International Universities Press, 1951.

———— (1938), The Child and the Symbol. *Scientia* (Milan), 64:21-26.

———— & WECHSLER, D. (1935), What Do Children Know about the Interior of the Body? *Int. J. Psycho-Anal.*, 16:355-360.

SCHOENBERGER, M., *see* MAHLER, M. S.

SCHUR, M. (1958), The Ego and the Id in Anxiety. *The Psychoanalytic Study of the Child*, 13:190-220.

————(1960a), Discussion of Dr. John Bowlby's Paper (1960a). *The Psychoanalytic Study of the Child*, 15:63-84.

———— (1960b), Introductory Remarks to Panel on Psychoanalysis and Ethology, rep. M. Ostow. *J. Amer. Psychoanal. Assn.*, 8:526.

———— (1966), *The Id and the Regulatory Principles of Mental Functioning.* New York: International Universities Press.

SEARLES, H. F. (1960), *The Nonhuman Environment in Normal Development and in Schizophrenia.* New York: International Universities Press.

———— (1965), *Collected Papers on Schizophrenia and Related Subjects.* New York: International Universities Press.

SECHEHAYE, M. A. (1947), *Symbolic Realization: A New Method of Psychotherapy Applied to a Case of Schizophrenia.* New York: International Universities Press, 1951.

———— (1950), *Reality Lost and Regained: Autobiography of a Schizophrenic Girl.* New York: Grune & Stratton, 1951.

———— (1956a), *A New Psychotherapy in Schizophrenia: Relief of Frustrations by Symbolic Realization.* New York: Grune & Stratton.

———— (1956b), The Transference in Symbolic Realization. *Int. J. Psycho-Anal.*, 37:270-277.

SETTLAGE, C. F. (1964), Psychoanalytic Theory in Relation to the Nosology of Childhood Psychic Disorders. *J. Amer. Psychoanal. Assn.*, 12:776-801.

SHUGART, G. (1956), History Taking in Infantile Psychosis. *Soc. Work*, 1:84-93.

SILBERPFENNIG, I., *see* KESTENBERG, J. S.

SPEERS, R. W. & LANSING, C. (1965), *Group Therapy in Childhood Psychosis.* Chapel Hill: University of North Carolina Press.

SPERLING, M. (1951), The Neurotic Child and His Mother: A Psychoanalytic Study. *Amer. J. Orthopsychiat.*, 21:351-364.

———— (1954), Childhood Schizophrenia [Round Table, 1953]: Reactive Schizophrenia in Children. *Amer. J. Orthopsychiat.*, 24:506-512.

SPIEGEL, L. A. (1959), The Self, the Sense of Self, and Perception. *The Psychoanalytic Study of the Child*, 14:81-109.

SPITZ, R. A. (1945a), Diacritic and Coenesthetic Organizations: The Psychiatric Significance of a Functional Division of the Nervous System into a Sensory and Emotive Part. *Psychoanal. Rev.*, 32:146-162.

———— (1945b), Hospitalism: An Inquiry into the Genesis of Psychiatric Conditions in Early Childhood. *The Psychoanalytic Study of the Child*, 1:53-74.

———— (1946a), Hospitalism: A Follow-up Report. *The Psychoanalytic Study of the Child*, 2:113-117.

———— (1946b), Anaclitic Depression. *The Psychoanalytic Study of the Child*, 2:313-342.

———— (1950), Relevancy of Direct Infant Observation. *The Psychoanalytic Study of the Child*, 5:66-73.

———— (1951), The Psychogenic Diseases in Infancy: An Attempt at Their Etiologic Classification. *The Psychoanalytic Study of the Child*, 6:255-275.

———— (1953), Contribution to a symposium on "Basic Problems in Early Childhood." Annual Meeting of the American Psychoanalytic Association, Los Angeles.

———— (1955), The Primal Cavity: A Contribution to the Genesis of Perception and Its Role for Psychoanalytic Theory. *The Psychoanalytic Study of the Child*, 10:215-240.

———— (1957), *No and Yes: On the Genesis of Human Communication*. New York: International Universities Press.

———— (1959), *A Genetic Field Theory of Ego Formation*. New York: International Universities Press.

———— (1960), Discussion of Dr. John Bowlby's Paper (1960a). *The Psychoanalytic Study of the Child*, 15:85-94.

———— (1965), *The First Year of Life: A Psychoanalytic Study of Normal and Deviant Development of Object Relations*. New York: International Universities Press.

———— & WOLF, K. (1946), The Smiling Response. *Genet. Psychol. Monogr.*, 34:57-125.

SPOCK, B. (1963), The Striving for Autonomy and Regressive Object Relationships. *The Psychoanalytic Study of the Child*, 18:361-364.

STÄRKE, A. (1919), The Reversal of the Libido-Sign in Delusions of Persecution. *Int. J. Psycho-Anal.*, 1:231-234, 1920.

STARR, P. H. (1954), Psychoses in Children: Their Origin and Structure. *Psychoanal. Quart.*, 23:544-565.

STERN, M. (1951), Pavor Nocturnus. *Int. J. Psycho-Anal.*, 32:302-309.

———— (1961), Blank Hallucinations: Remarks about Trauma and Perceptual Disturbances. *Int. J. Psycho-Anal.*, 42:205-215.

———— (1968), Fear of Death and Neurosis. *J. Amer. Psychoanal. Assn.*, 16:3-31.

STIRNIMANN, F. (1947), Das Kind und seine früheste Umwelt. *Psychologische Praxis*, 6. Basel: Karger.

STOLLER, R. J. (1966a), The Analysis of the Mother of a Transvestite Boy. *Bull. Phila. Assn. Psychoanal.*, 16:50-54.

———— (1966b), The Mother's Contribution to Infantile Transvestic Behavior. *Int. J. Psycho-Anal.*, 47:384-395.

STONE, L. (1961), *The Psychoanalytic Situation*. New York: International Universities Press.

——— (1967), The Psychoanalytic Situation and Transference: Postscript to an Earlier Communication. *J. Amer. Psychoanal. Assn.*, 15:3-58.

SZASZ, T. (1957), *Pain and Pleasure: A Study of Bodily Feelings.* New York: Basic Books.

SZUREK, S. A. (1956), Psychotic Episodes and Psychotic Maldevelopment. *Amer. J. Orthopsychiat.*, 26:519-543.

TANNER, J. M. & INHELDER, B., eds. (1953), *Discussions on Child Development*, Vol. I [First Meeting of the World Health Organization Study Group on the Psychobiological Development of the Child, Geneva, 1953]. New York: International Universities Press.

TARTAKOFF, H. H. (1966), The Normal Personality in Our Culture and the Nobel Prize Complex. In: *Psychoanalysis—A General Psychology: Essays in Honor of Heinz Hartmann*, ed. R. M. Loewenstein, L. M. Newman, M. Schur, & A. J. Solnit. New York: International Universities Press, pp. 222-252.

TAUSK, V. (1919), On the Origin of the "Influencing Machine" in Schizophrenia. In: *The Psychoanalytic Reader*, ed. R. Fliess. New York: International Universities Press, 1948, pp. 52-85.

VON MONAKOW, C. (1923), *The Emotions, Morality and the Brain.* Washington & New York: Nervous and Mental Disease Publishing Co., 1924.

VAN OPHUIJSEN, J. H. (1920), On the Origin of the Feeling of Persecution. *Int. J. Psycho-Anal.*, 1:235-239.

WAELDER, R. (1960), *Basic Theory of Psychoanalysis.* New York: International Universities Press.

WEIL, A. P. (1953a), Clinical Data and Dynamic Considerations in Certain Cases of Childhood Schizophrenia. *Amer. J. Orthopsychiat.*, 23:518-529.

——— (1953b), Certain Severe Disturbances of Ego Development in Childhood. *The Psychoanalytic Study of the Child*, 8:271-287.

——— (1956), Some Evidences of Deviational Development in Infancy and Childhood. *The Psychoanalytic Study of the Child*, 11: 292-299.

WEILAND, I. H. (1966), Considerations on the Development of Symbiosis, Symbiotic Psychosis, and the Nature of Separation Anxiety. *Int. J. Psycho-Anal.*, 47:1-5.

WERNER, H. (1948), *Comparative Psychology of Mental Development.* New York: International Universities Press, 1957.

WINNICOTT, D. W. (1953a), Psychoses and Child Care. *Brit. J. Med. Psychol.*, 26:68-74.

——— (1953b), Transitional Objects and Transitional Phenomena: A Study of the First Not-Me Possession. *Int. J. Psycho-Anal.*, 34: 89-97.

———— (1956), Primary Maternal Preoccupation. *Collected Papers.* New York: Basic Books, 1958, pp. 300-305.

———— (1960), The Theory of the Parent-Infant Relationship. *Int. J. Psycho-Anal.,* 41:585-595.

———— (1965), *The Maturational Processes and the Facilitating Environment.* New York: International Universities Press.

WOLFF, P. H. (1959), Observations on Newborn Infants. *Psychosom. Med.,* 21:110-118.

YAZMAJIAN, R. V. (1967), Biological Aspects of Infantile Sexuality and the Latency Period. *Psychoanal. Quart.,* 36:203-229.

ZAZZO, R. (1953), In: *Discussions on Child Development,* Vol. I. [First Meeting of the World Health Organization Study Group on Psychobiological Development of the Child, Geneva, 1953], ed. J. M. Tanner & B. Inhelder. New York: International Universities Press.

Bibliographical Notes

CHAPTER I, ON THE CONCEPTS OF SYMBIOSIS AND SEPARATION-INDIVIDUATION, is based on "On Human Symbiosis and the Vicissitudes of Individuation: An Overview of Human Symbiosis and Individuation," presented at the Plenary Session of the Annual Meeting of the American Psychoanalytic Association, Detroit, Michigan, May 7, 1967, and published in the *Journal of the American Psychoanalytic Association*, 15:740-763, 1967.

CHAPTER II, THE SYMBIOSIS THEORY OF INFANTILE PSYCHOSIS, is based on the following papers: "On Child Psychosis and Schizophrenia: Autistic and Symbiotic Infantile Psychoses," presented at the 17th International Psycho-Analytical Congress, Amsterdam, August 6, 1951, and published in *The Psychoanalytic Study of the Child*, 7:286-305, 1952; "On Symbiotic Child Psychosis: Genetic, Dynamic and Restitutive Aspects" by Margaret S. Mahler and Bertram J. Gosliner, presented at the New York Psychoanalytic Society, February 22, 1955, and later at the Philadelphia Psychoanalytic Society and the Austen Riggs Center, Stockbridge, Mass., and published in *The Psychoanalytic Study of the Child*, 10:195-212, 1955; "Autism and Symbiosis, Two Extreme Disturbances of Identity," presented at the 20th Congress of the International Psycho-Analytical Association, Paris, July 29, 1957, and published in *The International Journal of Psycho-Analysis*, 39:77-83, 1958; "On Two Crucial Phases of Integration of the Sense of Identity: Separation-Individuation and Bisexual Identity," presented at the American Psychoanalytic Association Meeting, Chicago, May, 1957, and abstracted in Panel Report: "Problems of Identity," reported by D. L. Rubinfine in *Journal of the American Psychoanalytic Association*, 6:131-142, 1958; "Severe Emotional Disturbances in Childhood: Psychosis" by Margaret S. Mahler, Manuel Furer, and Calvin F. Settlage, published in *American Handbook of Psychiatry*, edited by S. Arieti, New York: Basic Books, 1959, pp. 816-839; "Perceptual Dedifferentiation and Psychotic 'Object Relationship,' " presented at the 21st Congress of the International Psycho-Analytical Association, Copenhagen, July, 1959, as part of the Symposium on Psychotic Object Relationships, and published in *The International Journal of Psycho-Analysis*, 41:548-553, 1960; "On Sadness and Grief in Infancy and Childhood: Loss and Restoration of the Symbiotic Love Object," presented at the Tenth Anniversary Symposium, the Child Psychiatry Unit, Massachusetts Mental Health Center, Harvard Medical School, and published in *The Psychoanalytic Study of the Child*, 16:332-351, 1961; "Development of Symbiosis, Symbiotic Psychosis, and the Nature of Separation Anxiety: Remarks on Weiland's Paper" by Margaret S. Mahler and Manuel Furer, published in *The International Journal of Psycho-Analysis*, 47:559-560, 1966. Several sections of Chapter II have not been published previously.

CHAPTER III, DIAGNOSTIC CONSIDERATIONS, is based on the following papers: "On Child Psychosis and Schizophrenia: Autistic and Symbiotic Infantile Psychoses," published in *The Psychoanalytic Study of the Child*, 7:286-305, 1952; "Severe Emotional Disturbances in Childhood: Psychosis" by Margaret S. Mahler, Manuel Furer, and Calvin F. Settlage, published in *American Handbook of Psychiatry*, edited by S. Arieti, New York: Basic Books, 1959, pp. 816-839. The final section of this Chapter, "The Relative Relevance of Anamnestic Data," has not been published previously.

CHAPTER IV, CLINICAL CASES OF CHILD PSYCHOSIS, is based on the following papers: "On Child Psychosis and Schizophrenia: Autistic and Symbiotic Infantile Psychoses," published in *The Psychoanalytic Study of the Child*, 7:286-305, 1952; "Some Observations on Disturbances of the Ego in a Case of Infantile Psychosis" by Margaret S. Mahler and Paula Elkisch, published in *The Psychoanalytic Study of the Child*, 8:252-261, 1953; "On Symbiotic Child Psychosis: Genetic, Dynamic and Restitutive Aspects" by Margaret S. Mahler and Bertram J. Gosliner, published in *The Psychoanalytic Study of the Child*, 10:195-212, 1955; "On Infantile Precursors of the 'Influencing Machine' (Tausk)" by Paula Elkisch and Margaret S. Mahler, presented at the Fall Meeting of the American Psychoanalytic Association, December 6, 1958, and published in *The Psychoanalytic Study of the Child*, 14:219-235, 1959; "Severe Emotional Disturbances in Childhood: Psychosis" by Margaret S. Mahler, Manuel Furer, and Calvin F. Settlage, published in *American Handbook of Psychiatry*, edited by S. Arieti, New York: Basic Books, 1959, pp. 816-839; "On Sadness and Grief in Infancy and Childhood: Loss and Restoration of the Symbiotic Love Object," published in *The Psychoanalytic Study of the Child*, 16:332-351, 1961.

CHAPTER V, PROTOTYPES OF MOTHER-CHILD INTER-ACTION, is based on the following papers: "On Symbiotic Child Psychosis: Genetic, Dynamic and Restitutive Aspects" by Margaret S. Mahler and Bertram J. Gosliner, published in *The Psychoanalytic Study of the Child*, 10:195-212, 1955; "On Infantile Precursors of the 'Influencing Machine' (Tausk)" by Paula Elkisch and Margaret S. Mahler, published in *The Psychoanalytic Study of the Child*, 14:219-235, 1959; "On Early Infantile Psychosis: The Symbiotic and Autistic Syndromes," presented to the Department of Psychiatry of New York University, School of Medicine, February 17, 1964, to a joint meeting of the Department of Psychiatry, Hadassah University Hospital, and the Albert and Mary Lasker Child Psychiatry Department of Hadassah Medical Organization in Jerusalem, March 24, 1964, to the Basic Sciences Conference series at McGill University, Department of Psychiatry, Montreal, February 4, 1965, and to the Chicago Psychoanalytic Society, February 23, 1965, and published in the *Journal of the American Academy of Child Psychiatry*, 4:554-568, 1965. Except for the illustrative case material, this Chapter is entirely new and has not been previously published.

CHAPTER VI, THERAPY, is based on the following papers: "On Child Psychosis and Schizophrenia: Autistic and Symbiotic Infantile Psychoses," published in *The Psychoanalytic Study of the Child,* 7:286-305, 1952; "Severe Emotional Disturbances in Childhood: Psychosis" by Margaret S. Mahler, Manuel Furer, and Calvin F. Settlage, published in *American Handbook of Psychiatry,* edited by S. Arieti, New York: Basic Books, 1959, pp. 816-839; "Observations on Research Regarding the 'Symbiotic Syndrome' of Infantile Psychosis" by Margaret S. Mahler and Manuel Furer, presented at the Pan-American Medical Congress, Mexico City, May, 1960, and published in *The Psychoanalytic Quarterly,* 29:317-327, 1960. Much of the material contained in this Chapter is new and published here for the first time. Many of the thoughts were formulated jointly with Manuel Furer in the course of our therapeutic action research, with considerable help by the senior therapist, Mrs. Anni Bergman.

CHAPTER VII, CONCLUSIONS, is entirely new and has not been published previously.

Author Index

263

Subject Index